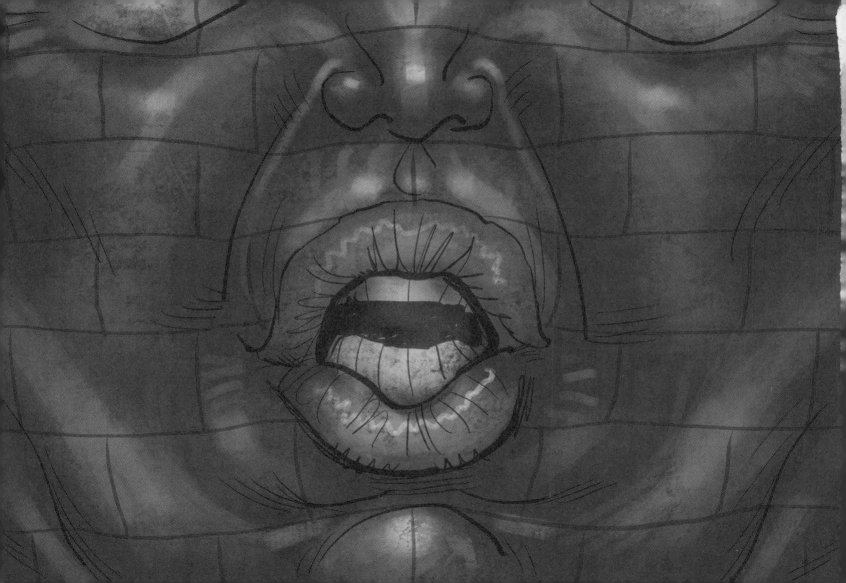

# UNPRESIDENTED

Cartoons of Chaos by
Kieron Dwyer

Introduction by
Shannon Wheeler

# Other Image books by Kieron Dwyer:

Last of the Independents HC, with Matt Fraction

LCD: Lowest Comic Denominator TPB

Sea of Red, with Rick Remender and Salgood Sam

XXXombies, with Rick Remender

CrawlSpace Collection, with Rick Remender and others

# Kieron Dwyer on the Web:

www.kierondwyer.com

Twitter: @Kierondwyer

IG: @Kierondwyer

www.unpresidented.me

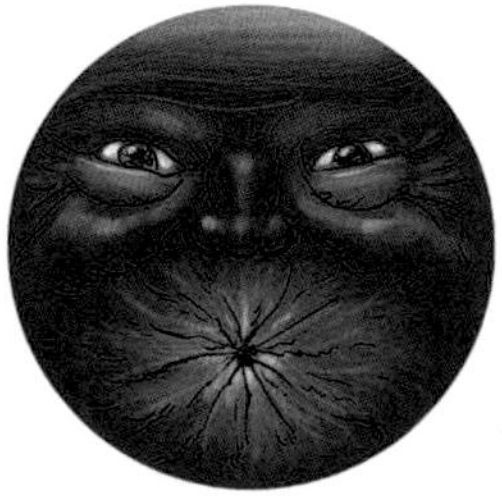

**IMAGE COMICS, INC.** • **Robert Kirkman:** Chief Operating Officer • **Erik Larsen:** Chief Financial Officer • **Todd McFarlane:** President • **Marc Silvestri:** Chief Executive Officer • **Jim Valentino:** Vic President • **Eric Stephenson:** Publisher / Chief Creative Officer • **Jeff Boison:** Director of Publishing Planning & Book Trade Sales • **Chris Ross:** Director of Digital Services • **Jeff Stang:** Director of Direct Marke Sales • **Kat Salazar:** Director of PR & Marketing • **Drew Gill:** Cover Editor • **Heather Doornink:** Production Director • **Nicole Lapalme:** Controller • **IMAGECOMICS.COM**

**UNPRESIDENTED.** First printing. June 2020. Published by Image Comics, Inc. Office of publication: 2701 NW Vaughn St., Suite 780, Portland, OR 97210.  Printed in Canada. For international rights, contact: foreignlicensing@imagecomics.com. ISBN: 978-1-5343-1587-7.

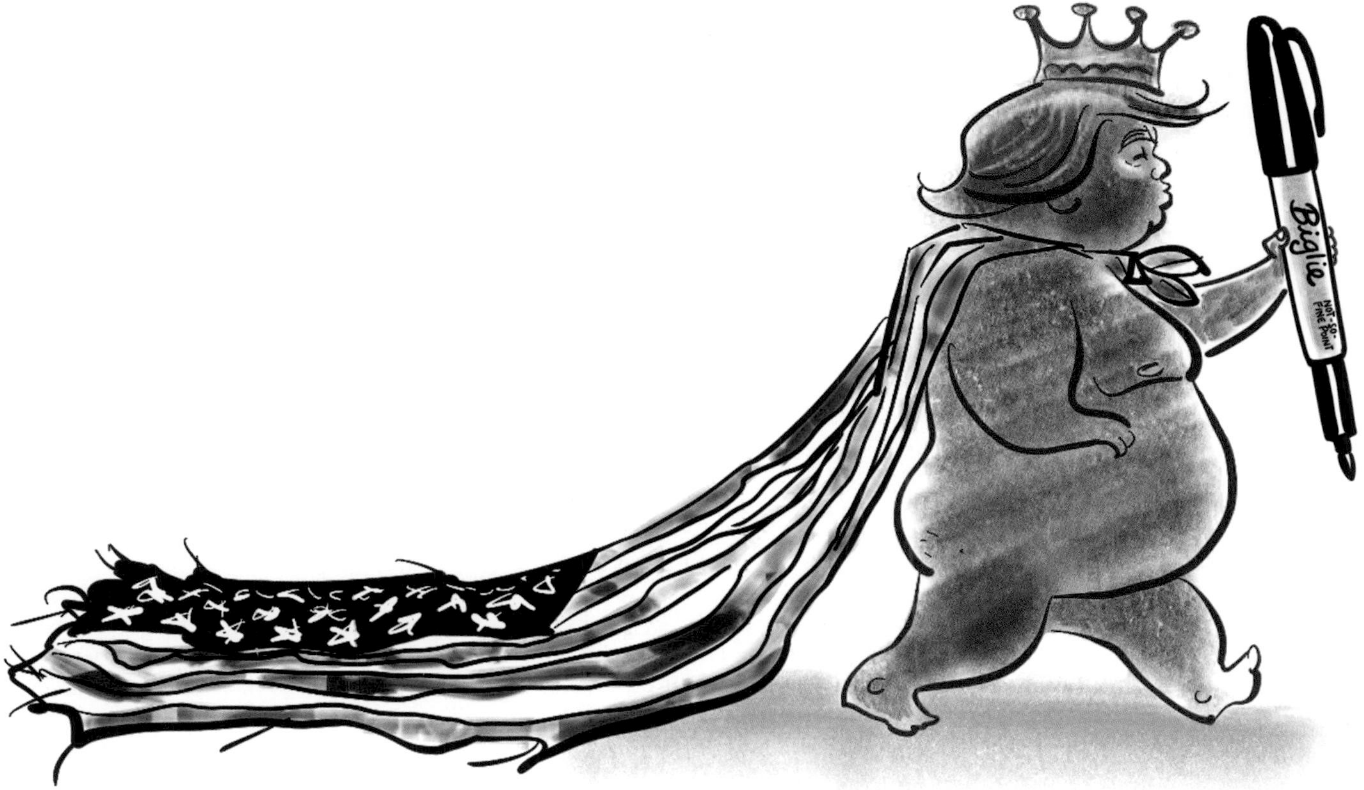
Biglie
NOT-SO-FINE POINT

# INTRODUCTION
## by Shannon Wheeler

Kieron visited Austin, Texas a million years ago. Even though he was the single most popular living comic book artist in the Western World drawing Batman, Superman, and most of the characters in what is now known as the Marvel Universe, he hung out with me and my small crew of underground cartoonists. I photocopied mini-comics for an audience of 23 people, and drew a college cartoon strip for an additional readership of 36. Kieron inked a three-panel comic strip of mine about a guy finding a quarter inside his own nose. Brilliant stuff. Kieron is a generous soul.

After dominating the mainstream market, Kieron self-published his ode to offensive humor, LCD: Lowest Comic Denominator, which exploded the underground scene. The comic ruthlessly took down celebrities and parodied corporate culture. Starbucks, not one to enjoy a joke, sued him for his gentle ribbing of their logo (he turned their mermaid into a Consumer Whore sex doll). Kieron is not allowed to discuss the terms of the settlement but it's worth googling. It's also worth pausing before giving your five bucks to a conglomerate that is willing to sue a cartoonist. Kieron remains undeterred, unafraid, and inspired.

Kieron is now diving into the world of editorial cartooning. If I had to guess his political leanings, I could open this book to any page and the drawings would rip my eyes out. I might guess he's a liberal-lefty. Though, to call it a political leaning is unfair. It's really the same thing that Kieron did with his mainstream and underground efforts: Fight evil. The superheroes fought a symbolic representation of evil by fighting supervillains. The underground comics exaggerate hypocrisy, greed, stupidity, and the villainous corporations with outrageous aplomb. And these political cartoons fall right in line with his previous efforts.

Unpresidented is a not-so-subtle attack on Trump. Kieron doesn't binge watch Netflix from behind an apathetic mass of belly fat. He picks up his pen and attacks modern injustices. He fights with the talent of a veteran cartoonist. It's ruthless. The GOP elephant is a predatory pedophile, Kellyanne Conway cooks turds in a cookie tin, and Trump has a swastika tattooed on the small of his back. None of these portraits are flattering but they are all drawn well. I wince, groan, shudder, and I'm grossed out. I'm jealous of Kieron's talent to go for the jugular. Sometimes he attacks with a sledgehammer - a dumb pun and a gross image. Sometimes he comes in fast and slices with a rapier-sharp wit, insight, and unique metaphor. It's always a shockingly good drawing. He is fearless. At the end of the day, I am heartened that he uses his powers of nausea for good.

Shannon Wheeler is the award-winning creator of Too Much Coffee Man, and his cartoons are regularly featured in the New Yorker, MAD Magazine and The Onion newspaper. His numerous books include Sh*t My President Says, God Is Disappointed in You, Apocrypha Now, and I Thought You Would Be Funnier. Web: TMCM.com, Twitter: @muchcoffee, IG: @MuchCoffeeMan

# BEFOREWORD
## by Kieron Dwyer

2016. A year that will live in infamy.

I still remember how unfathomable everything was, every single day of that year as we marched slowly, inexorably towards our terrible fate. So many of us laughed at the absurdity of it, the absolute insane absurdity of Donald tRump running for President to begin with. He'd danced around it so many times, for so long, a perpetual laughingstock, it was ridiculous that he was actually committing to it, actually following through on something so YUGE.

Each day brought new lows, fresh new Hells for us to contemplate. But we still thought it was a crazy dream that would end. Surely, the other Republicans would knock him out. He'd tire of the effort, give up like the petulant man-baby he's always been. No way he'd get the nomination. No way he'd WIN.

Even before tRump secured the Republican nomination, I found myself sitting outside my neighborhood Peet's Coffee on a warm summer afternoon, sipping my iced tea, avoiding my actual work for the day. I had my iPad with me as usual, but it was almost exclusively a work tool up to this fateful day. Suddenly, I was struck with a notion of what an intelligent alien life form might think some day in the not-so-distant future, should the unthinkable occur and tRump become President. And the following cartoon just tumbled out, the simplest, easiest way possible. It's magical when that happens, and it made me so happy to have the ability to think it, draw it, color it, and send it out to the world instantaneously, all from one device. Truly a blessing.

However, like many blessings, this came with a price. Once bitten, I found myself on Twitter and Facebook every day, taking in the latest news developments and feasting on them, fodder for my new obsession of documenting this slow-moving disaster in real time through cartoons. It felt great to be back doing something personal and reflective of my personal vision, after so long working on other people's ideas. I hadn't had such a direct pipeline from my mind to an audience since my adult humor series, *LCD: Lowest Comic Denominator,* in the early 2000's.

So here we are, looking both backward and forward. The election of 2020 is approaching and carries all the oppressive weight and expectation of 2016. Every election feels like the biggest, most important, most historic one, but there's no denying the gravity of this tRumpian era. With or without him, things will never be the same. We're through the looking glass, people.

Truly, everything now is UNPRESIDENTED.

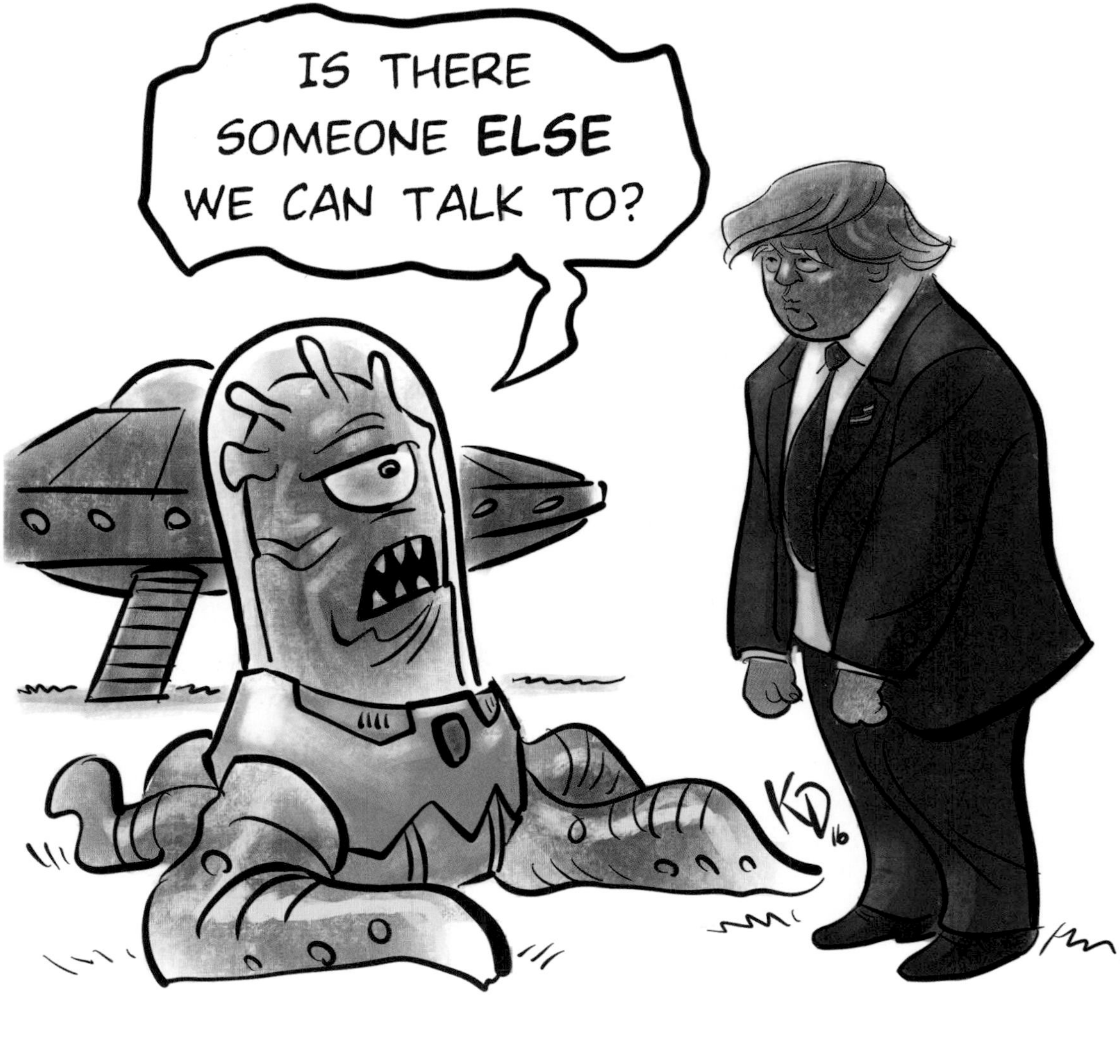
IS THERE SOMEONE **ELSE** WE CAN TALK TO?
KD 16

# THE EGO HAS LANDED

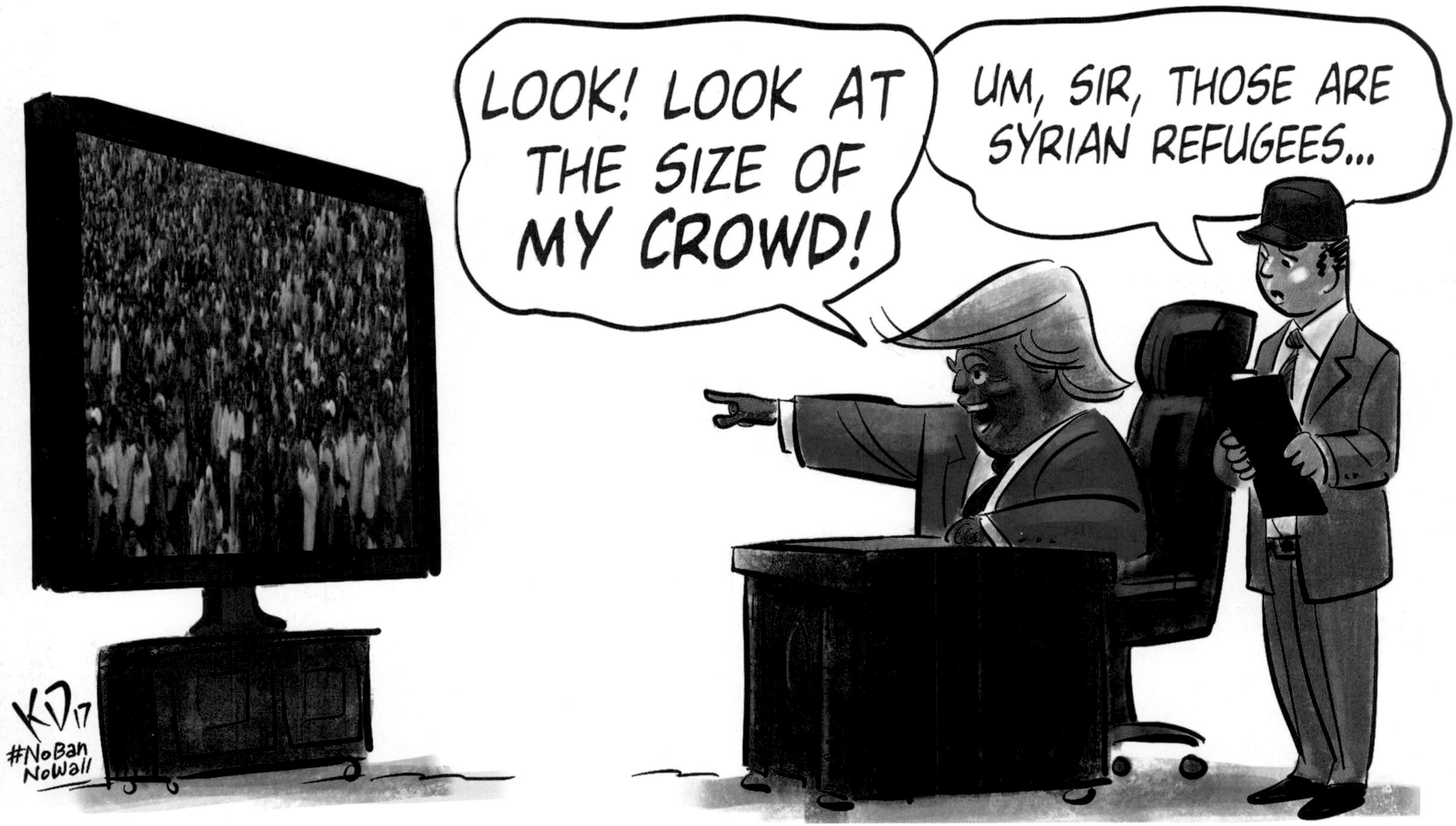
LOOK! LOOK AT THE SIZE OF MY CROWD!
UM, SIR, THOSE ARE SYRIAN REFUGEES...
KD 17
#NoBan NoWall

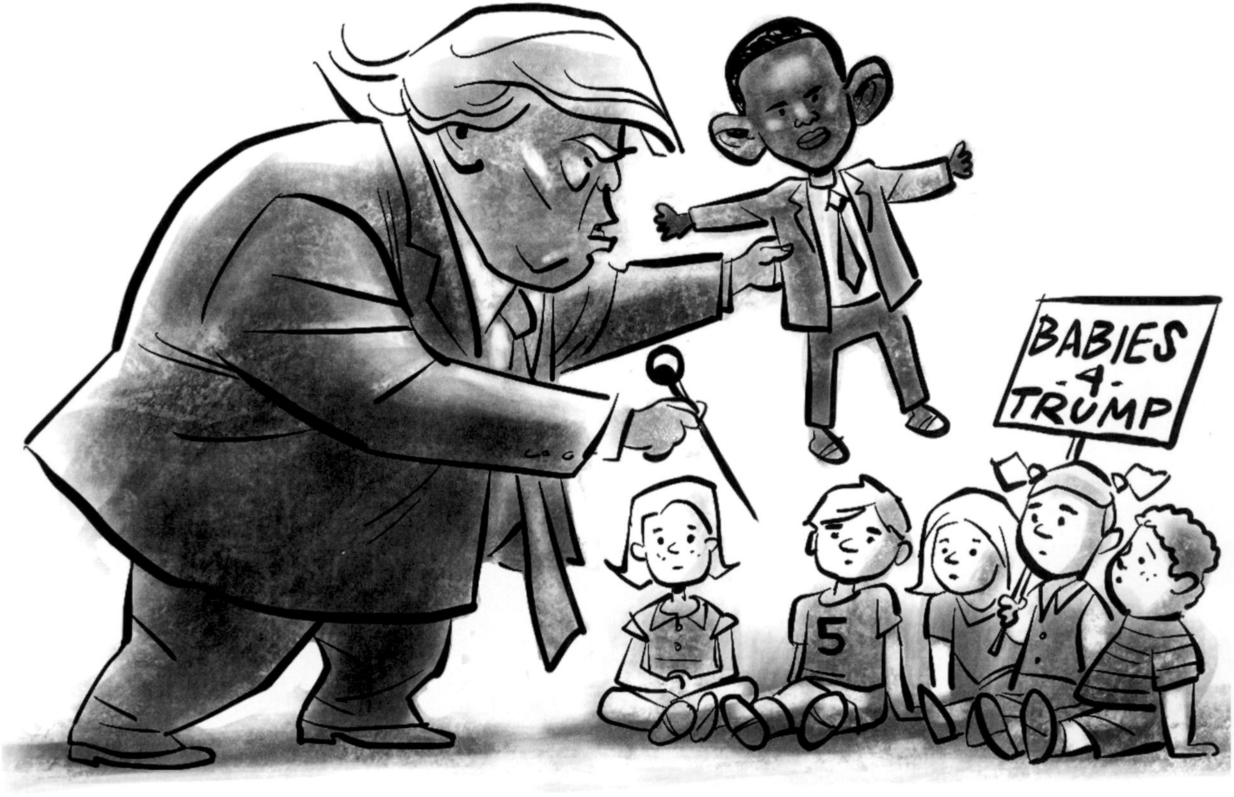
BABIES
-4-
TRUMP
5

*"Show me on the doll where the Black people hurt you."*

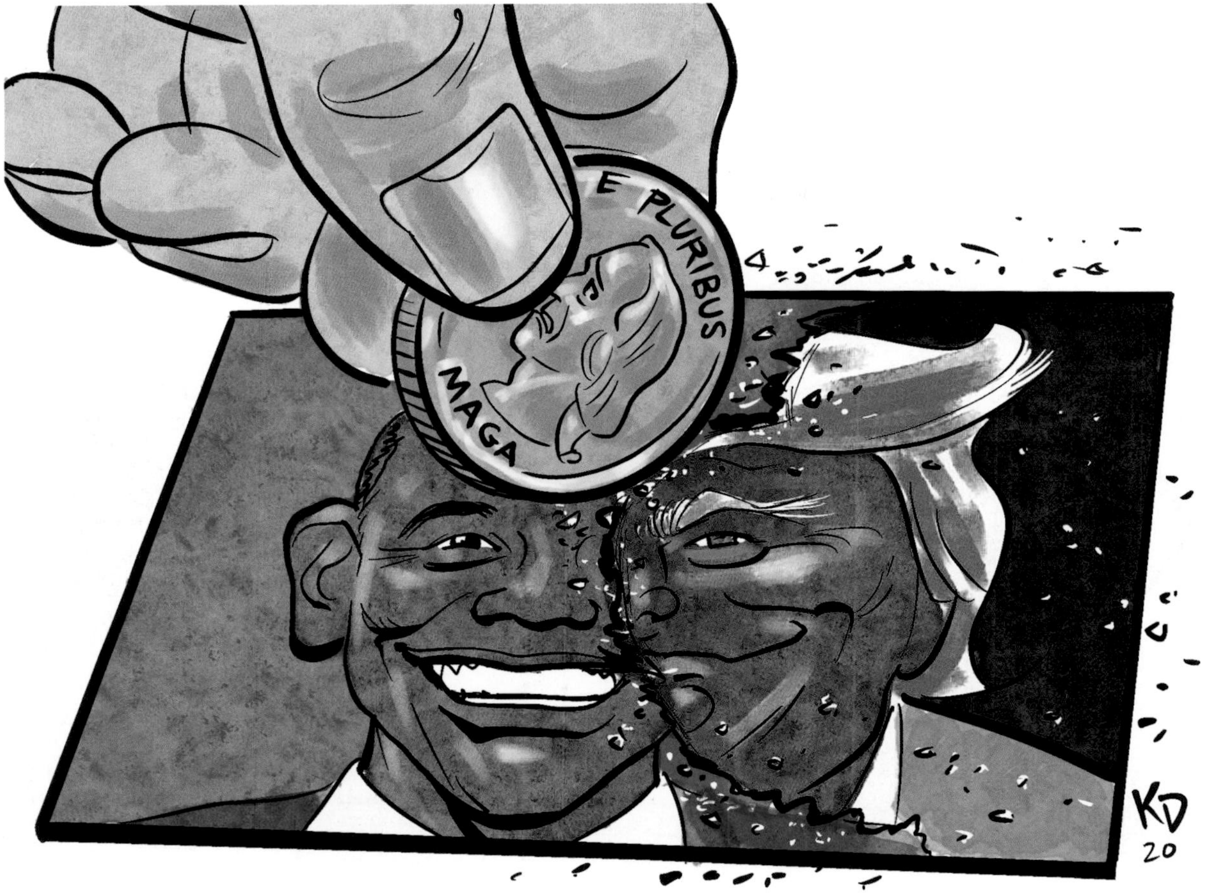
E PLURIBUS
MAGA
KD
20

*The Erase-ist Agenda*

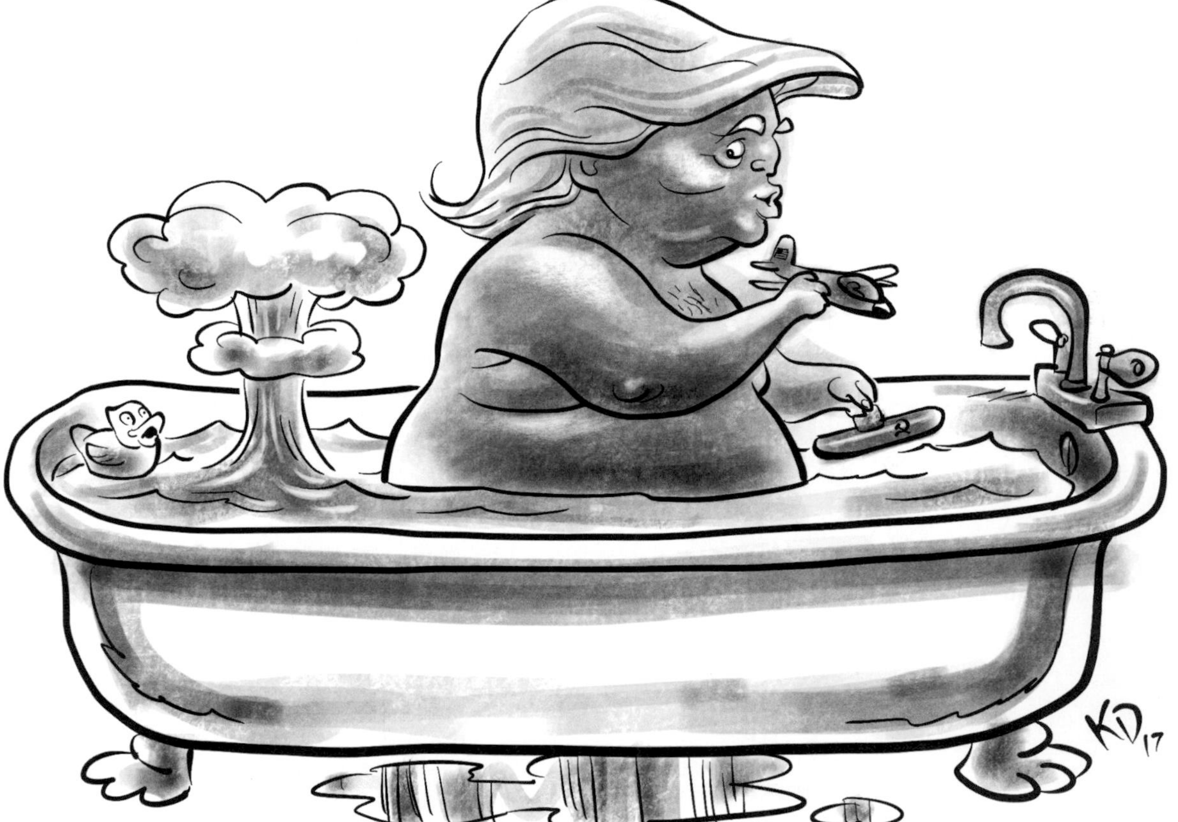
KD 17

*Emission Accomplished*

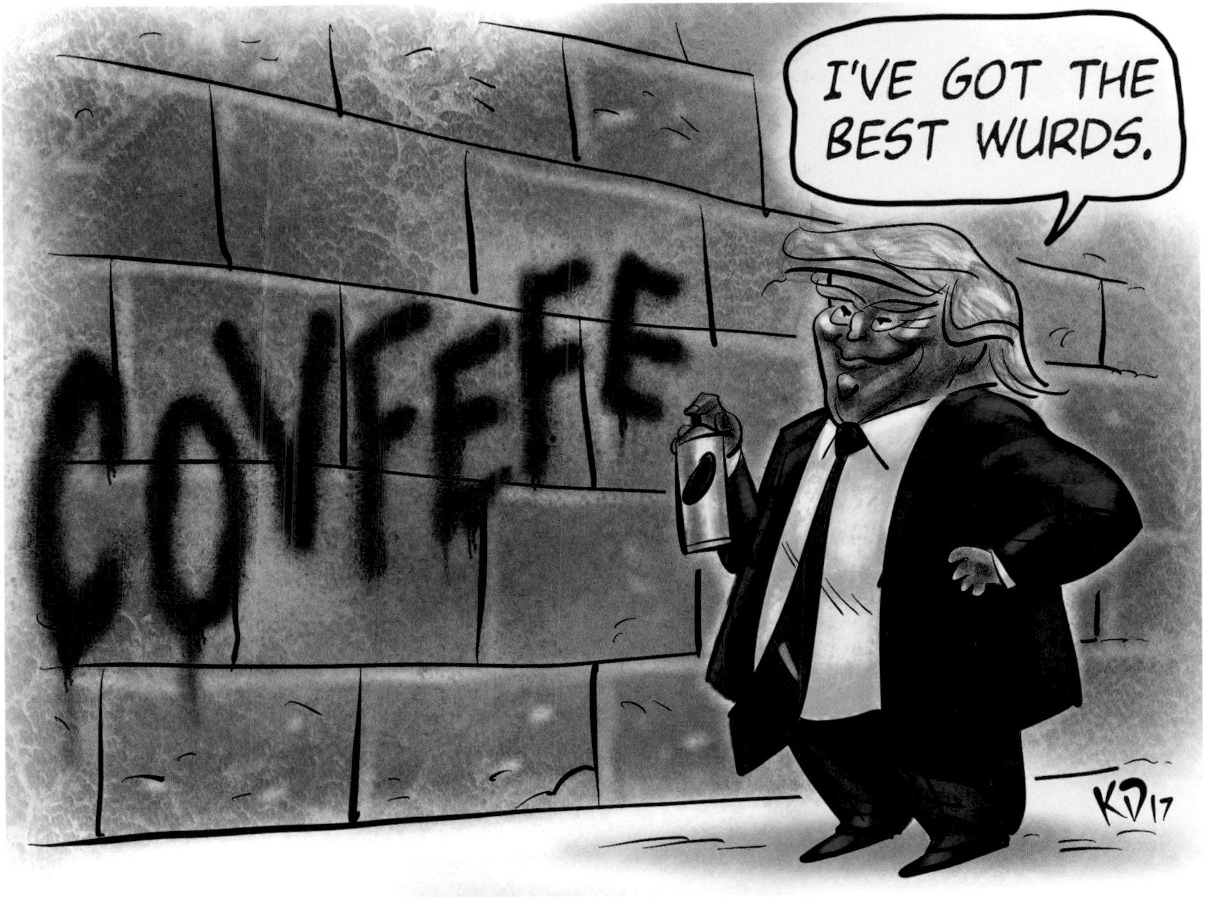
COVFEFE
I'VE GOT THE BEST WURDS.
KD17

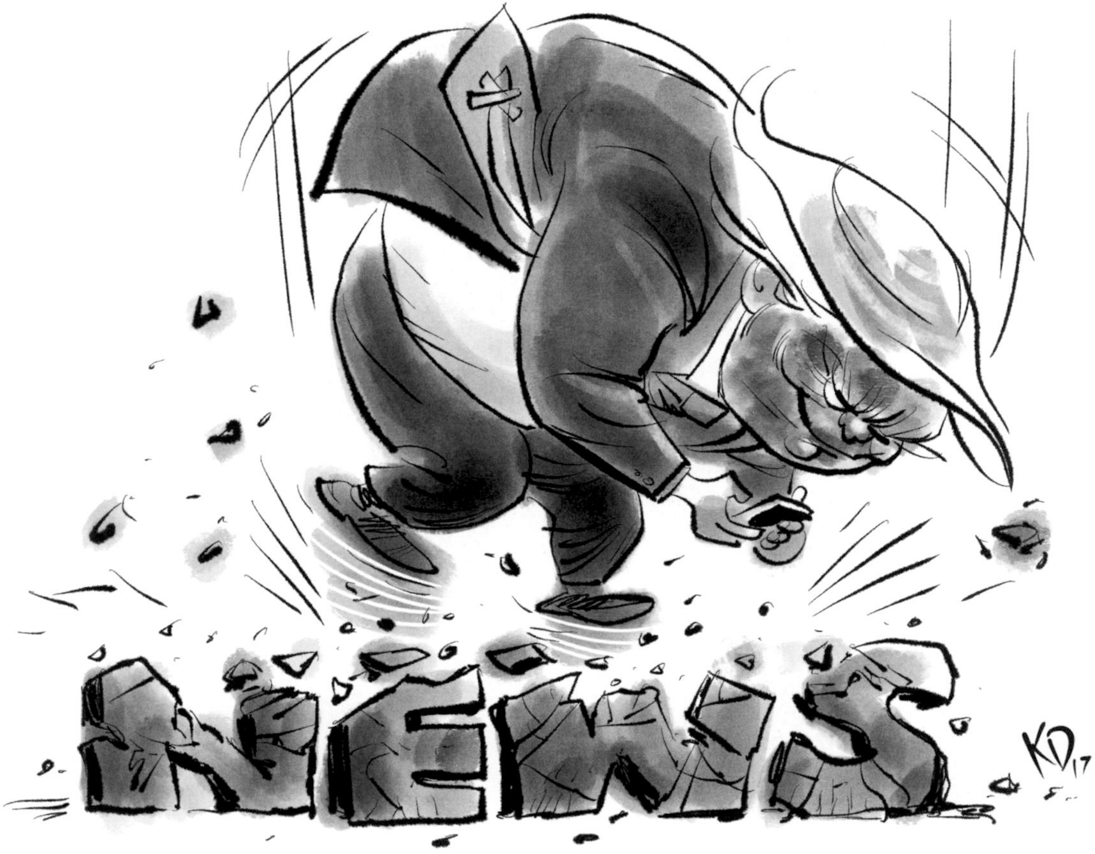
NEWS
KD17

*Breaking News*

# ORANGE BULL* GIVES YOU WINGS

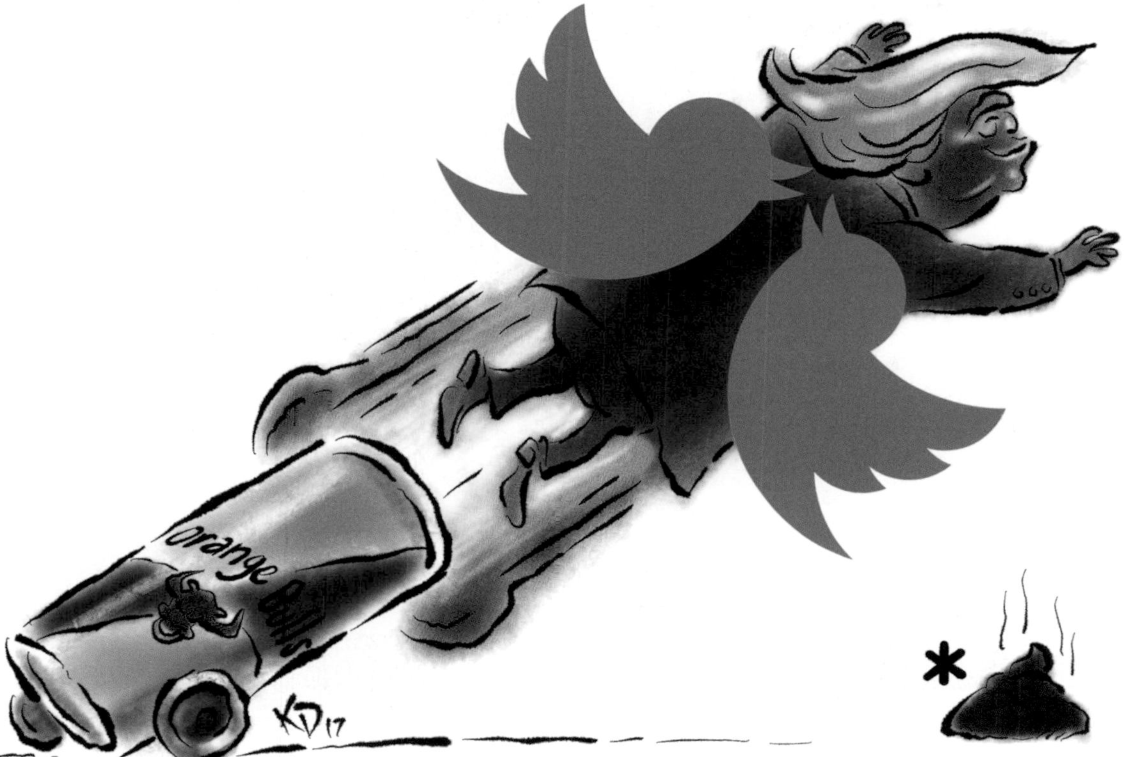
Orange Bulls
*

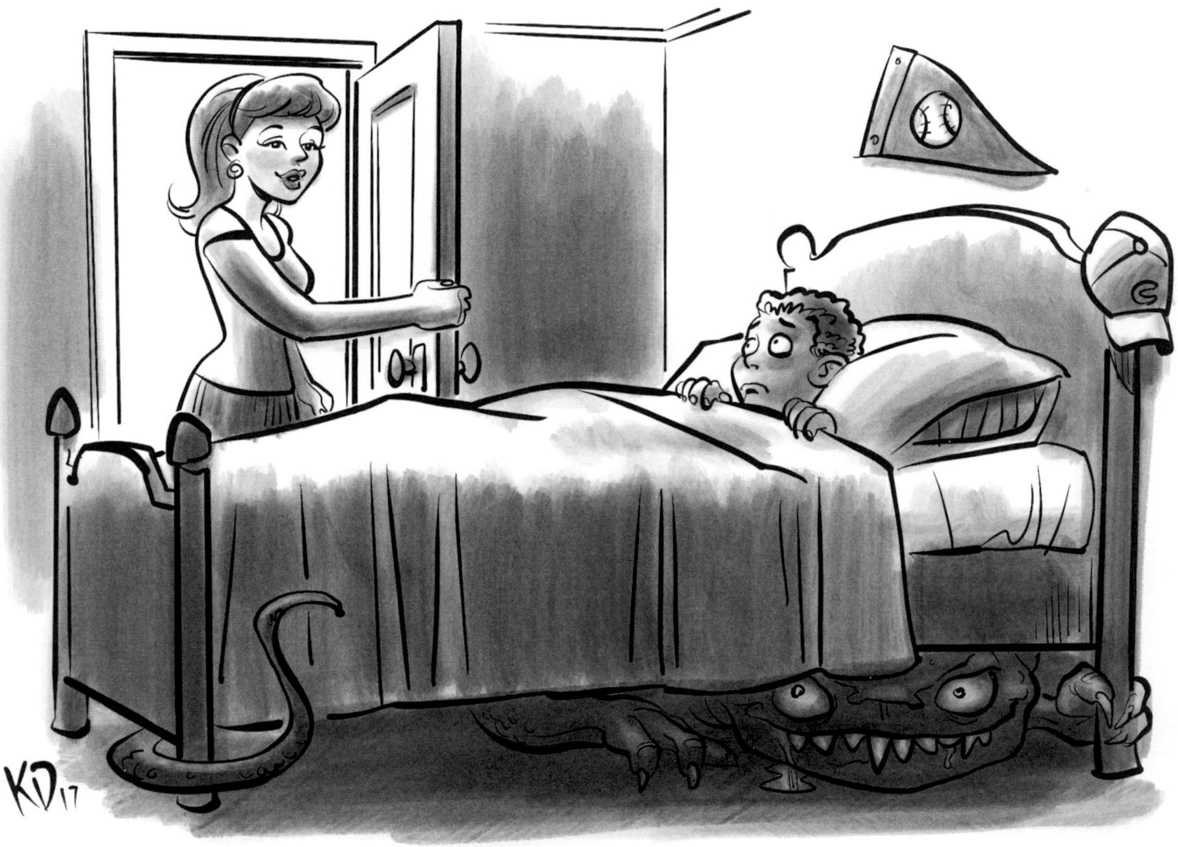

*"Honey, don't be silly. There's no such thing as Covfefe."*

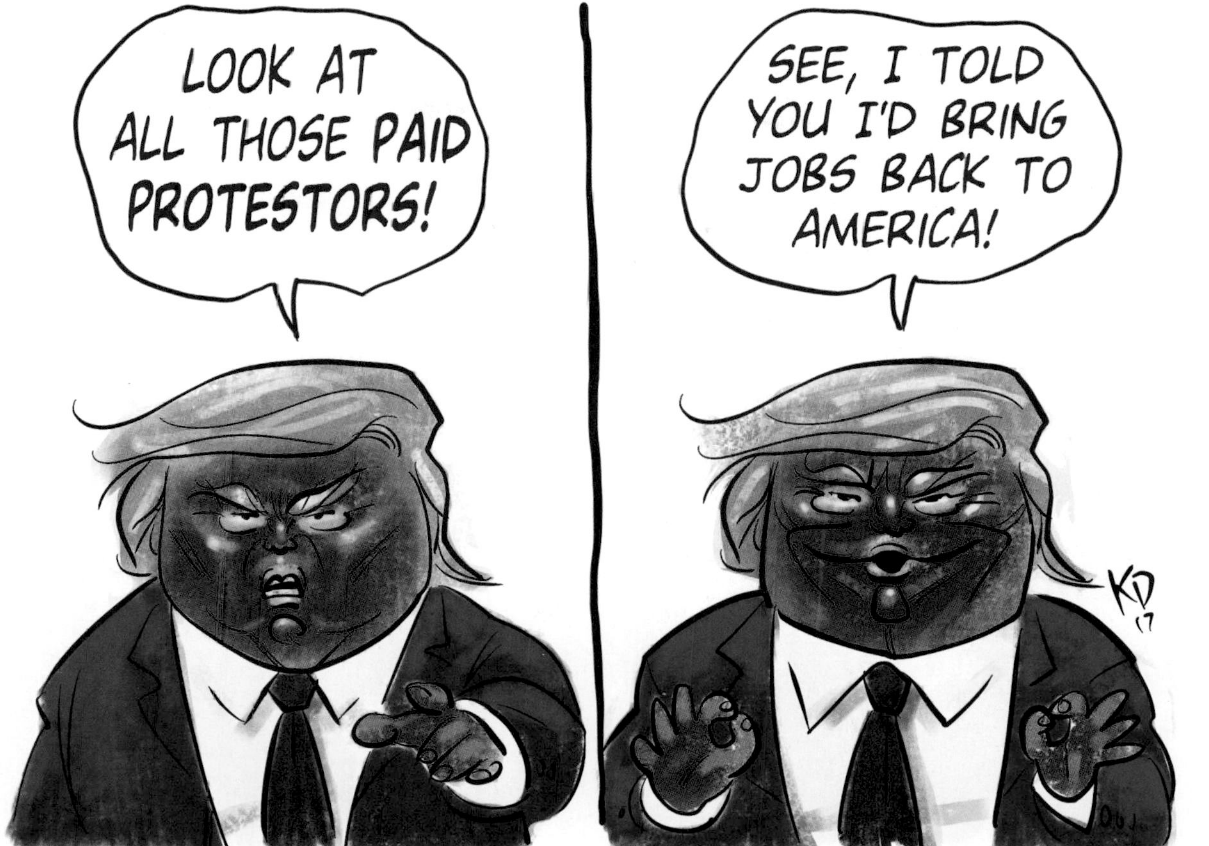
LOOK AT ALL THOSE PAID PROTESTORS!
SEE, I TOLD YOU I'D BRING JOBS BACK TO AMERICA!
KD 17

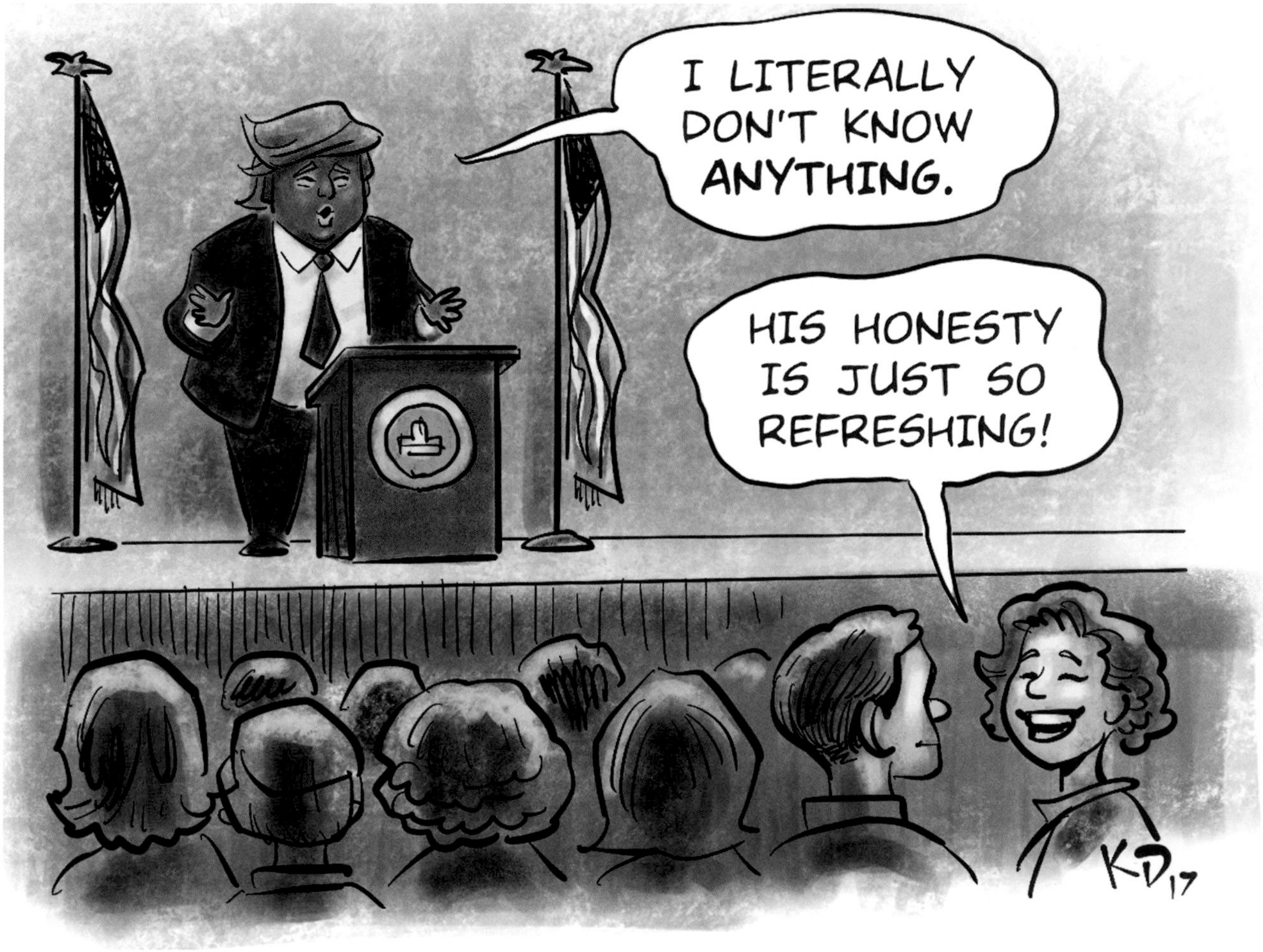
I LITERALLY DON'T KNOW ANYTHING.
HIS HONESTY IS JUST SO REFRESHING!
KD 17

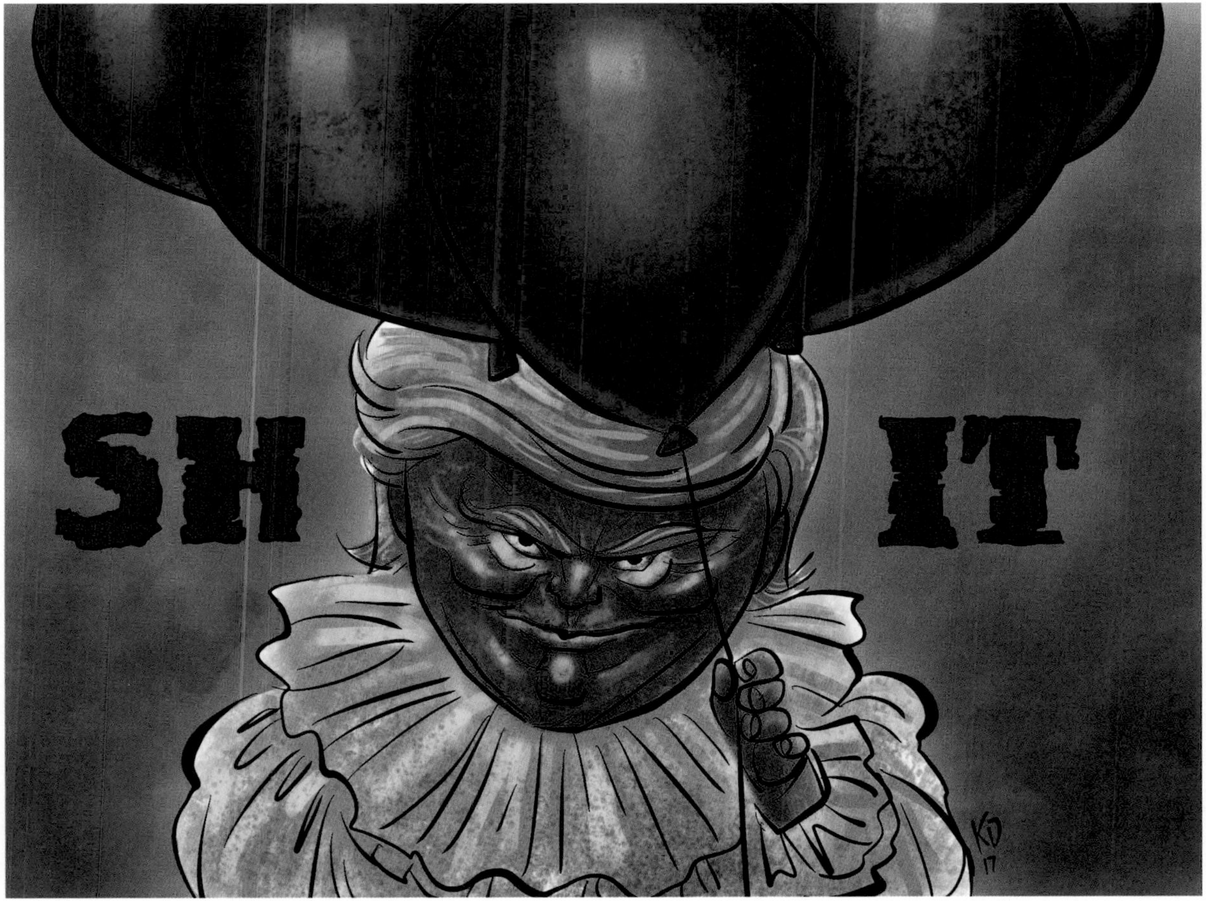
SH
IT
KD
17

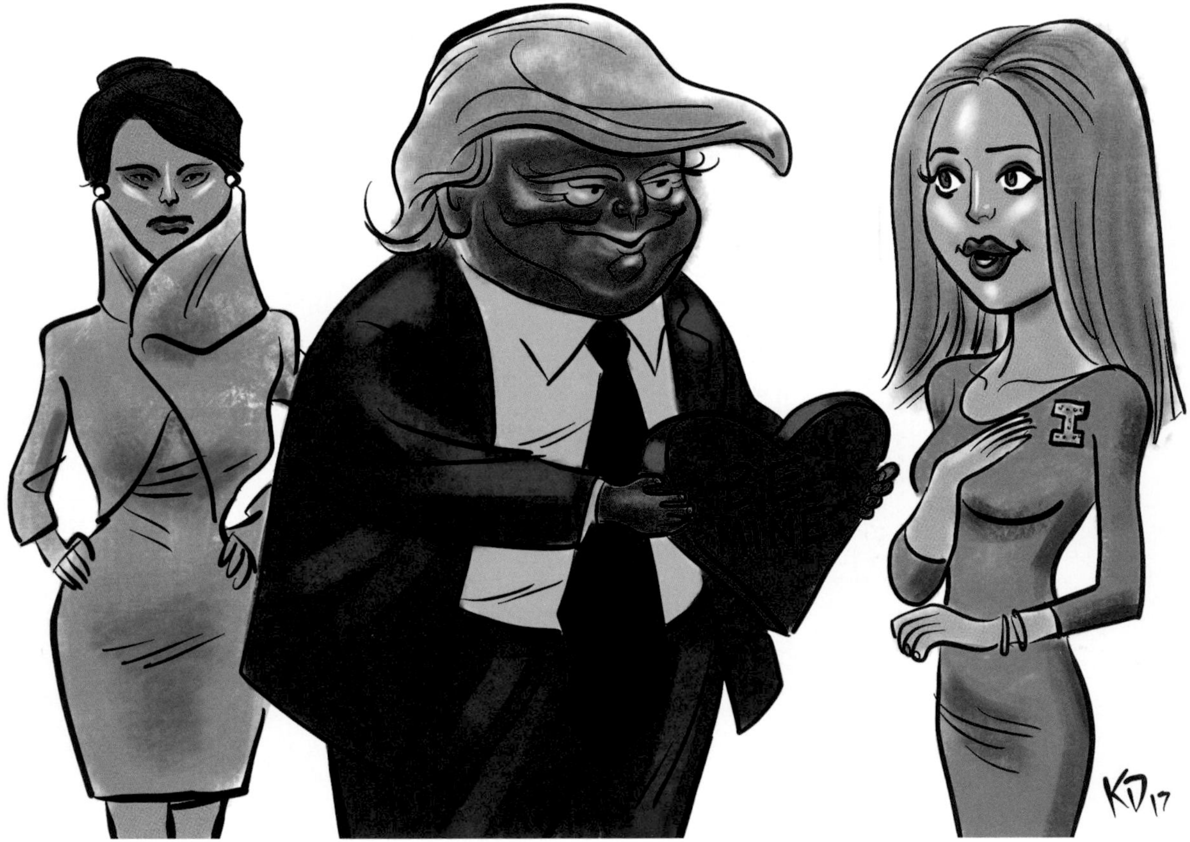
KD17

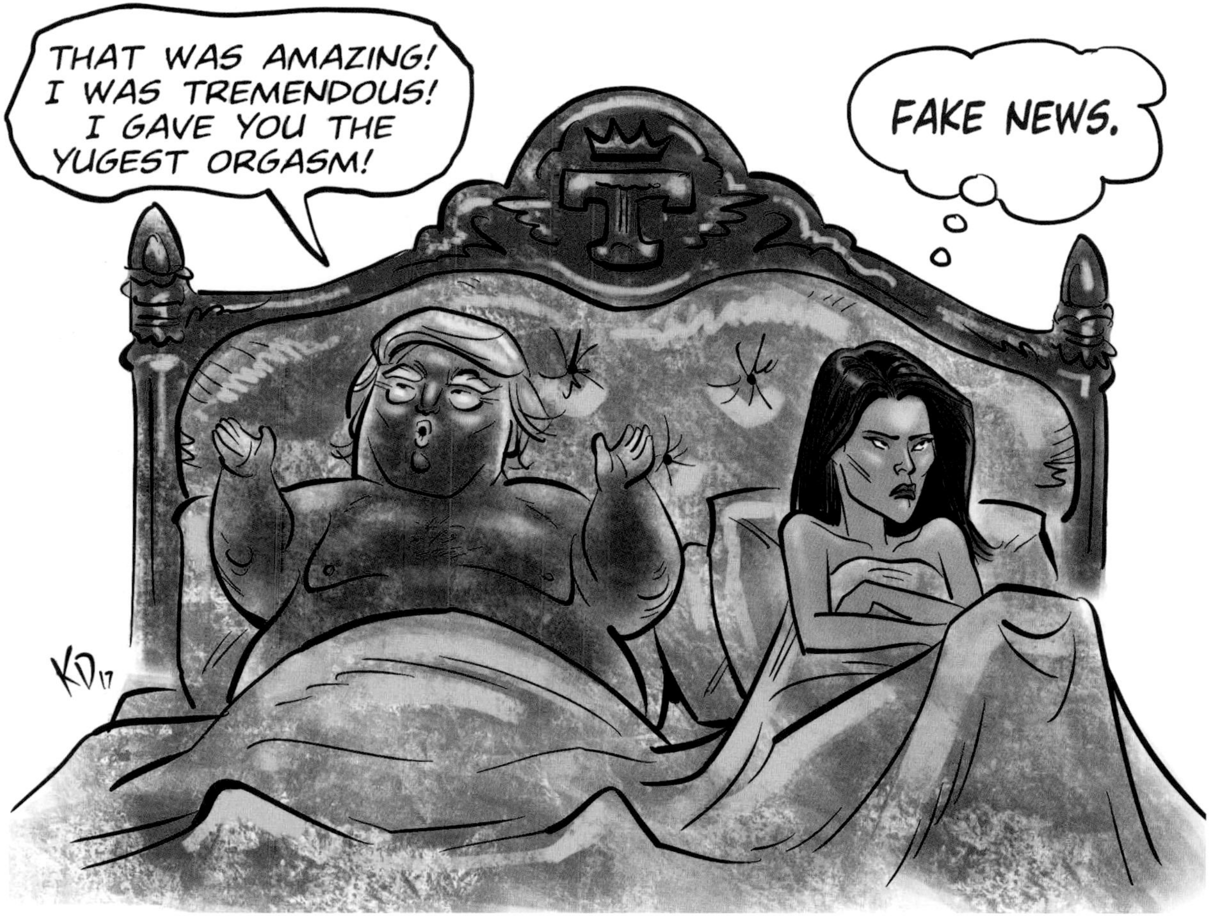
THAT WAS AMAZING! I WAS TREMENDOUS! I GAVE YOU THE YUGEST ORGASM!
FAKE NEWS.
KD 17

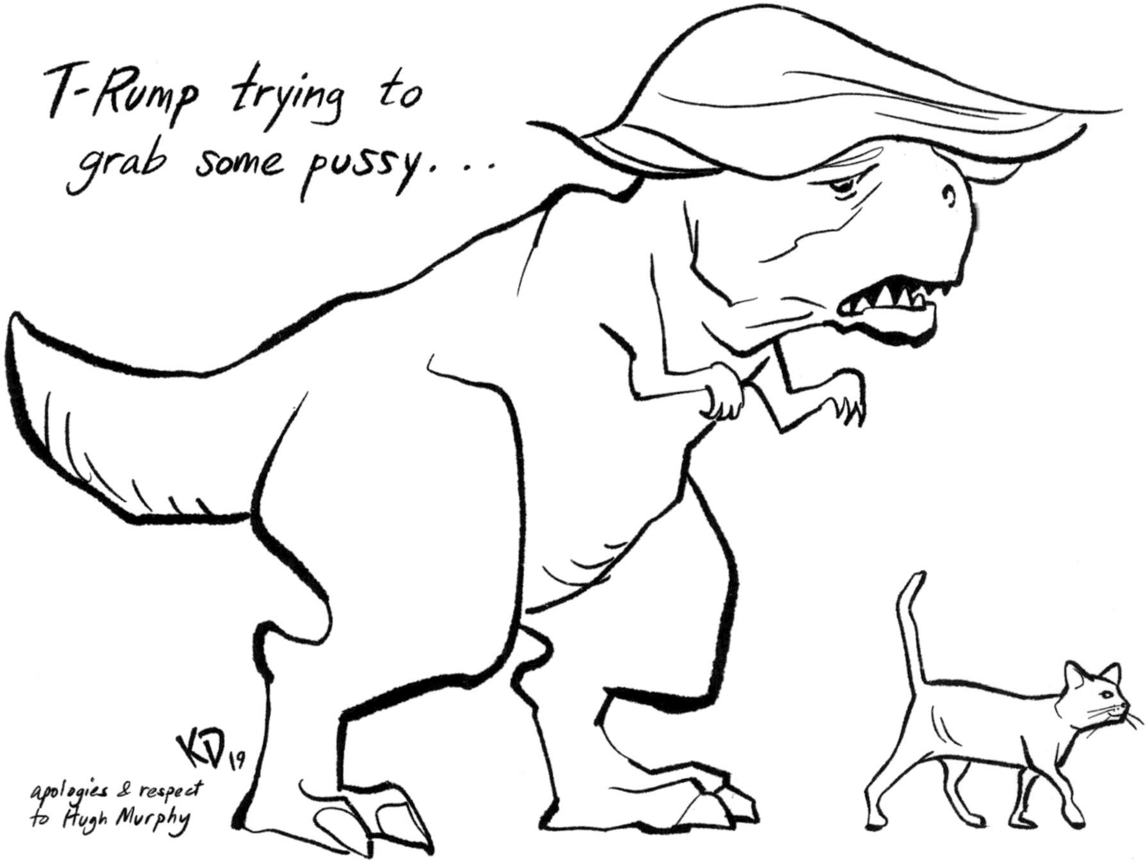
T-Rump trying to grab some pussy...
KD 19
apologies & respect to Hugh Murphy

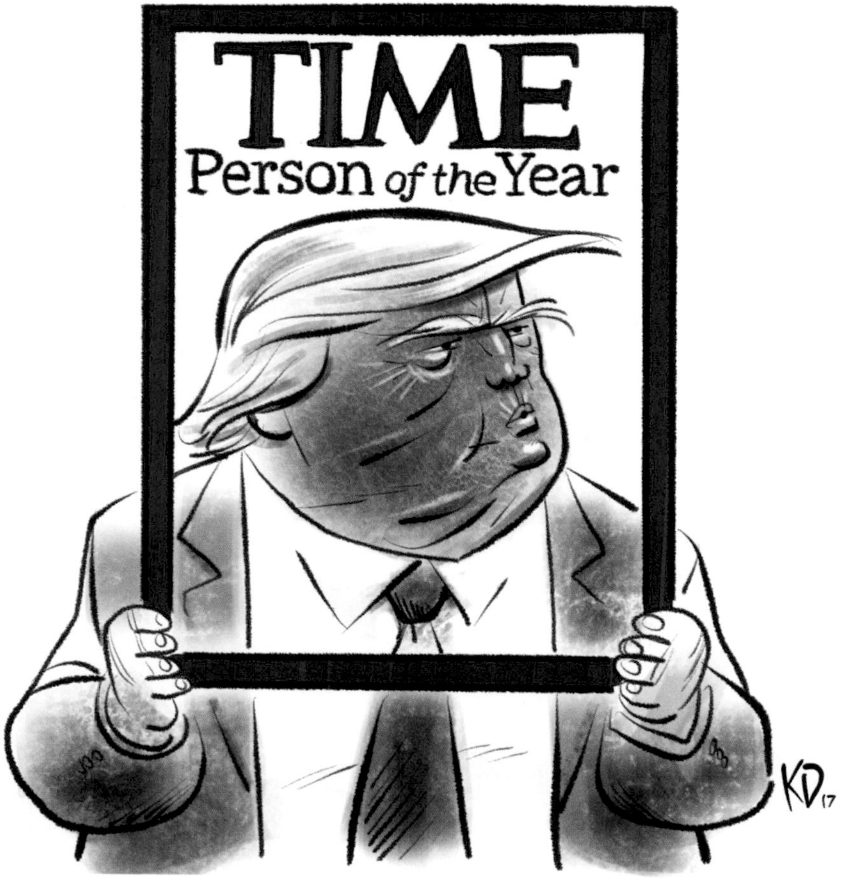
TIME
Person of the Year
KD 17

*Framed*

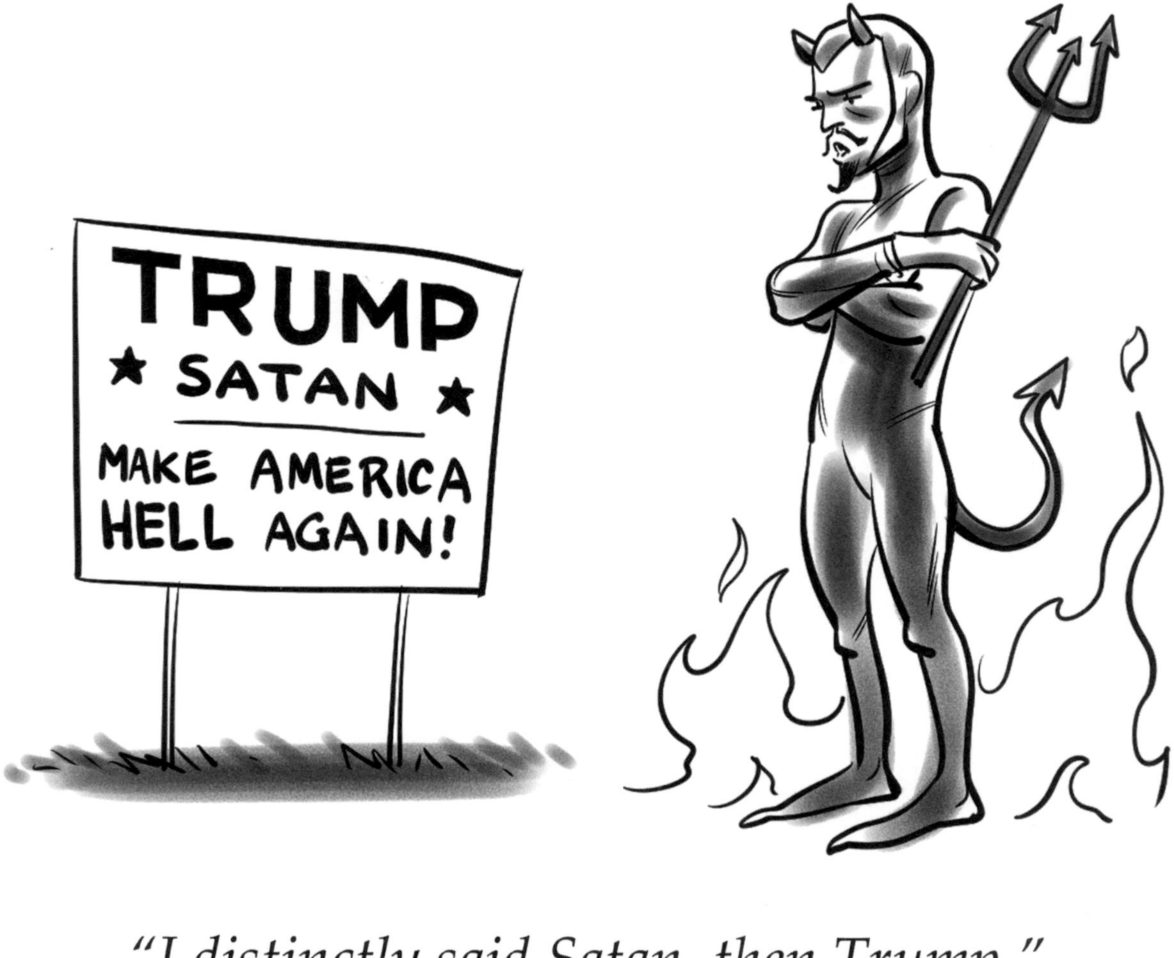
TRUMP
SATAN
MAKE AMERICA HELL AGAIN!

*"I distinctly said Satan, then Trump."*

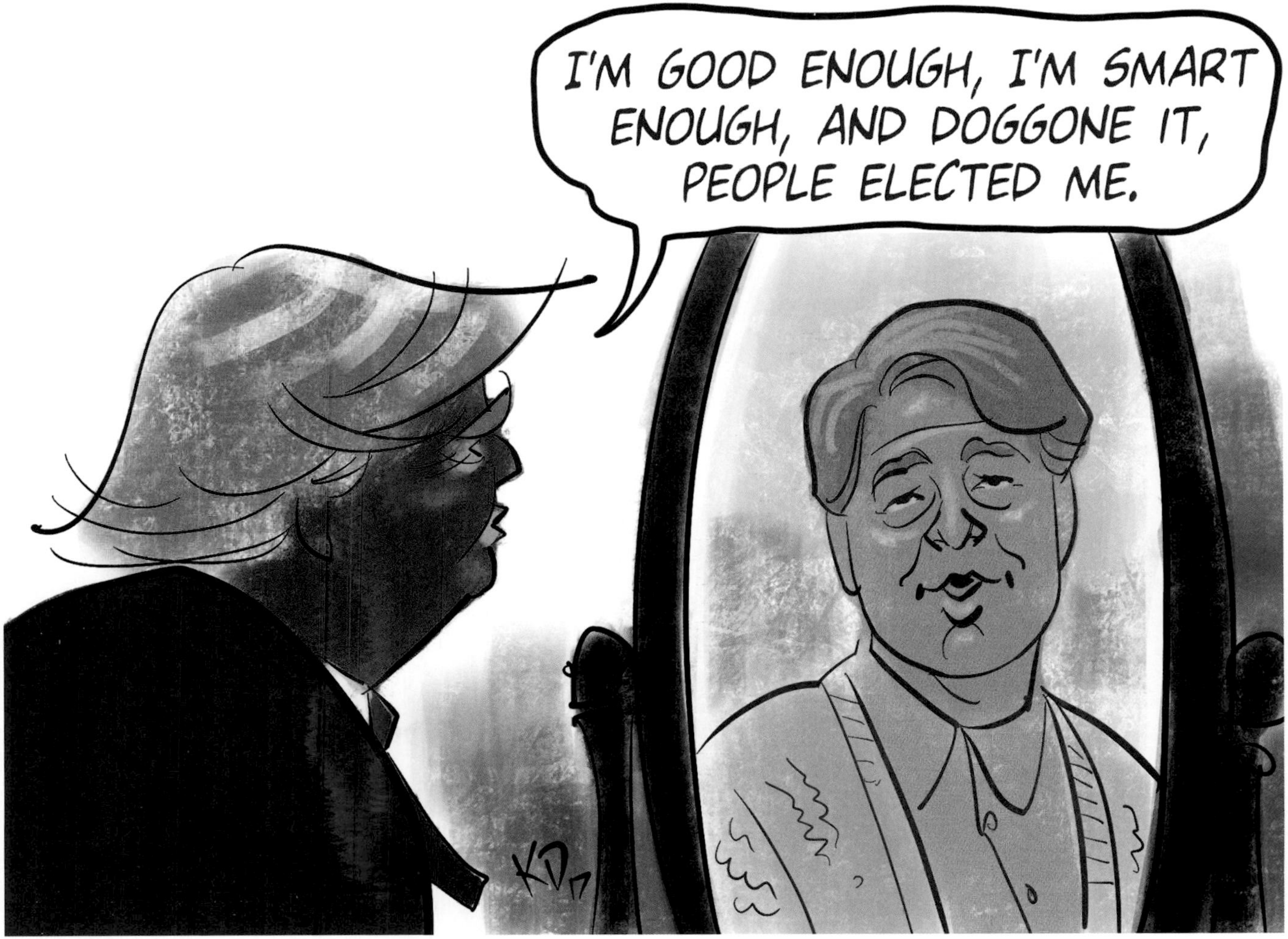
I'M GOOD ENOUGH, I'M SMART ENOUGH, AND DOGGONE IT, PEOPLE ELECTED ME.
KD

*President Stu Smiley*

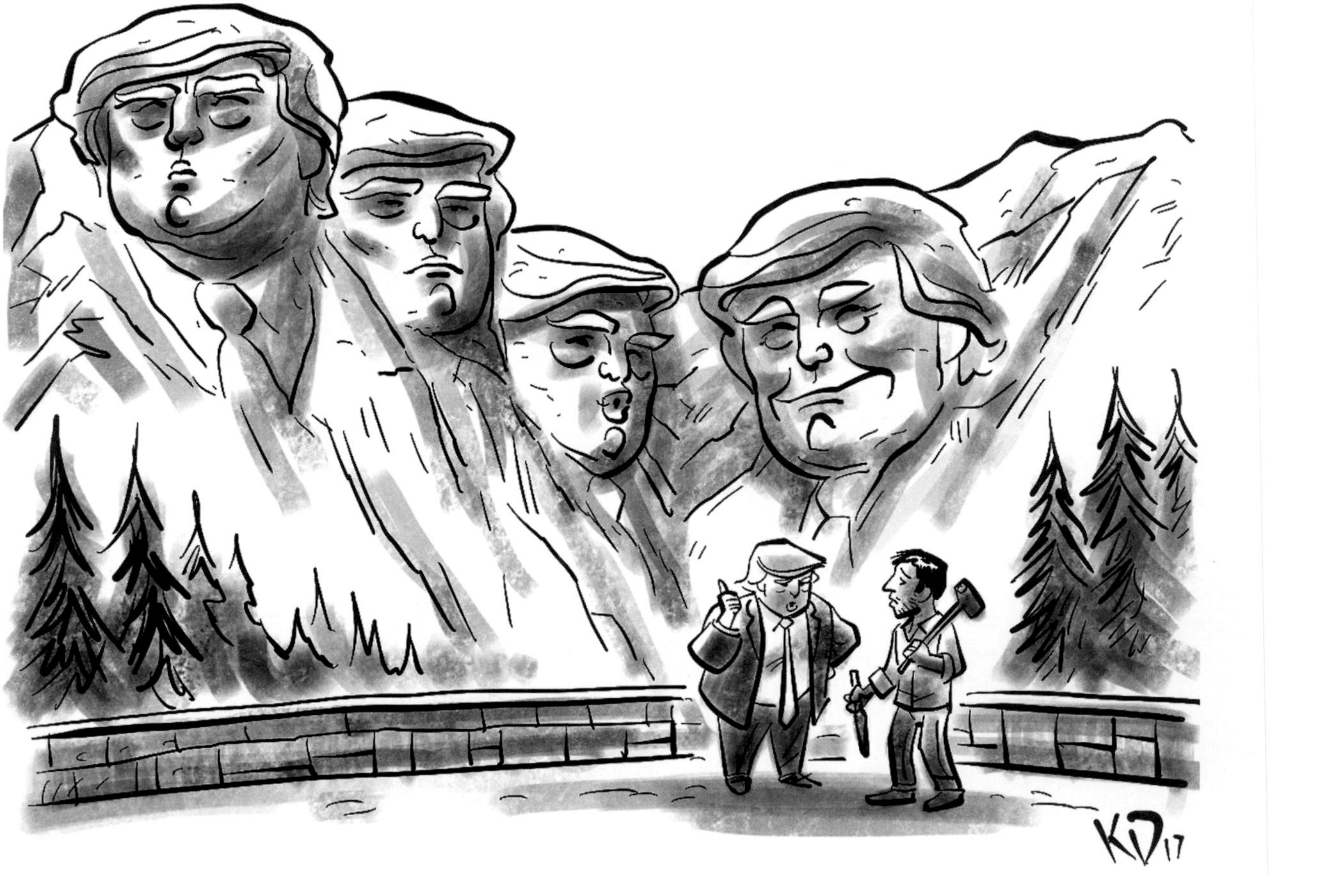

*"Yeah, let's go ahead and do a fifth one, for balance."*

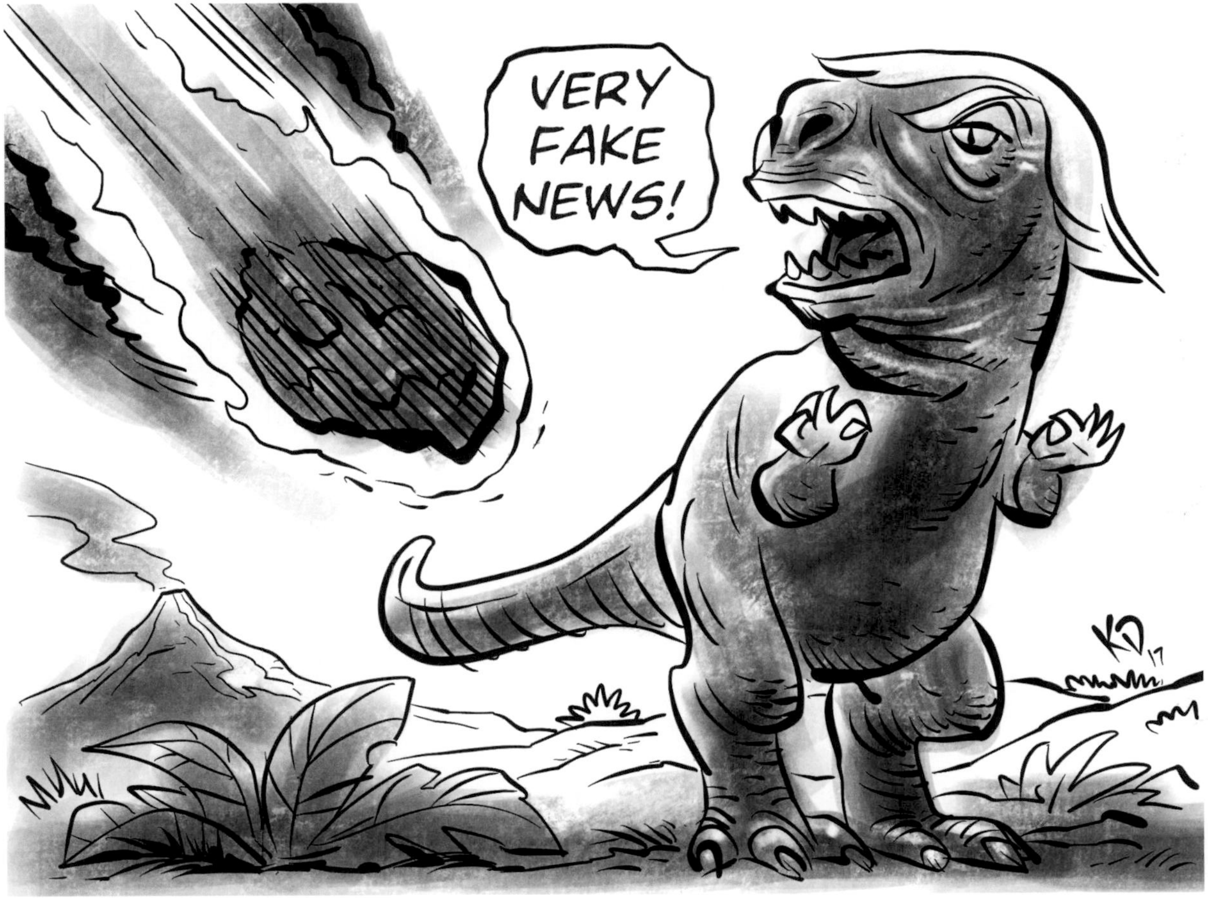
VERY FAKE NEWS!
KD 17

*Extinction Imminent*

ORANGE LIES MATTER

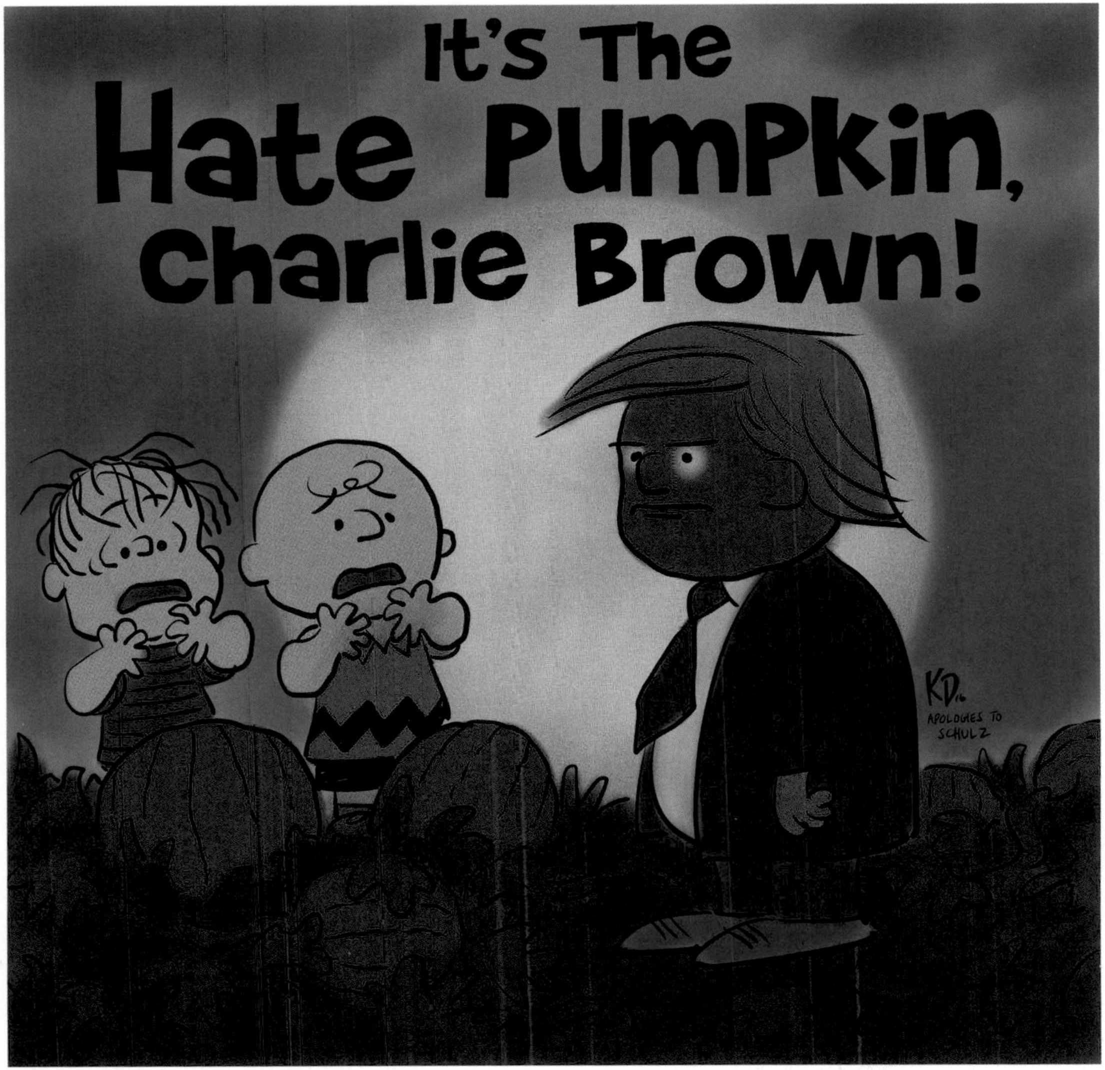
It's The
Hate Pumpkin,
Charlie Brown!
KD.16
APOLOGIES TO SCHULZ

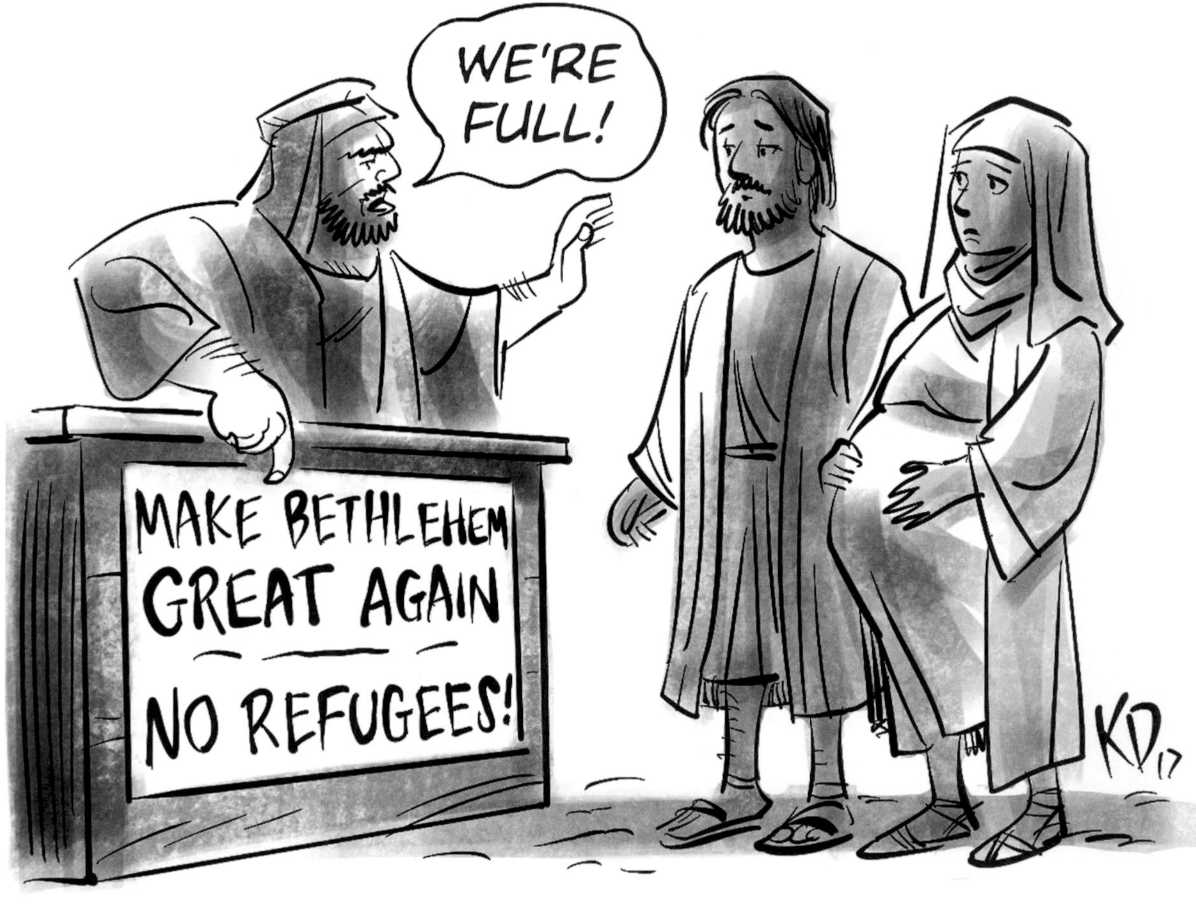
WE'RE FULL!
MAKE BETHLEHEM GREAT AGAIN
NO REFUGEES!
KD 17

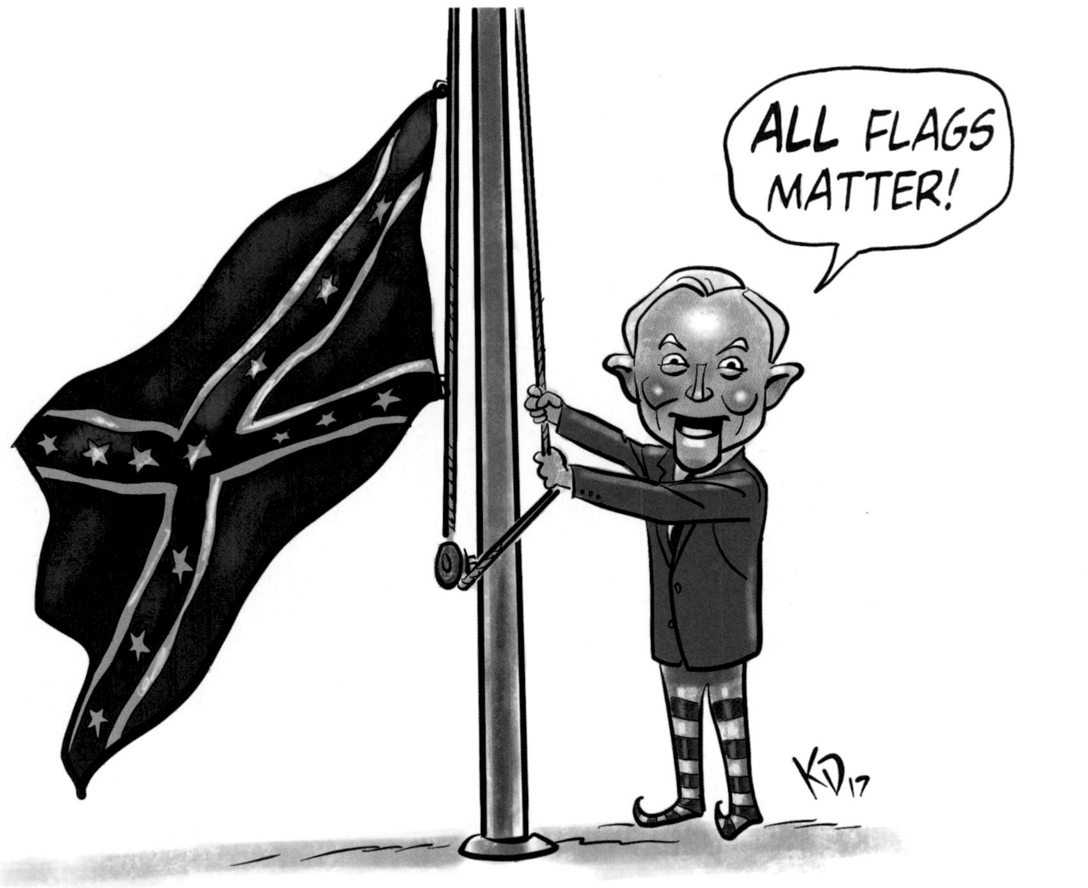
ALL FLAGS MATTER!
KD 17

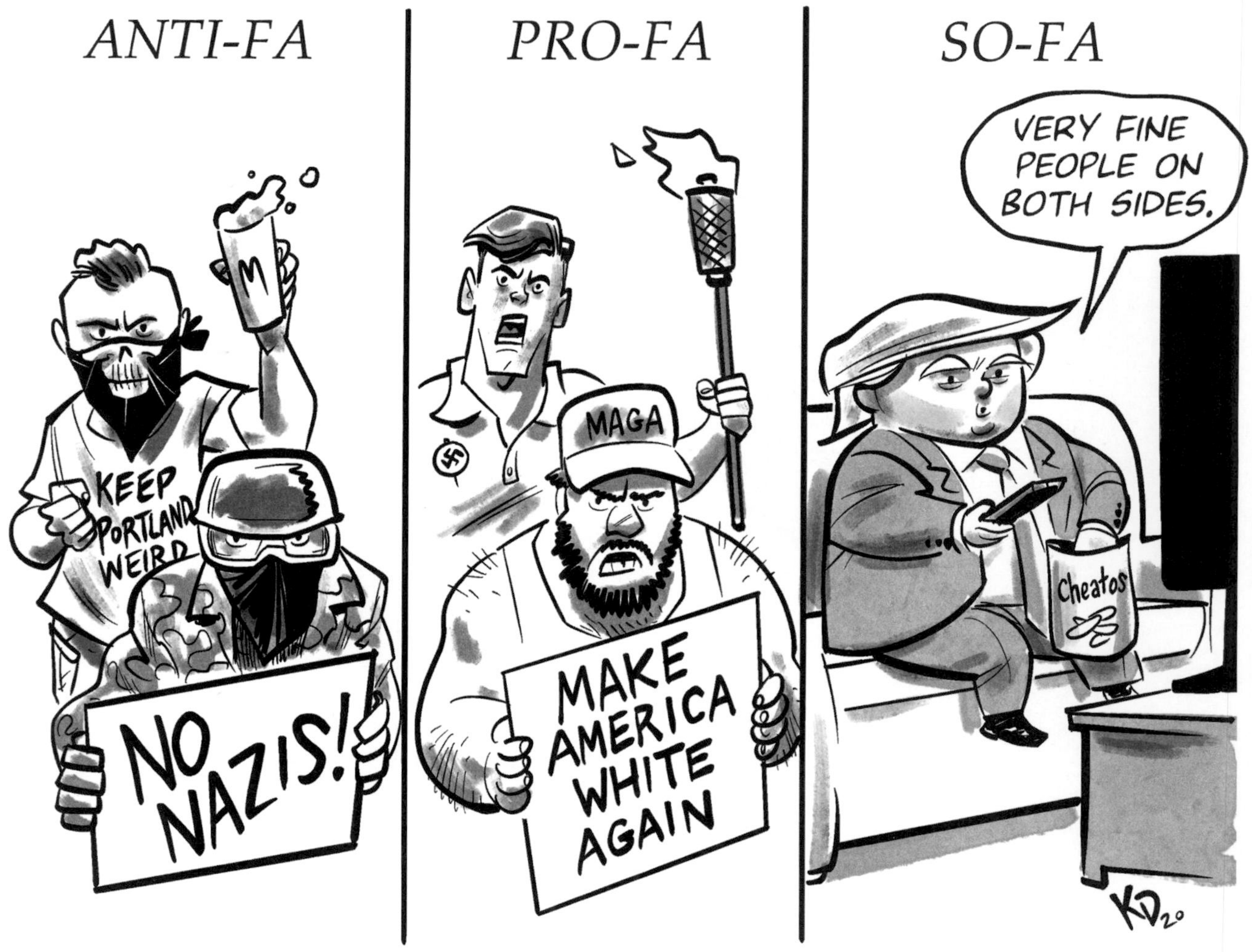
ANTI-FA
PRO-FA
SO-FA
M
KEEP PORTLAND WEIRD
NO NAZIS!
MAGA
MAKE AMERICA WHITE AGAIN
VERY FINE PEOPLE ON BOTH SIDES.
Cheatos
KD20

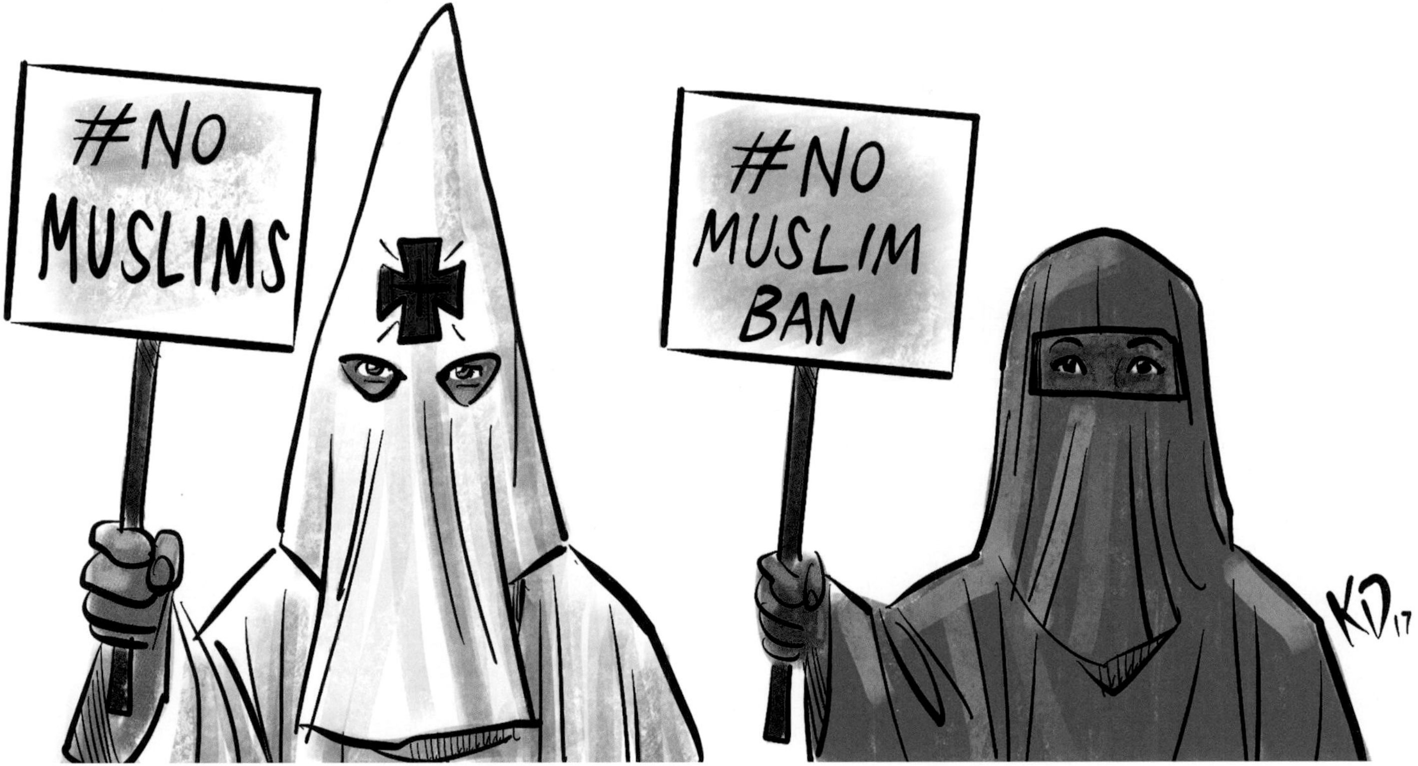
#NO MUSLIMS
#NO MUSLIM BAN
KD 17

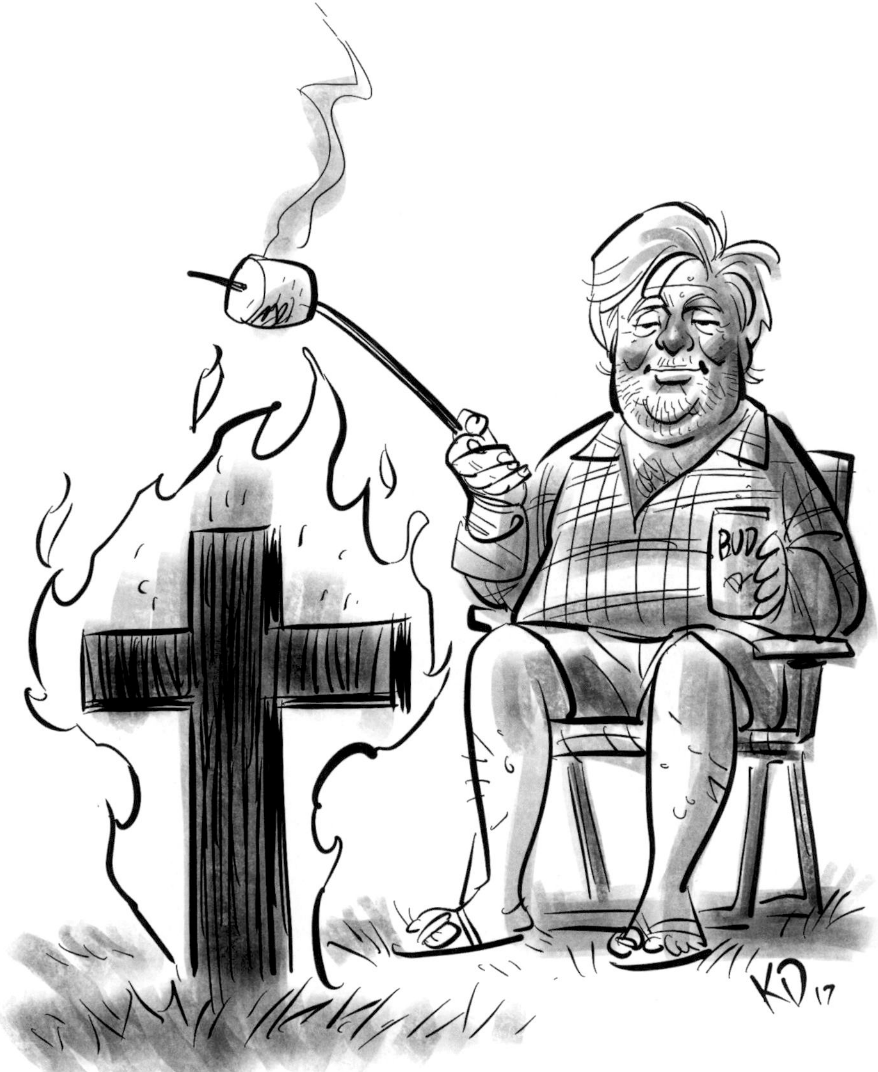
BUD
KD 17

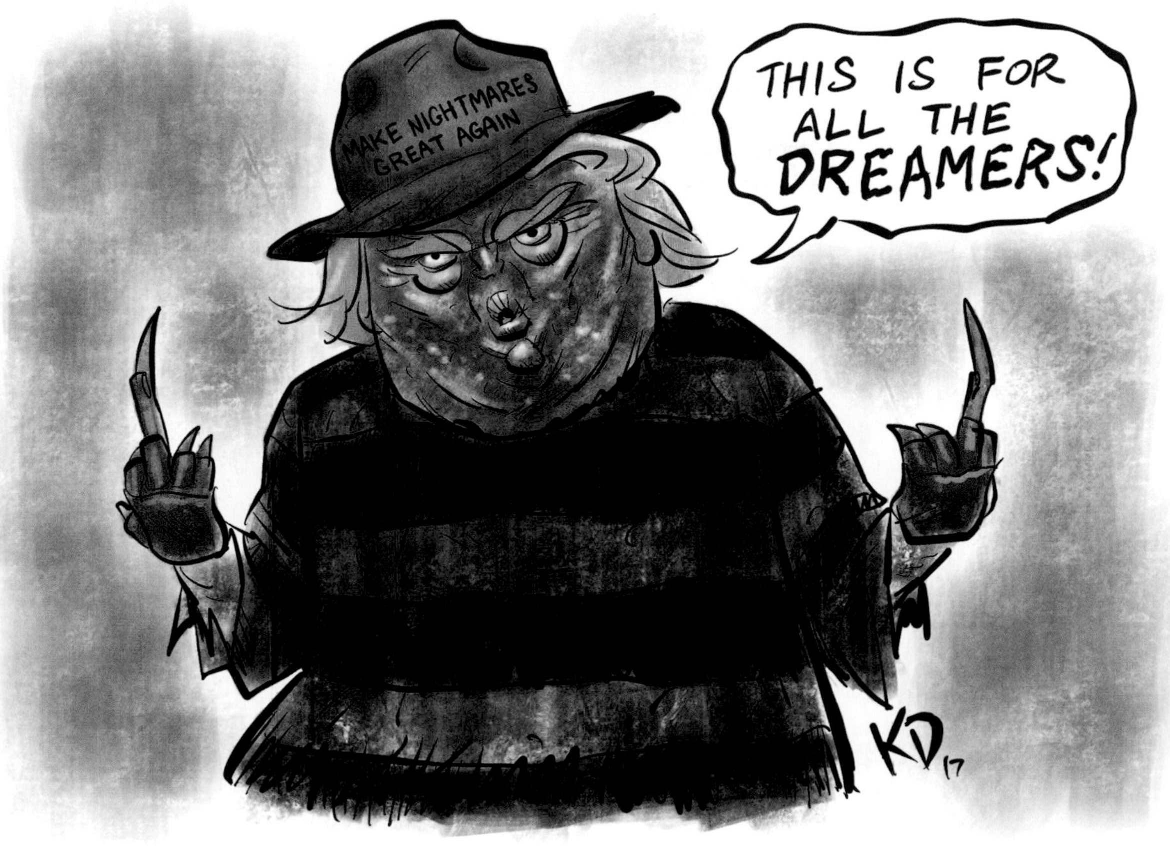
MAKE NIGHTMARES GREAT AGAIN
THIS IS FOR ALL THE DREAMERS!
KD 17

*Nightmare on Every Street*

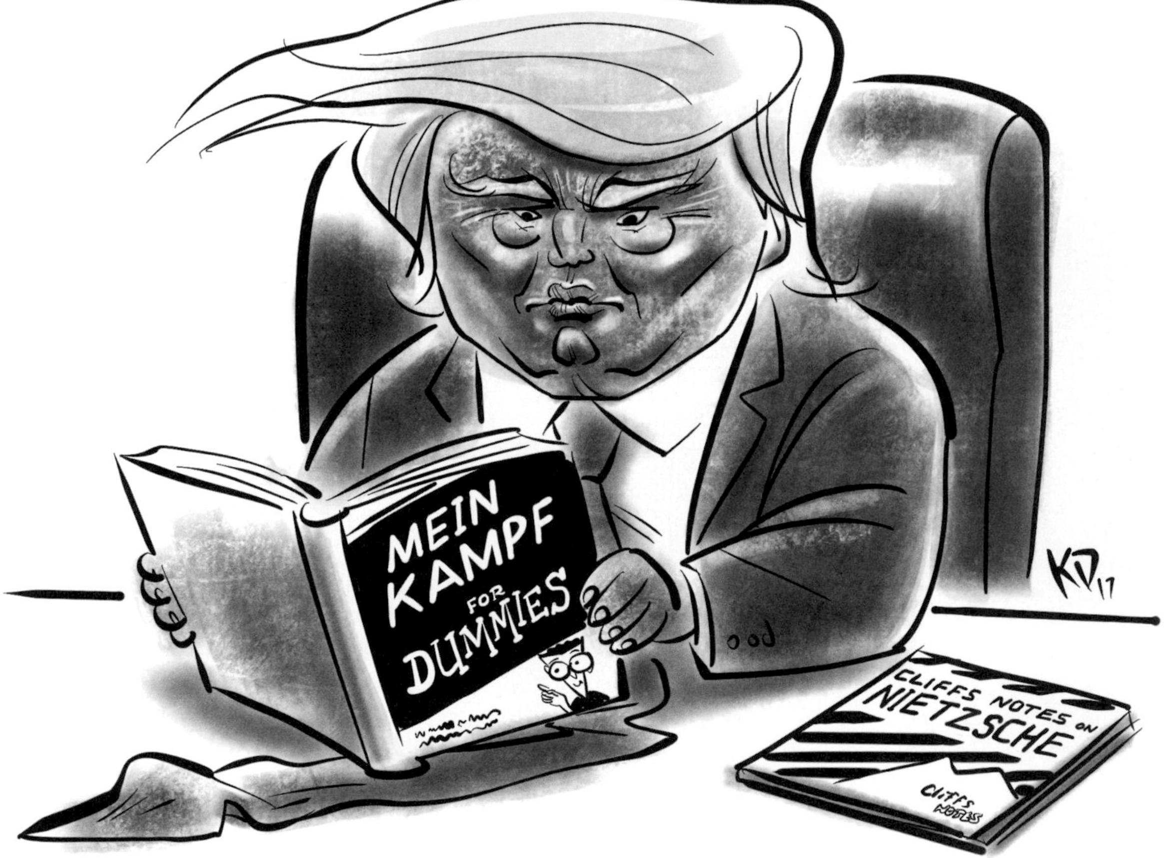
MEIN KAMPF FOR DUMMIES
CLIFFS NOTES ON NIETZSCHE
CLIFFS NOTES
KD 17

*"There is no Upside-Down. Period."*

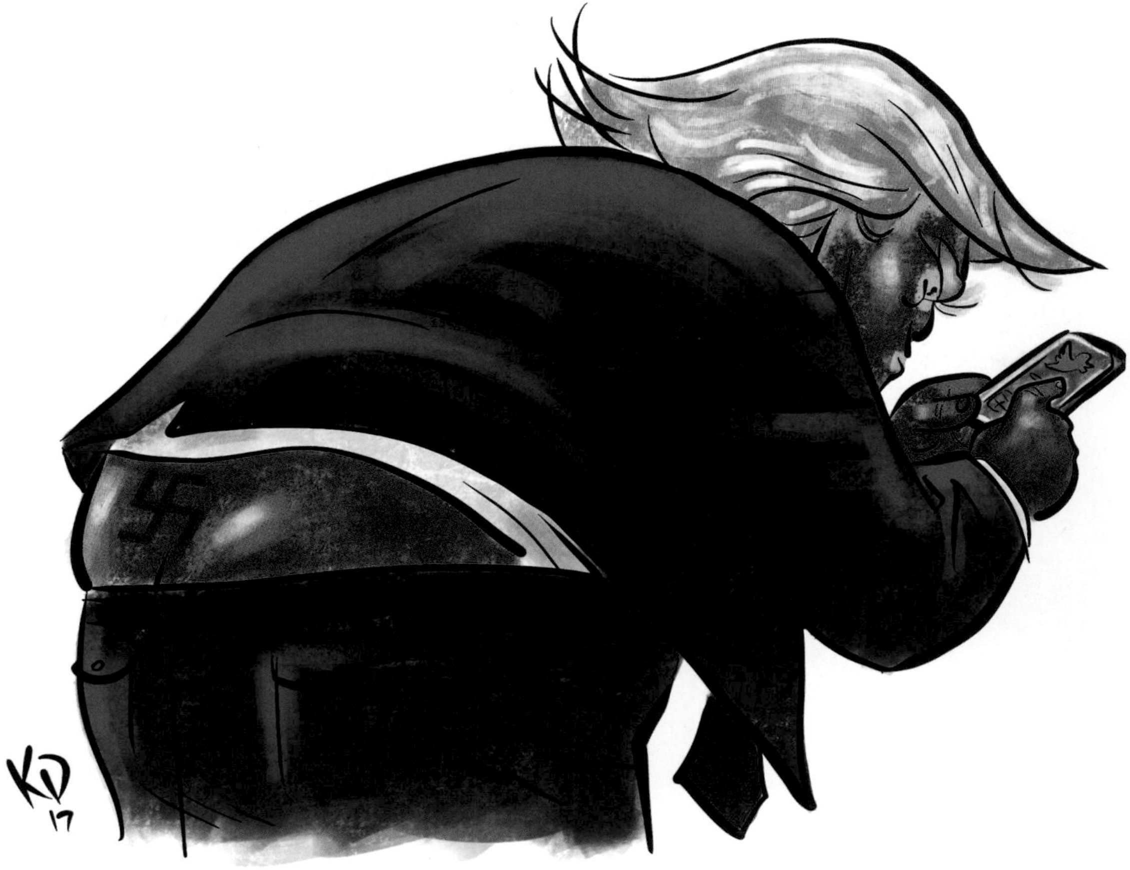
KD
17

*Trump Stamp*

1 2 3 4 5 6 7 8 9 10
NAZI
Punch
Card
Punch 19 and 20th is FREE!
11 12 13 14 15 16 17 18 19 20
© 2017 kierondwyer.com

# PUTIN'S PUPPET

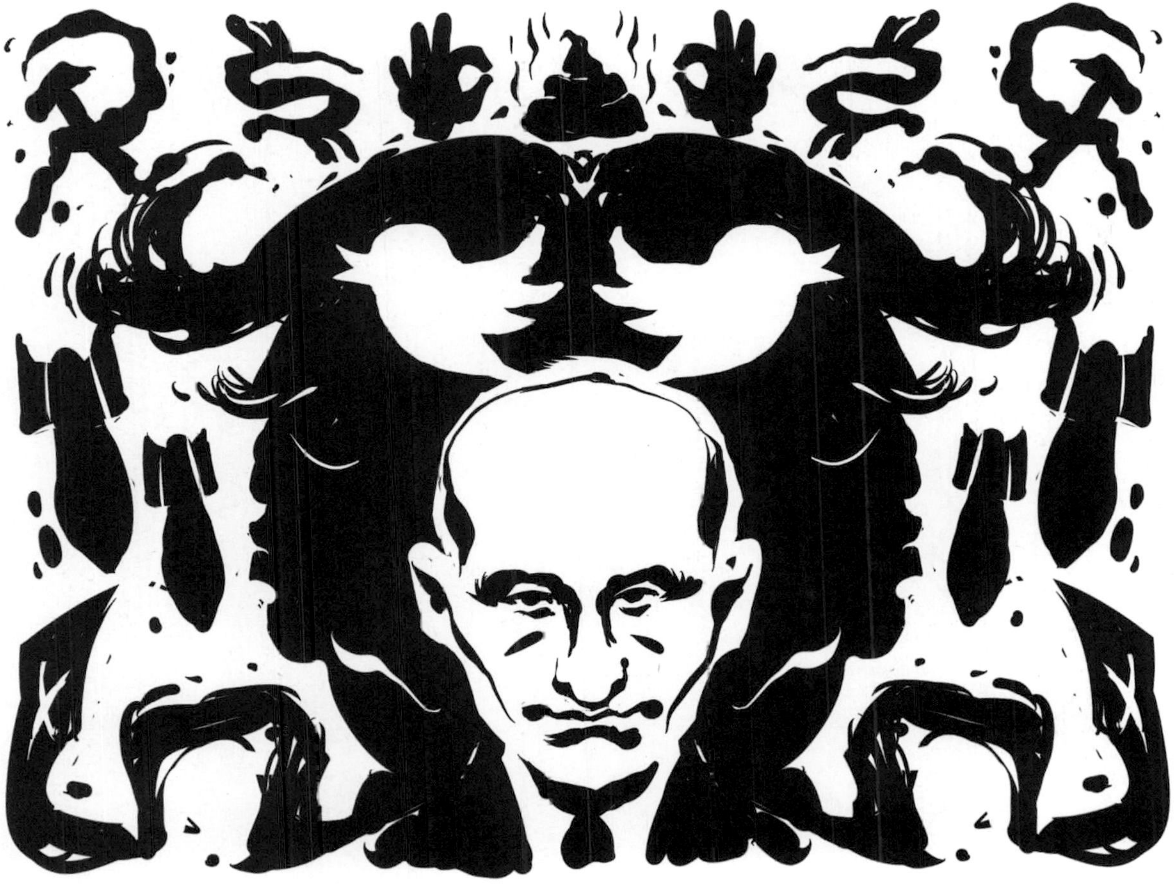

*Russian Rorschach Test*

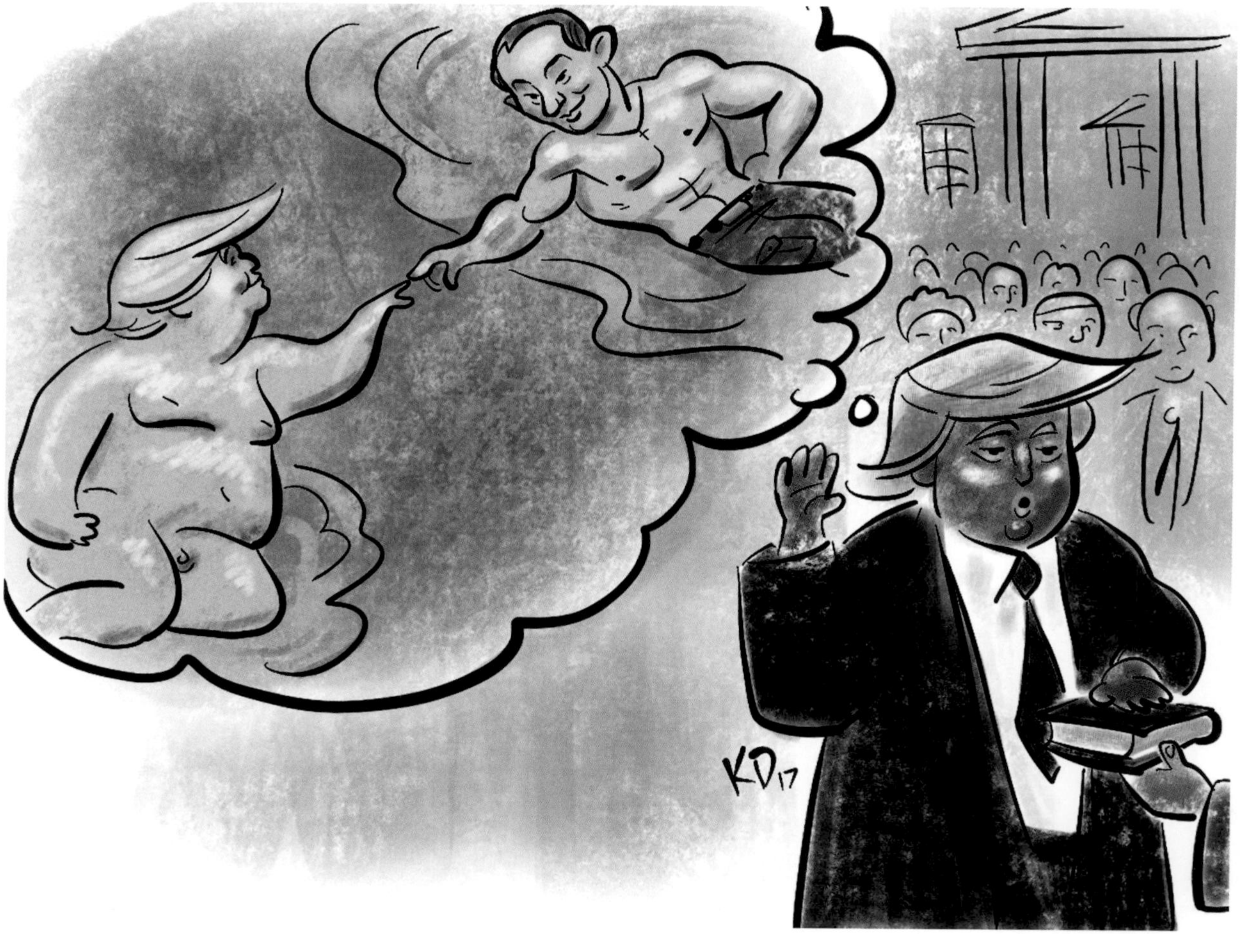
KD17

*"I swear to Pu -- err, God."*

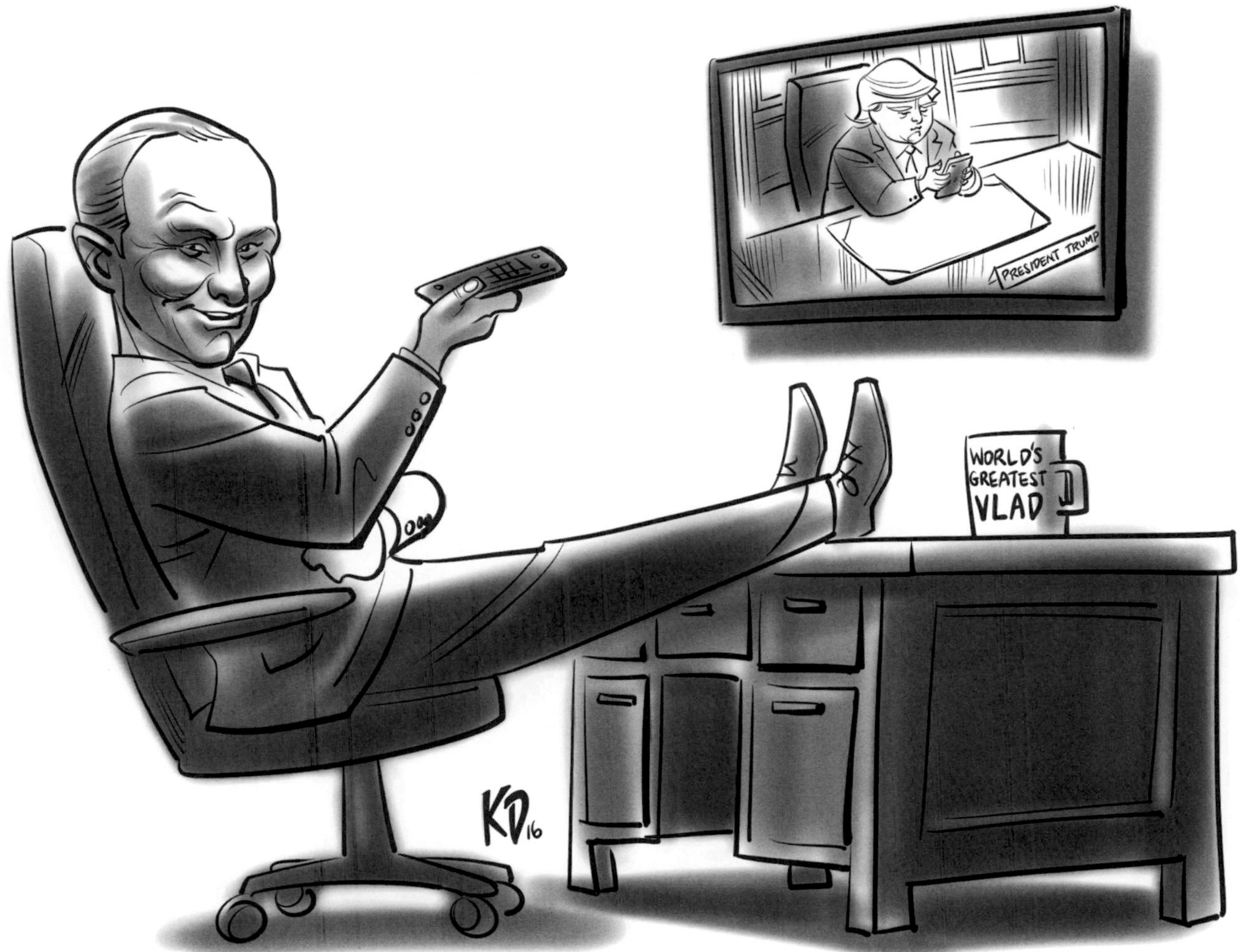
PRESIDENT TRUMP
WORLD'S GREATEST VLAD
KD16

*"I can see Washington from my house."*

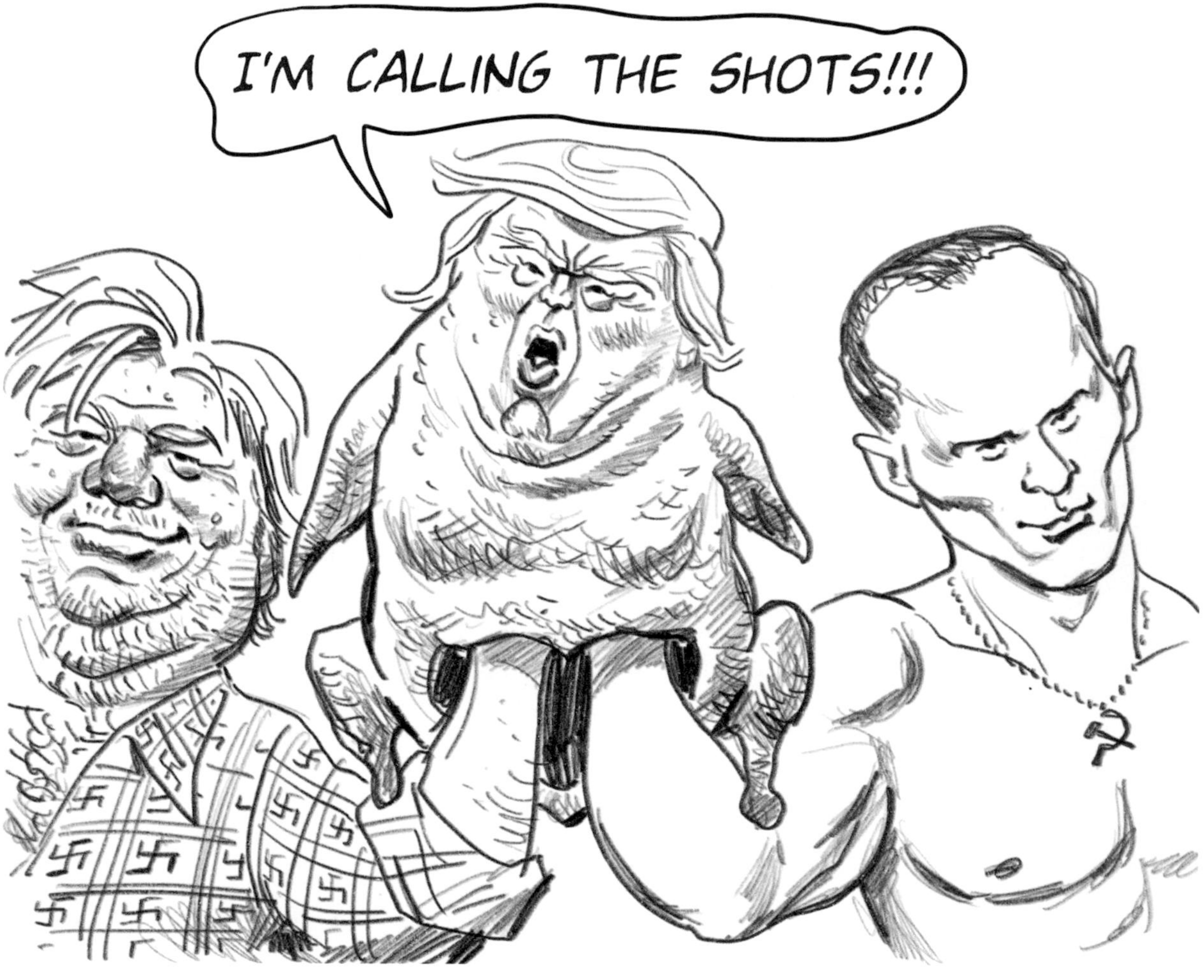
I'M CALLING THE SHOTS!!!

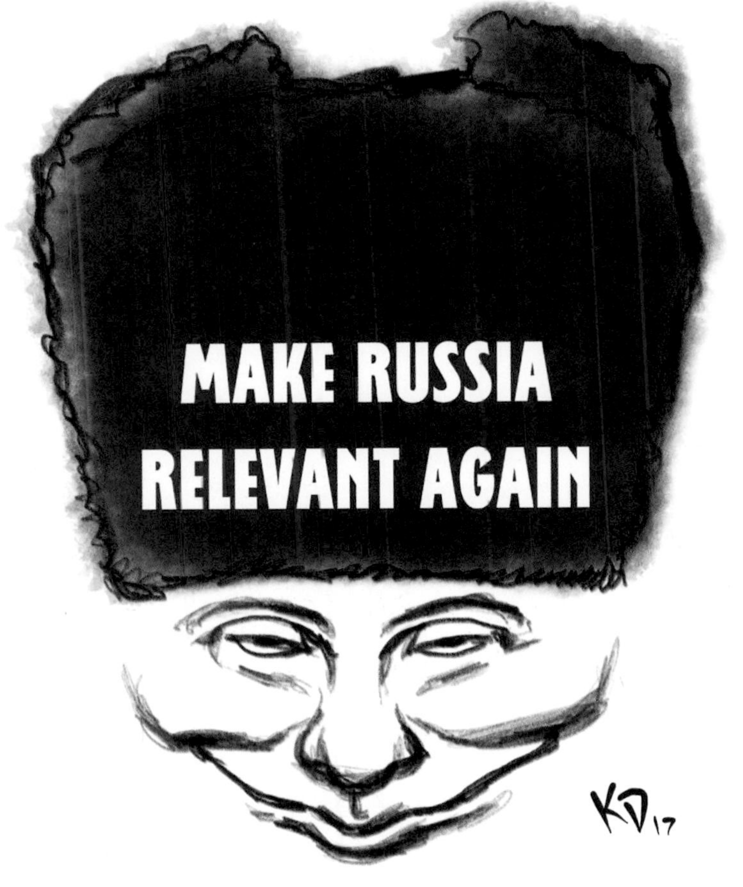
MAKE RUSSIA
RELEVANT AGAIN
KD 17

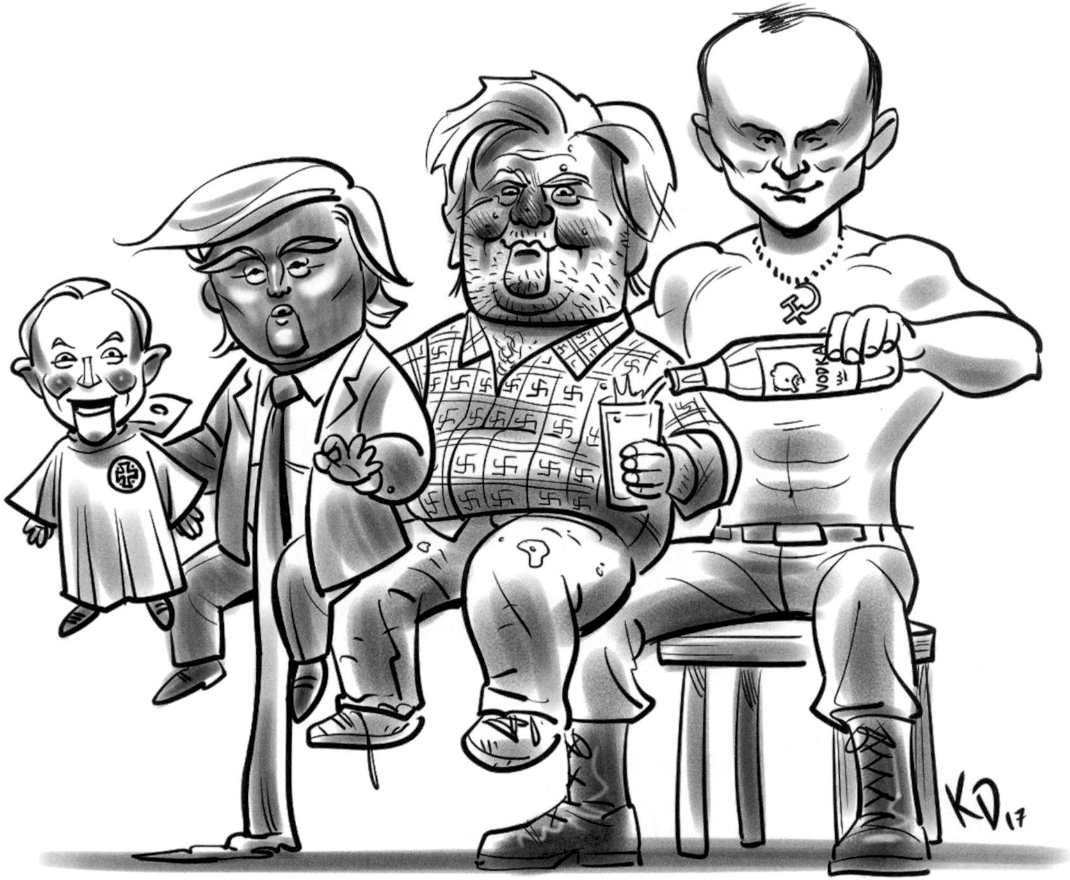
VODKA
KD 17

*Daisy Chain of Fools*

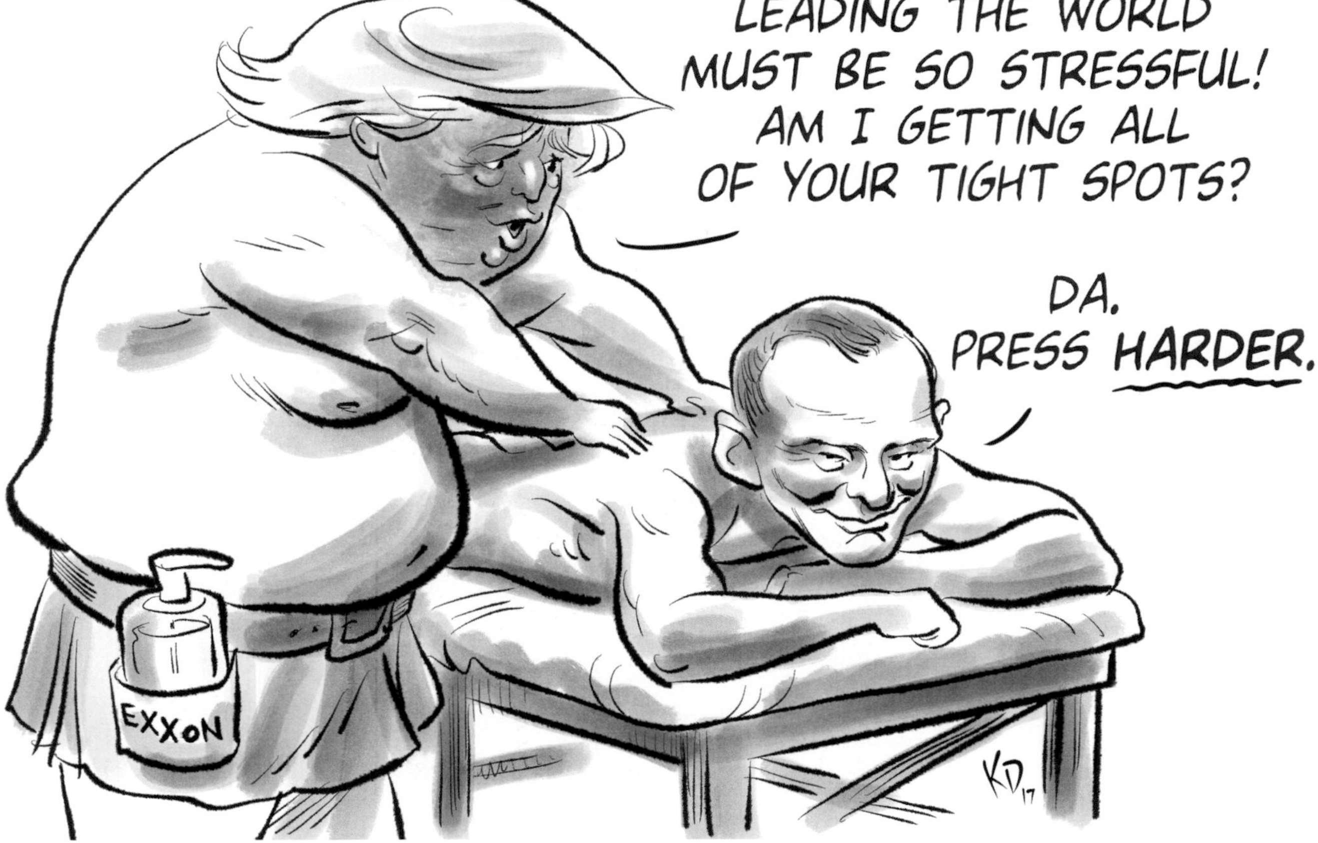
LEADING THE WORLD MUST BE SO STRESSFUL! AM I GETTING ALL OF YOUR TIGHT SPOTS?
DA. PRESS HARDER.
EXXON
KD 17

# TWEETSTORMS

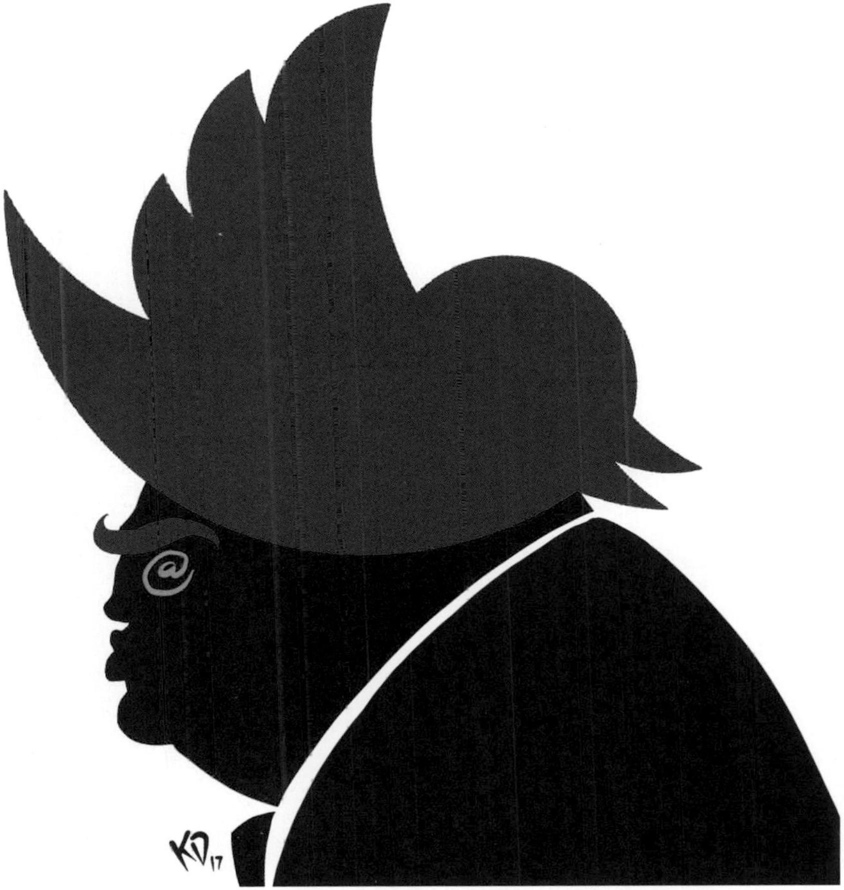
@
KD 17

*Commander-in-Tweet*

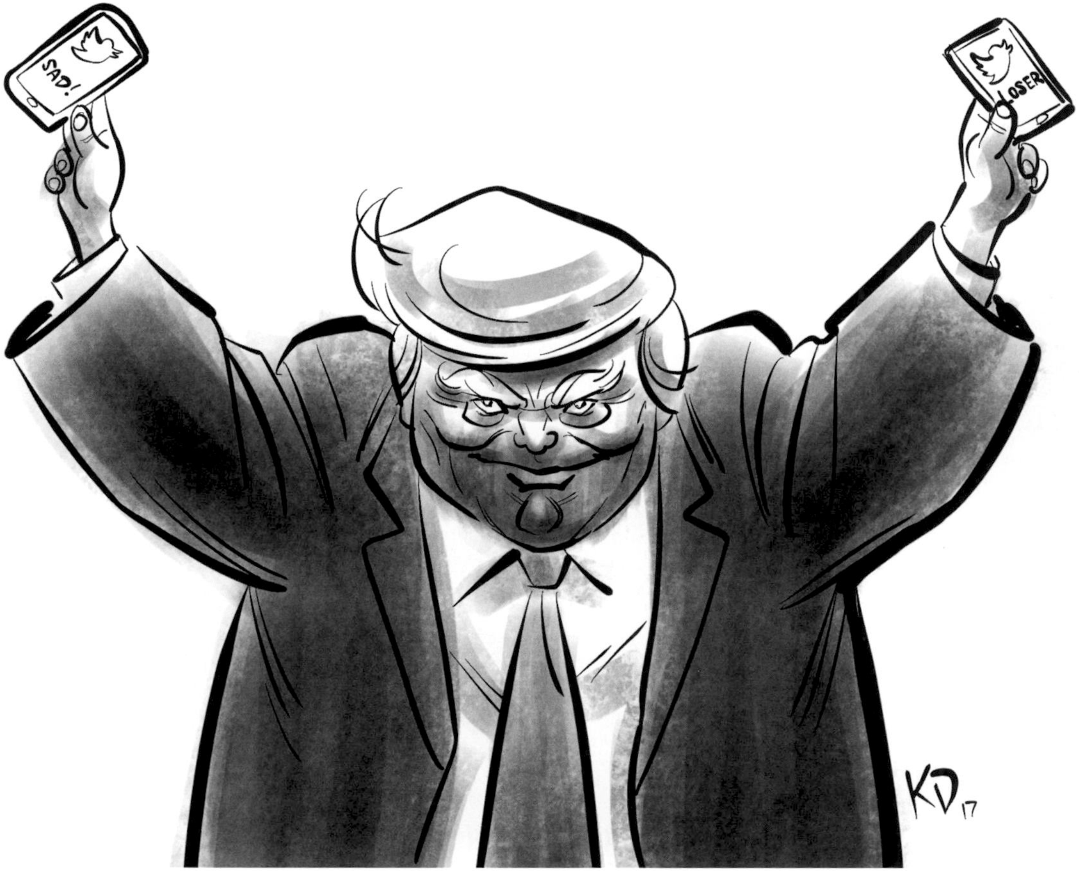
SAD!
LOSER
KD 17

*It's just History Retweeting*

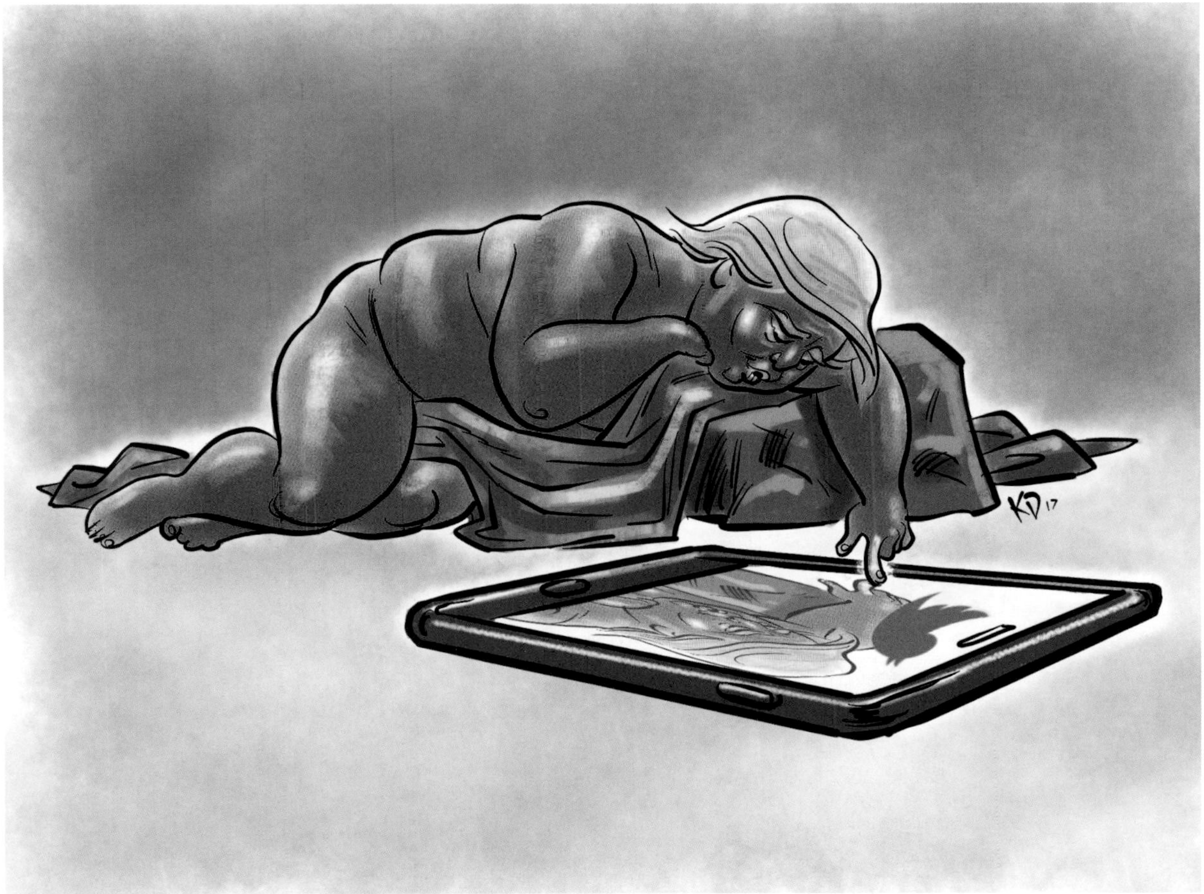
KD 17

*The Modern Narcissus*

*Not all heroes wear capes.*

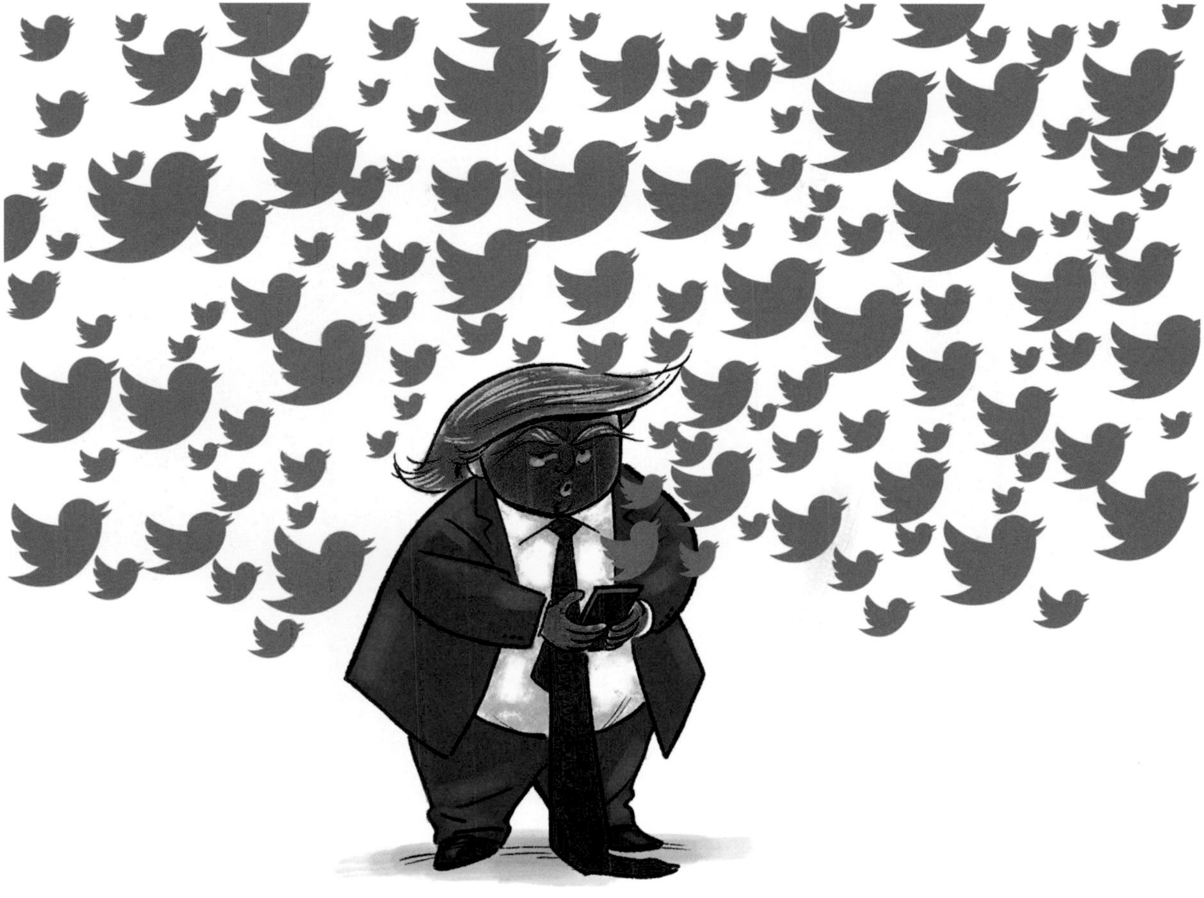

*"Eh, who cares if climate change is killing birds? I'll just make more."*

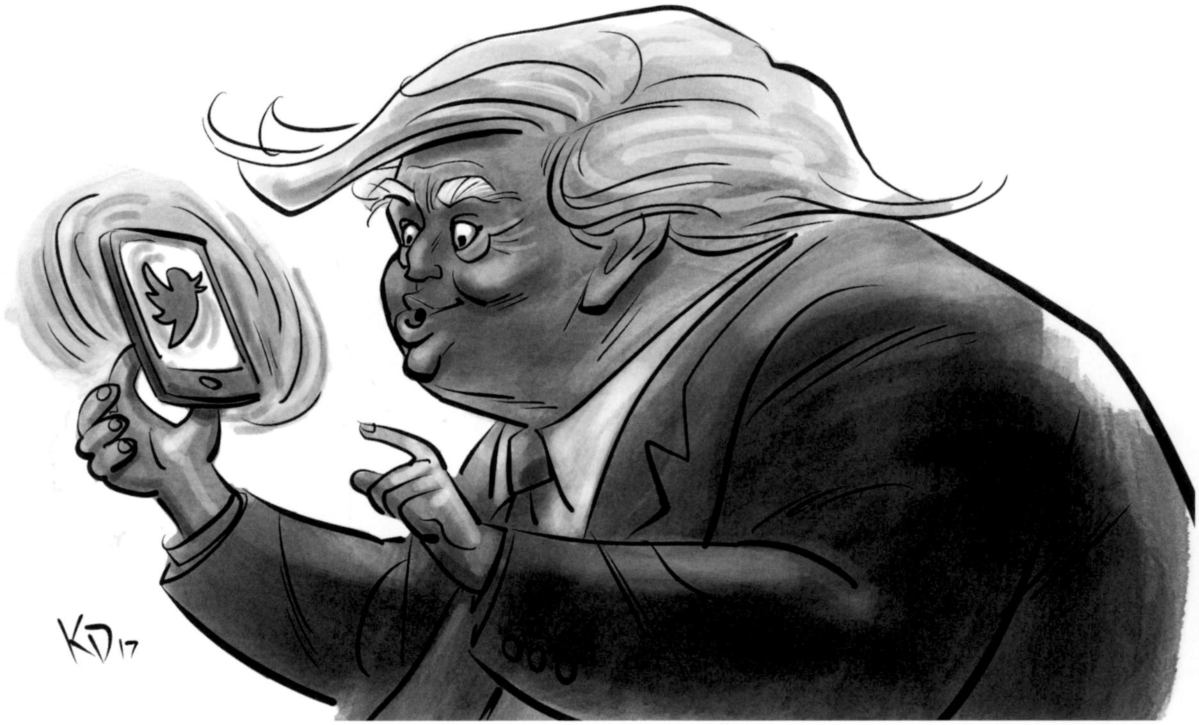
KD17

*Idget Spinner*

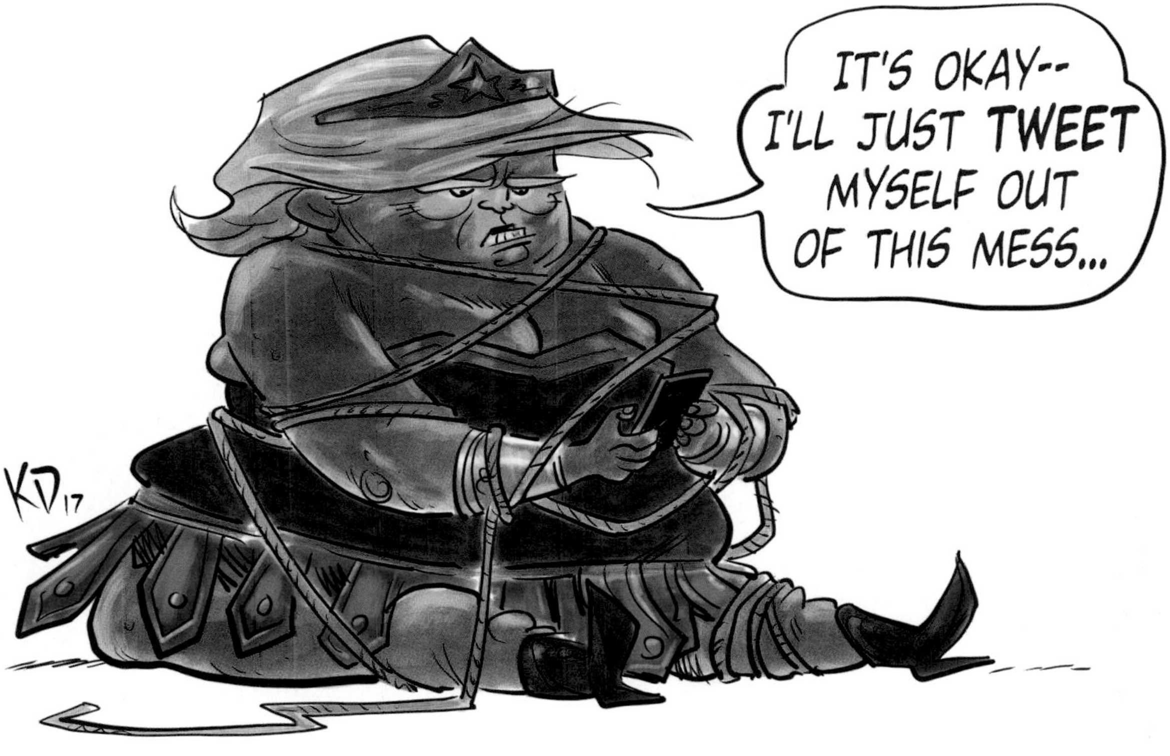
IT'S OKAY--
I'LL JUST TWEET
MYSELF OUT
OF THIS MESS...
KD17

*Blunder Man*

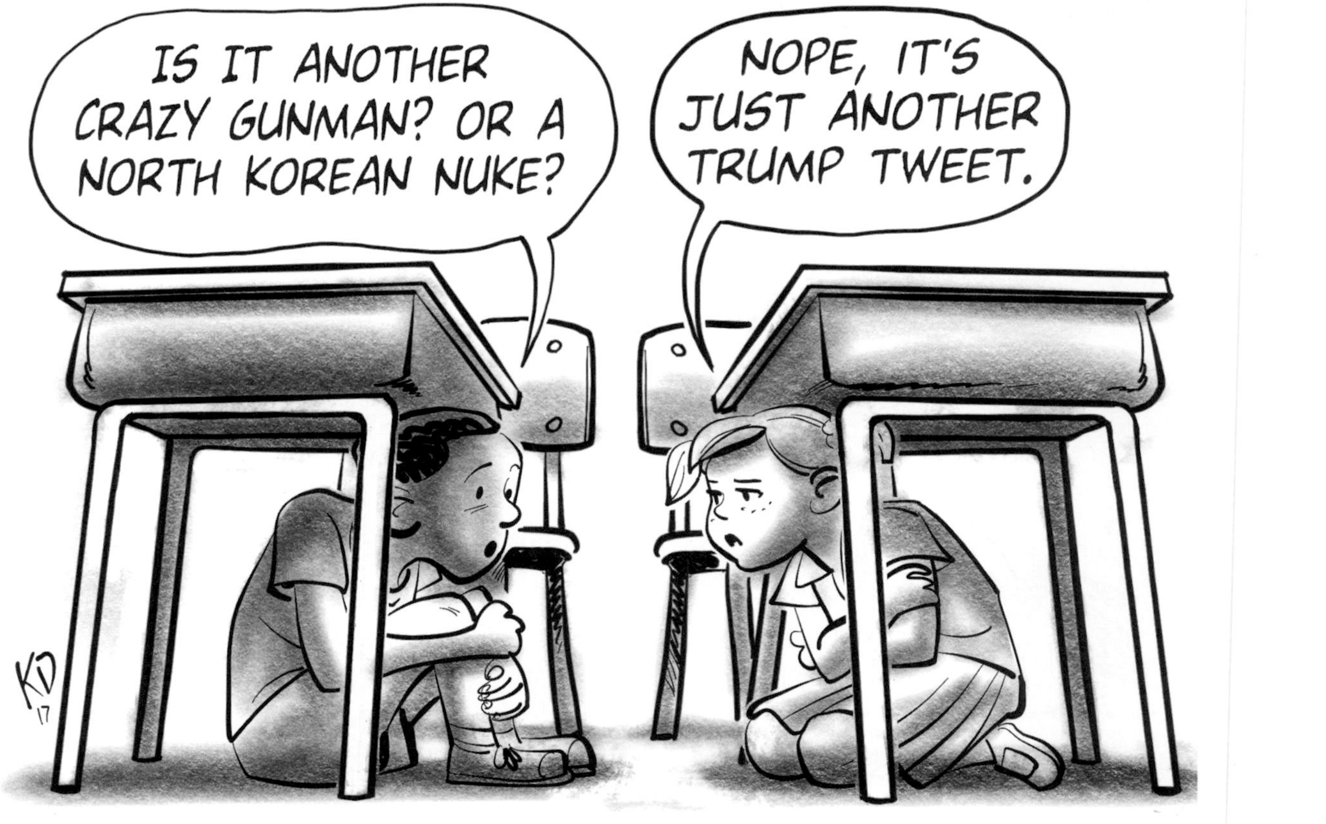
IS IT ANOTHER CRAZY GUNMAN? OR A NORTH KOREAN NUKE?
NOPE, IT'S JUST ANOTHER TRUMP TWEET.
KD 17

*Duck and Cover in the Trump Era*

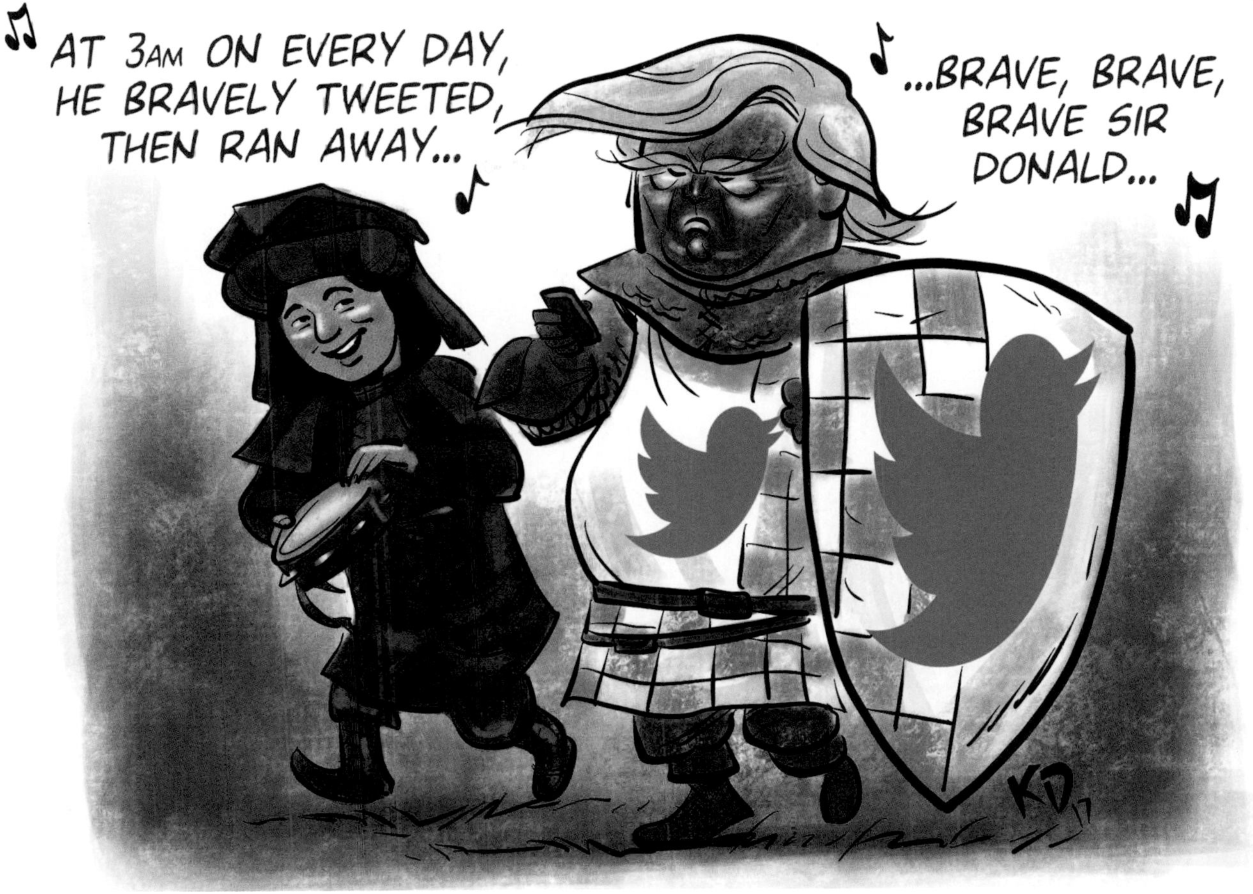
AT 3AM ON EVERY DAY, HE BRAVELY TWEETED, THEN RAN AWAY...
...BRAVE, BRAVE, BRAVE SIR DONALD...
KD 17

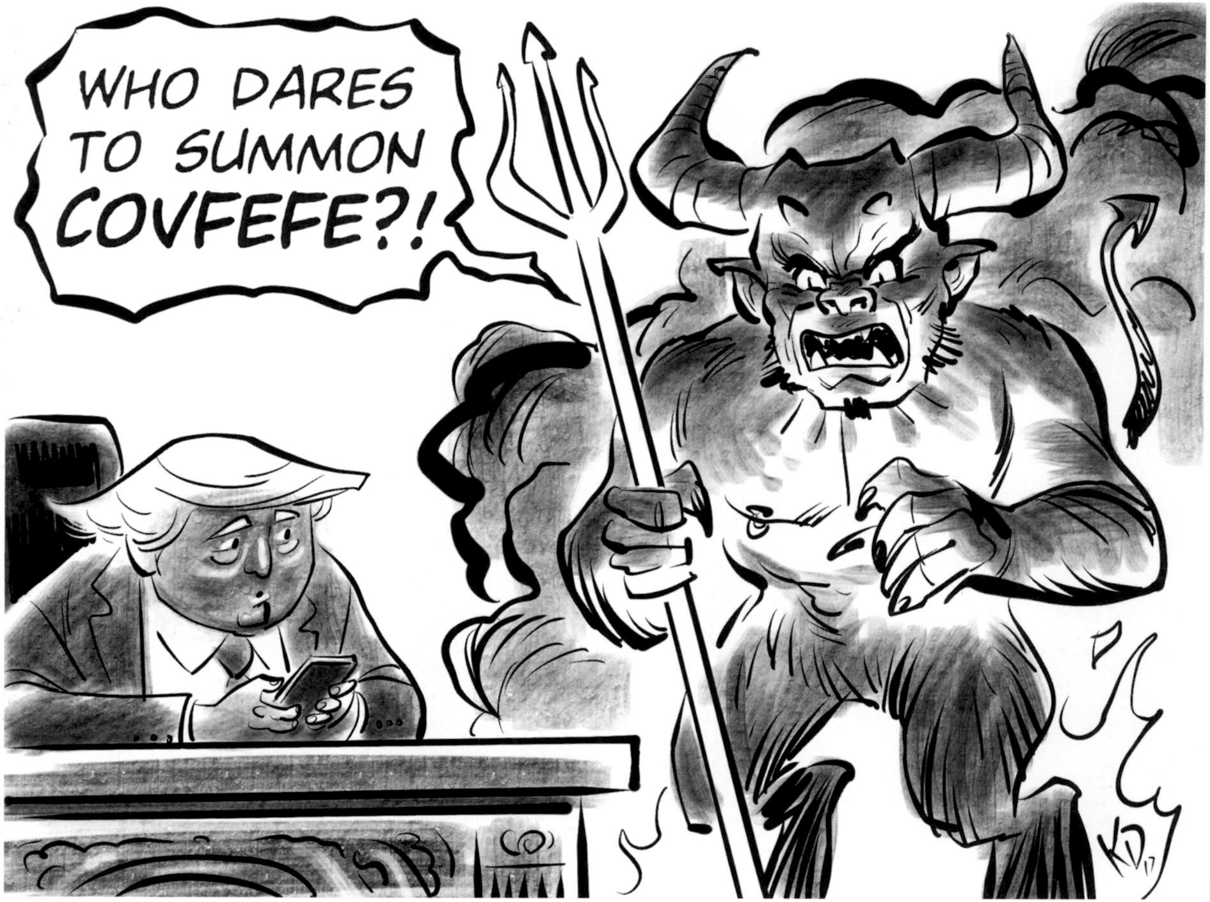
WHO DARES TO SUMMON COVFEFE?!

# Devolution is real.

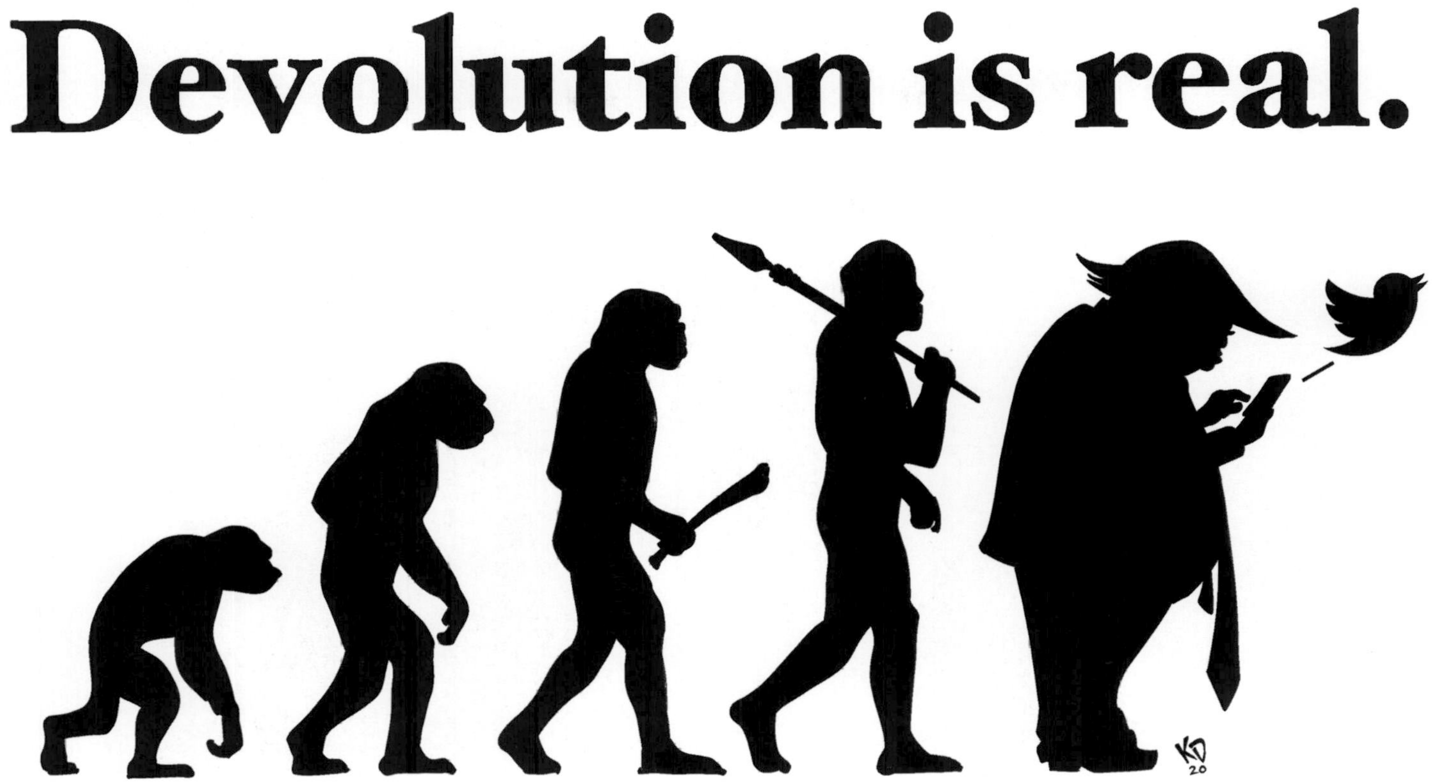
KD
20

MALFEASANTS

# WHAT'S COOKIN', KELLYANNE?

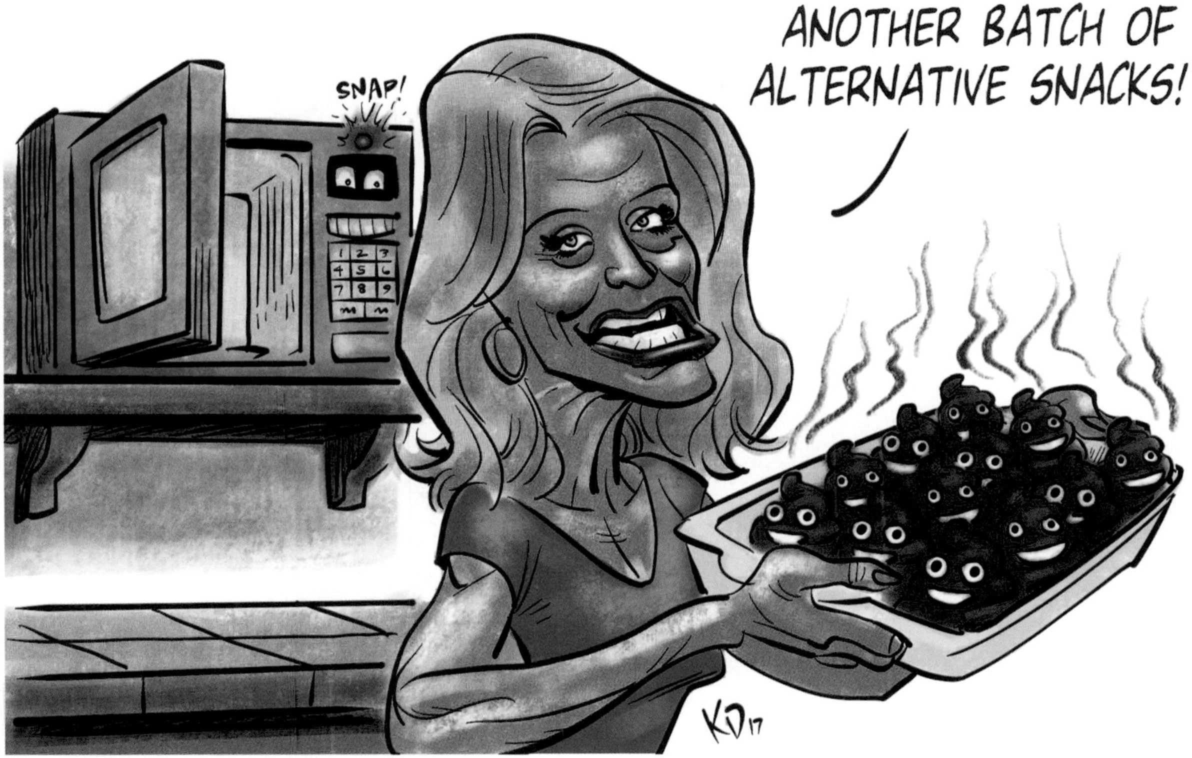
ANOTHER BATCH OF ALTERNATIVE SNACKS!
SNAP!
1 2 3
4 5 6
7 8 9

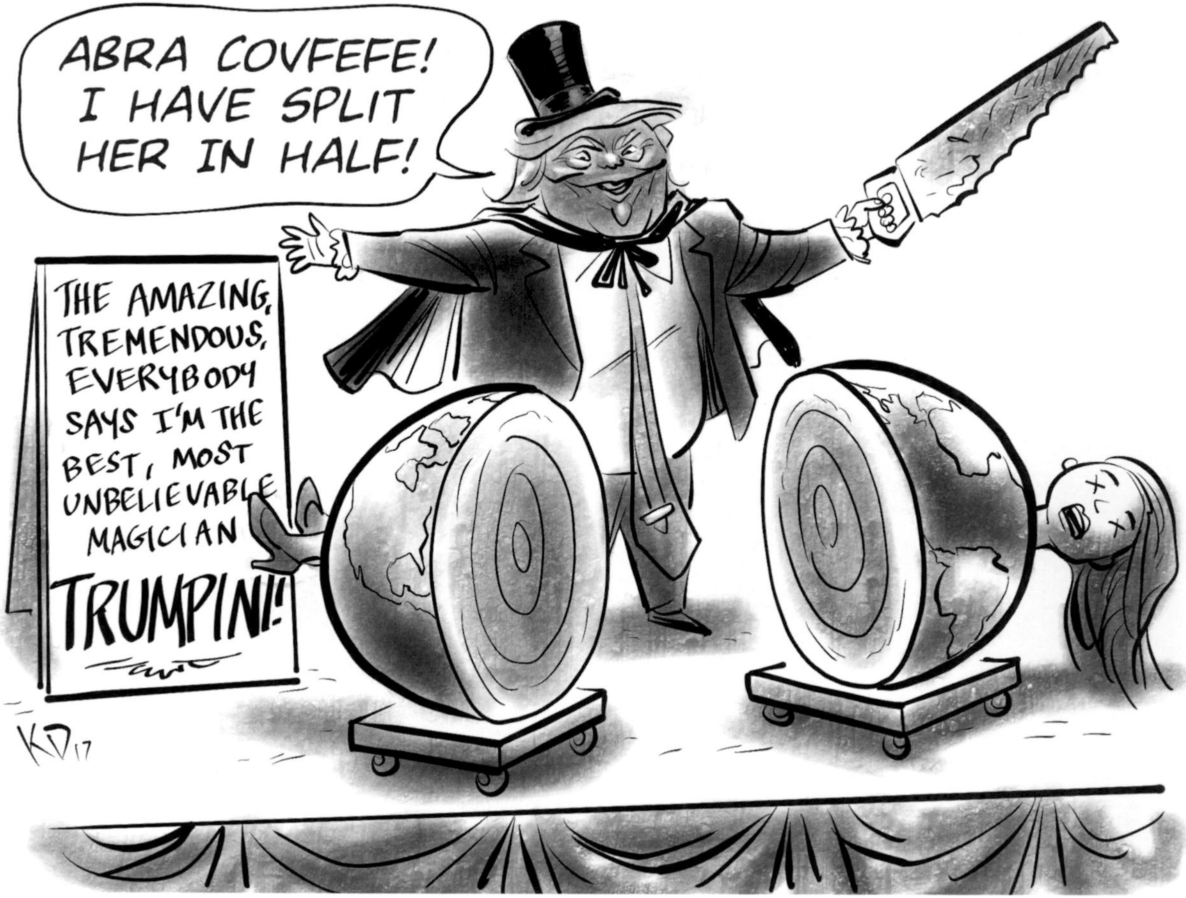
ABRA COVFEFE! I HAVE SPLIT HER IN HALF!
THE AMAZING, TREMENDOUS, EVERYBODY SAYS I'M THE BEST, MOST UNBELIEVABLE MAGICIAN
TRUMPINI!
KD 17

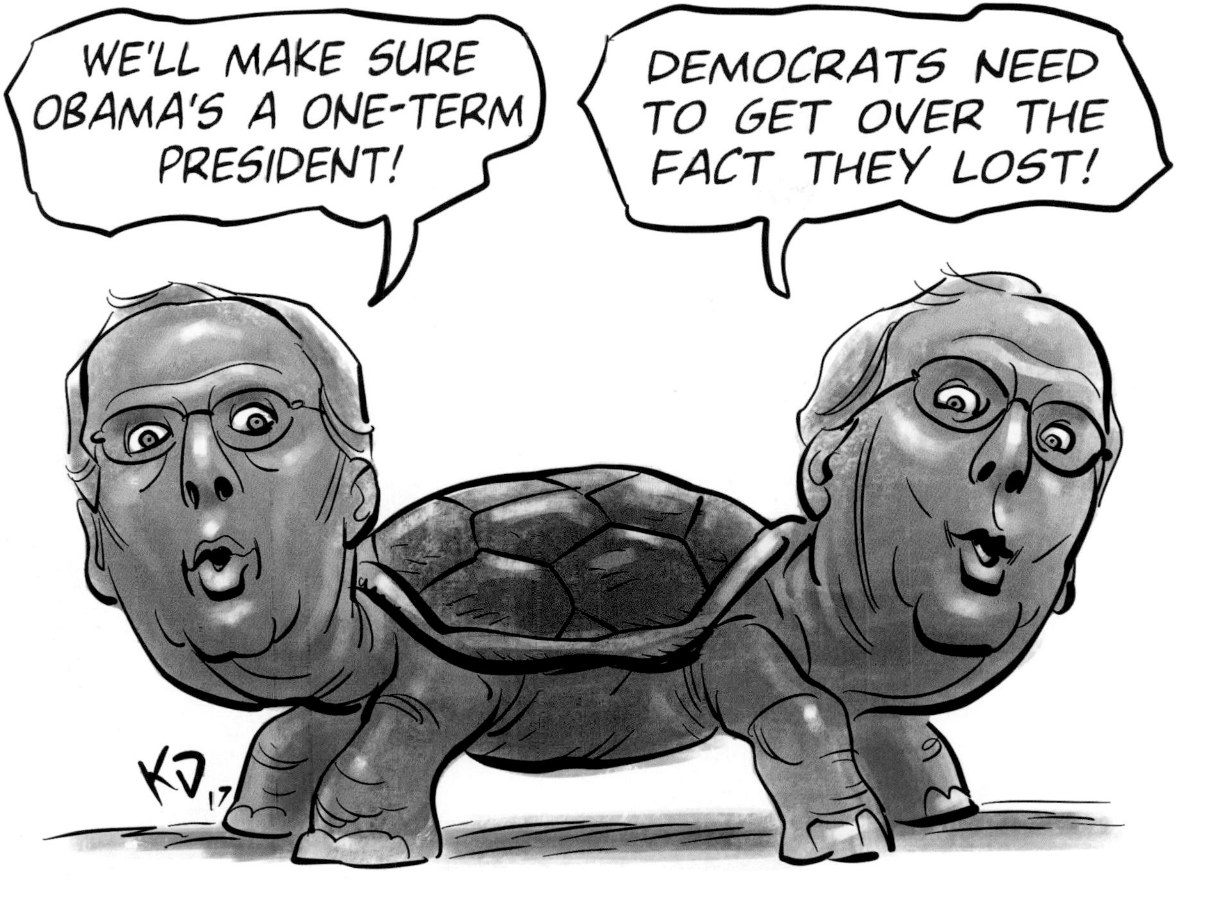
WE'LL MAKE SURE OBAMA'S A ONE-TERM PRESIDENT!
DEMOCRATS NEED TO GET OVER THE FACT THEY LOST!
KD 17

*Mitch McConnell, the Amazing Hypocritter*

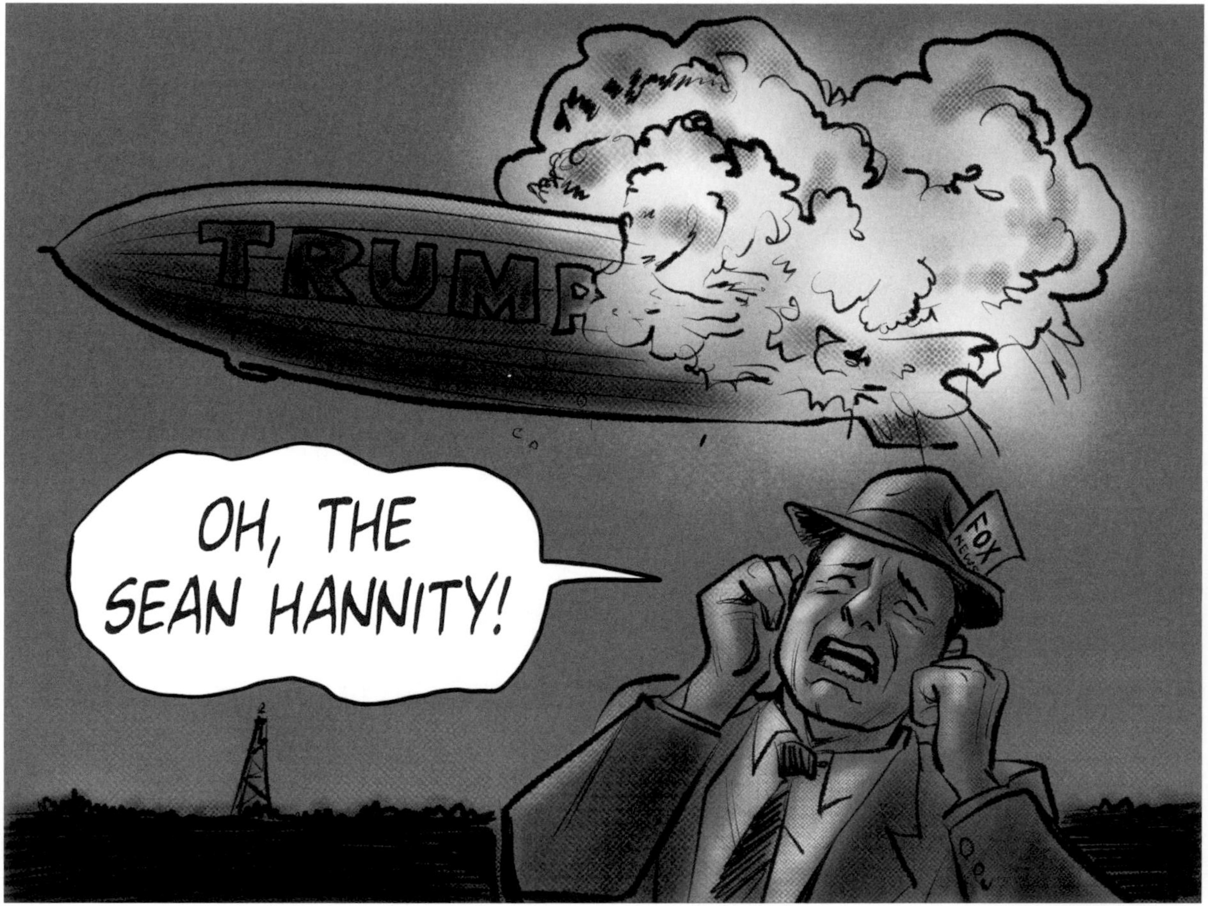
TRUMP
OH, THE SEAN HANNITY!
FOX NEWS

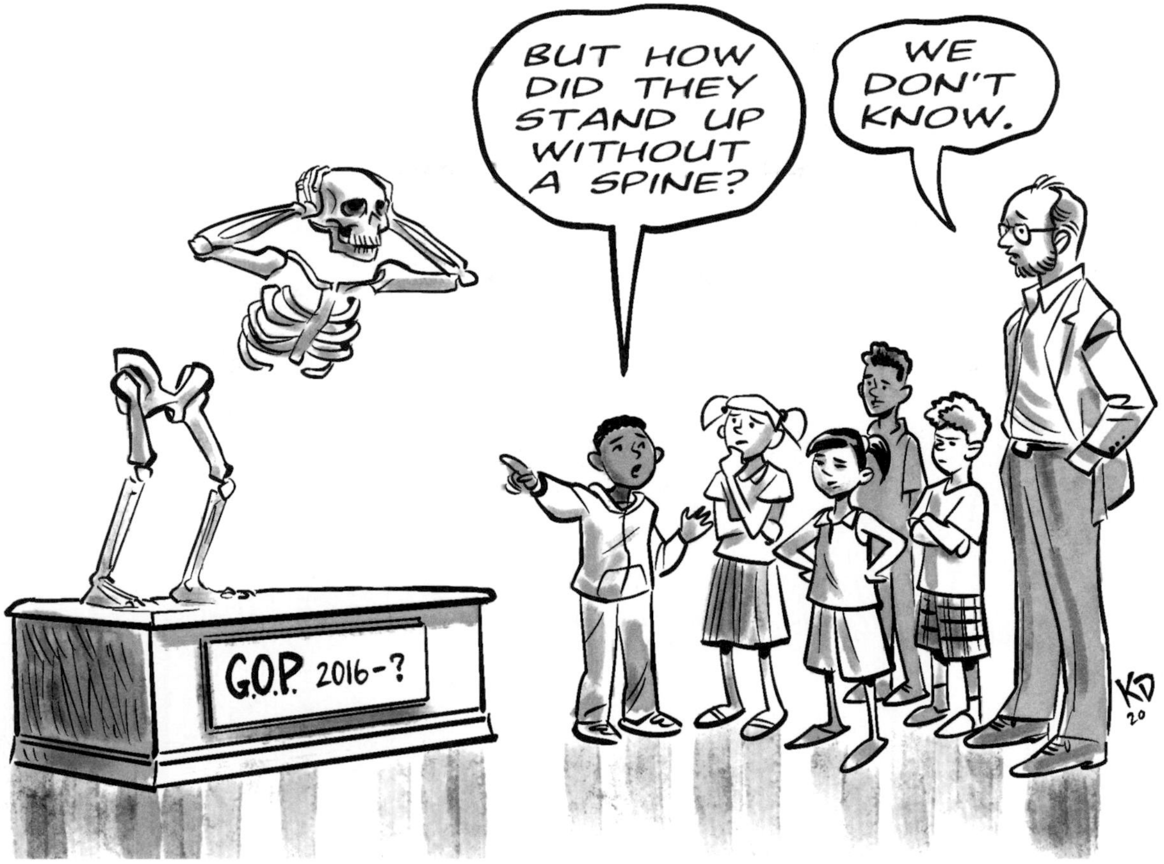
BUT HOW DID THEY STAND UP WITHOUT A SPINE?
WE DON'T KNOW.
G.O.P. 2016-?
KD 20

*In the Political Museum of the future*

# BIGLY

PLENTY OF ROOM LEFT IN THERE, SENATOR McCAIN!
COMPLIANTS

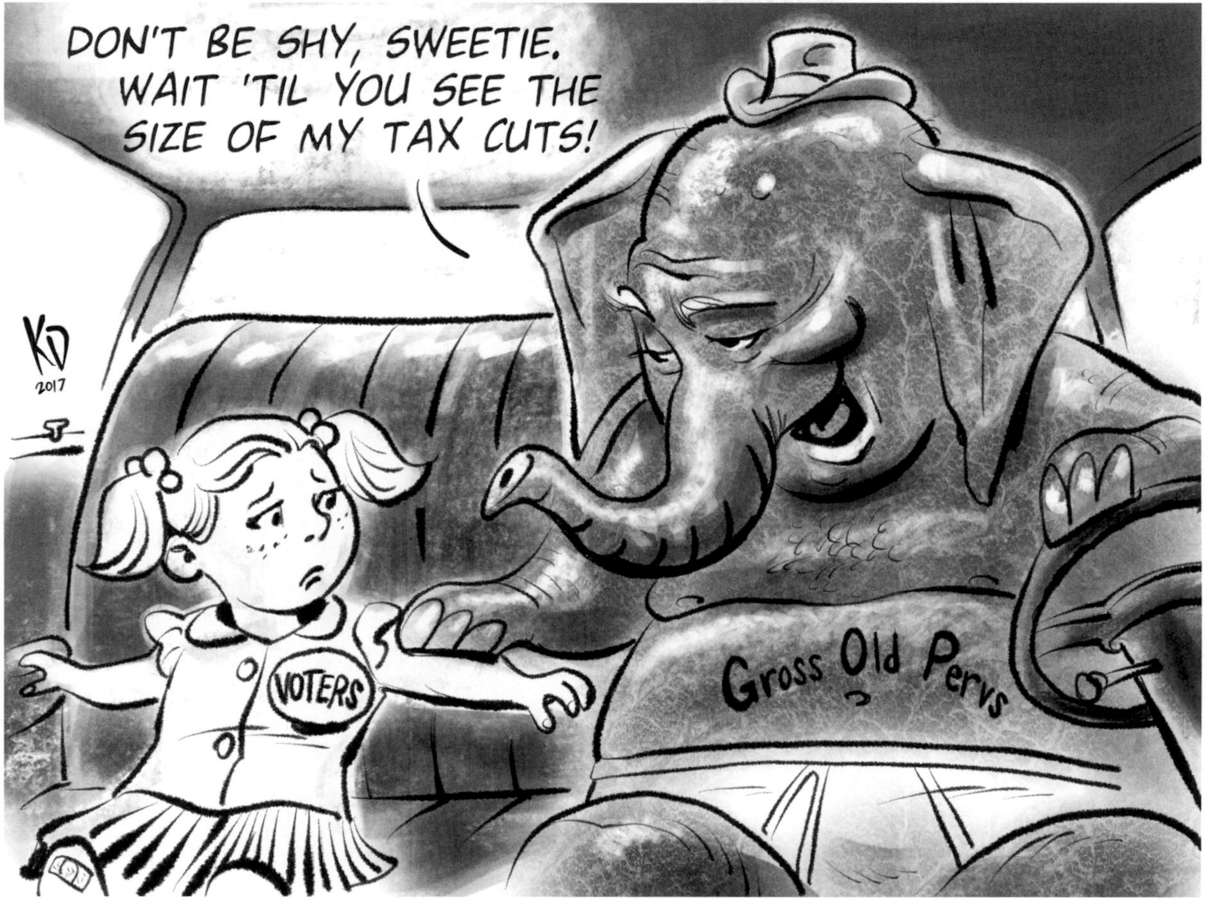
DON'T BE SHY, SWEETIE. WAIT 'TIL YOU SEE THE SIZE OF MY TAX CUTS!
KD 2017
VOTERS
Gross Old Pervs

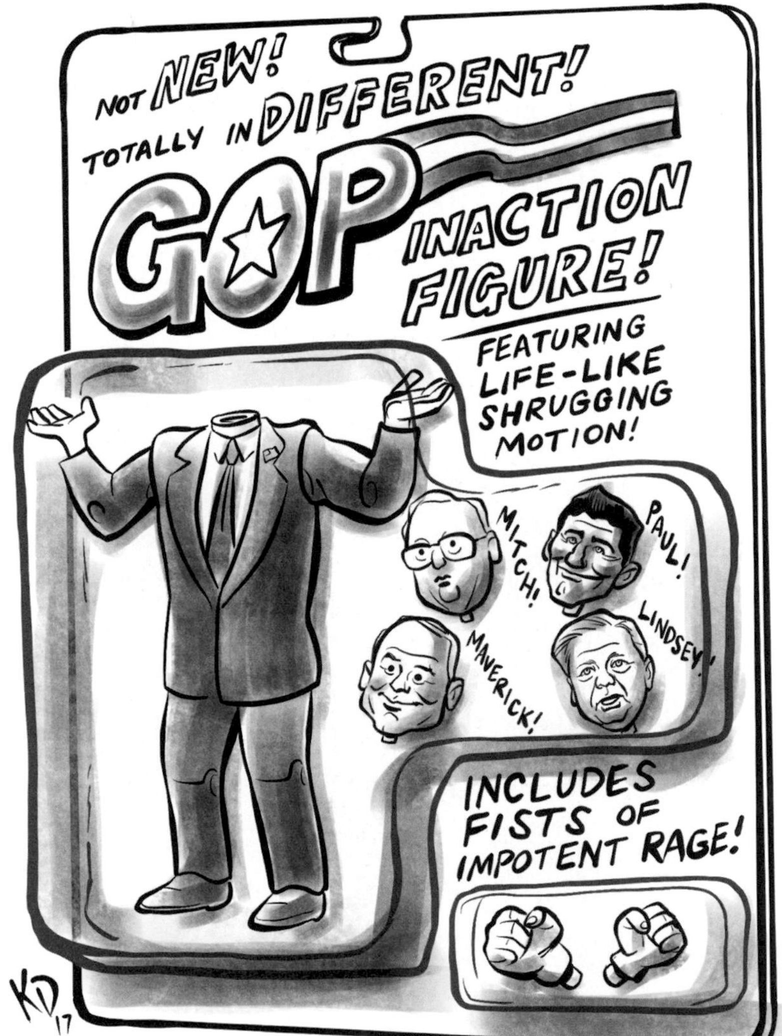
NOT NEW!
TOTALLY INDIFFERENT!
GOP INACTION FIGURE!
FEATURING LIFE-LIKE SHRUGGING MOTION!
MITCH!
PAUL!
MAVERICK!
LINDSEY!
INCLUDES FISTS OF IMPOTENT RAGE!
KD 17

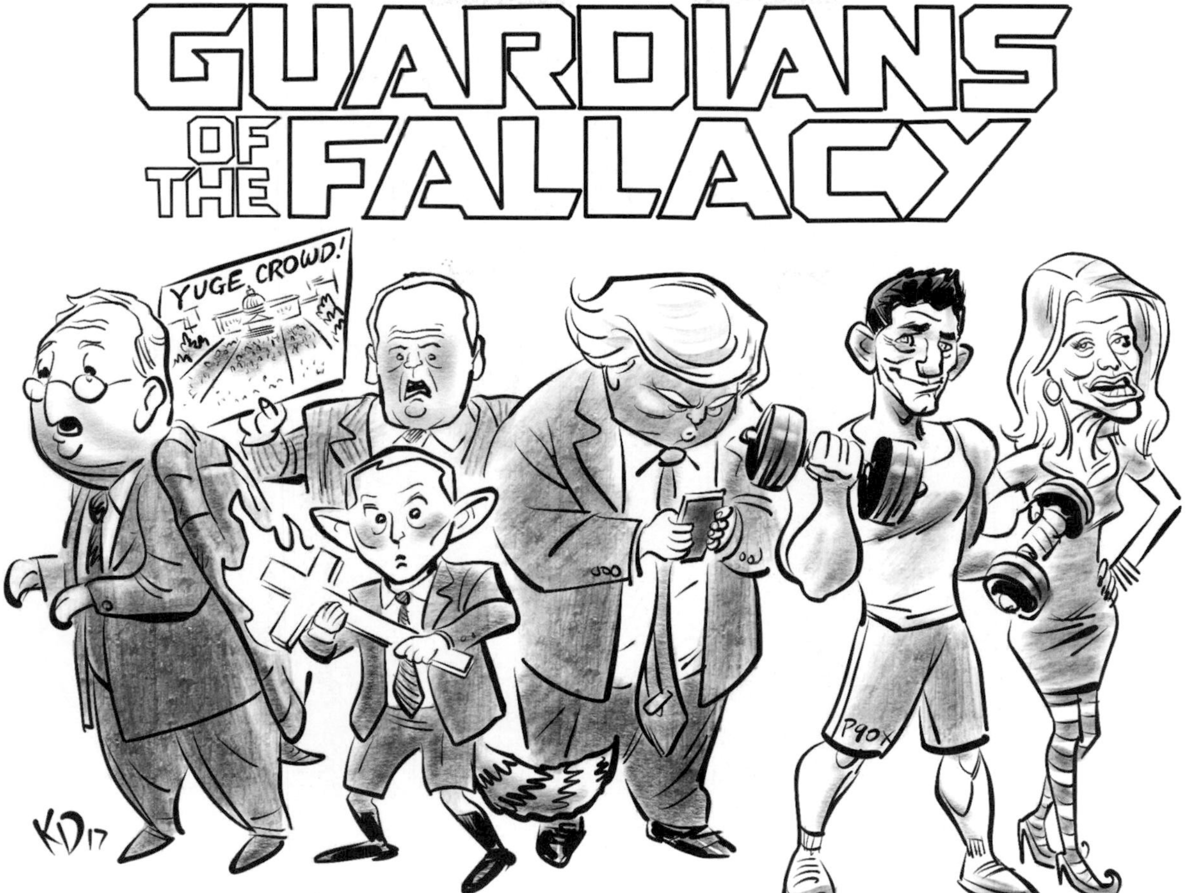
GUARDIANS OF THE FALLACY
YUGE CROWD!
P90X
KD 17

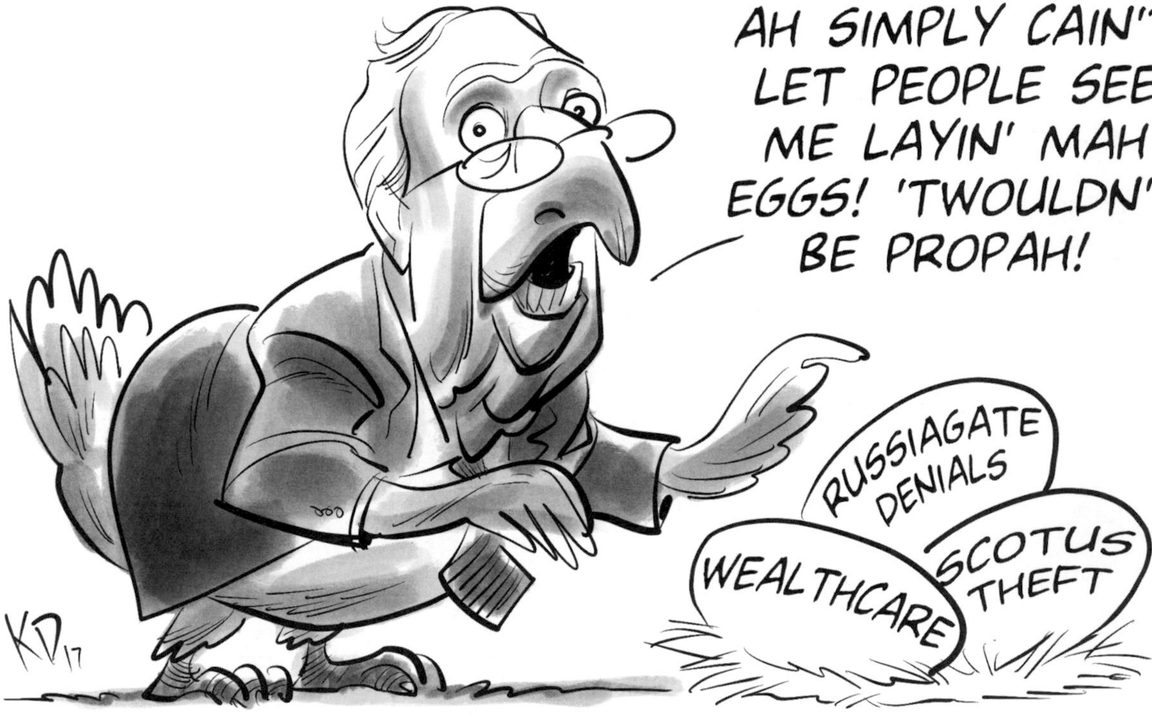
AH SIMPLY CAIN'T LET PEOPLE SEE ME LAYIN' MAH EGGS! 'TWOULDN'T BE PROPAH!
RUSSIAGATE DENIALS
WEALTHCARE
SCOTUS THEFT
KD 17

*Mitch McConnell: Kentucky Fraud, Chicken*

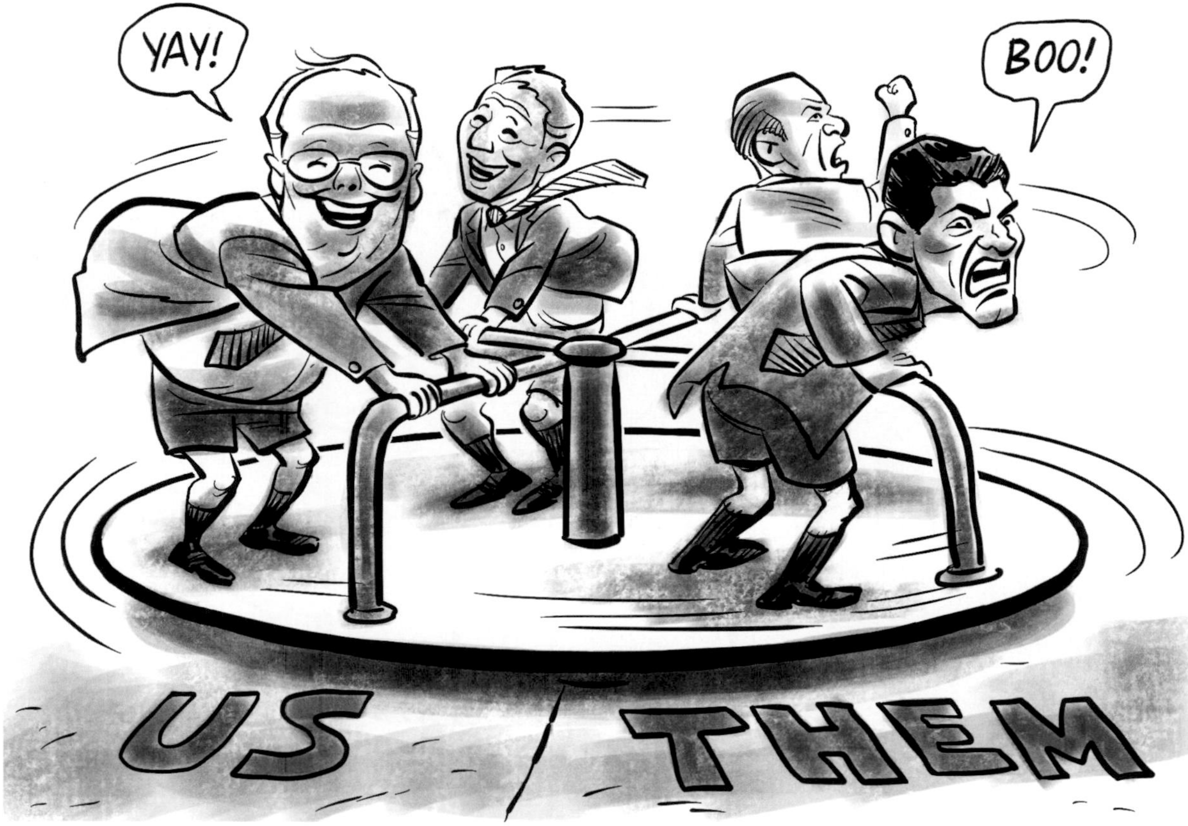
YAY!
BOO!
US
THEM

*Political Spin*

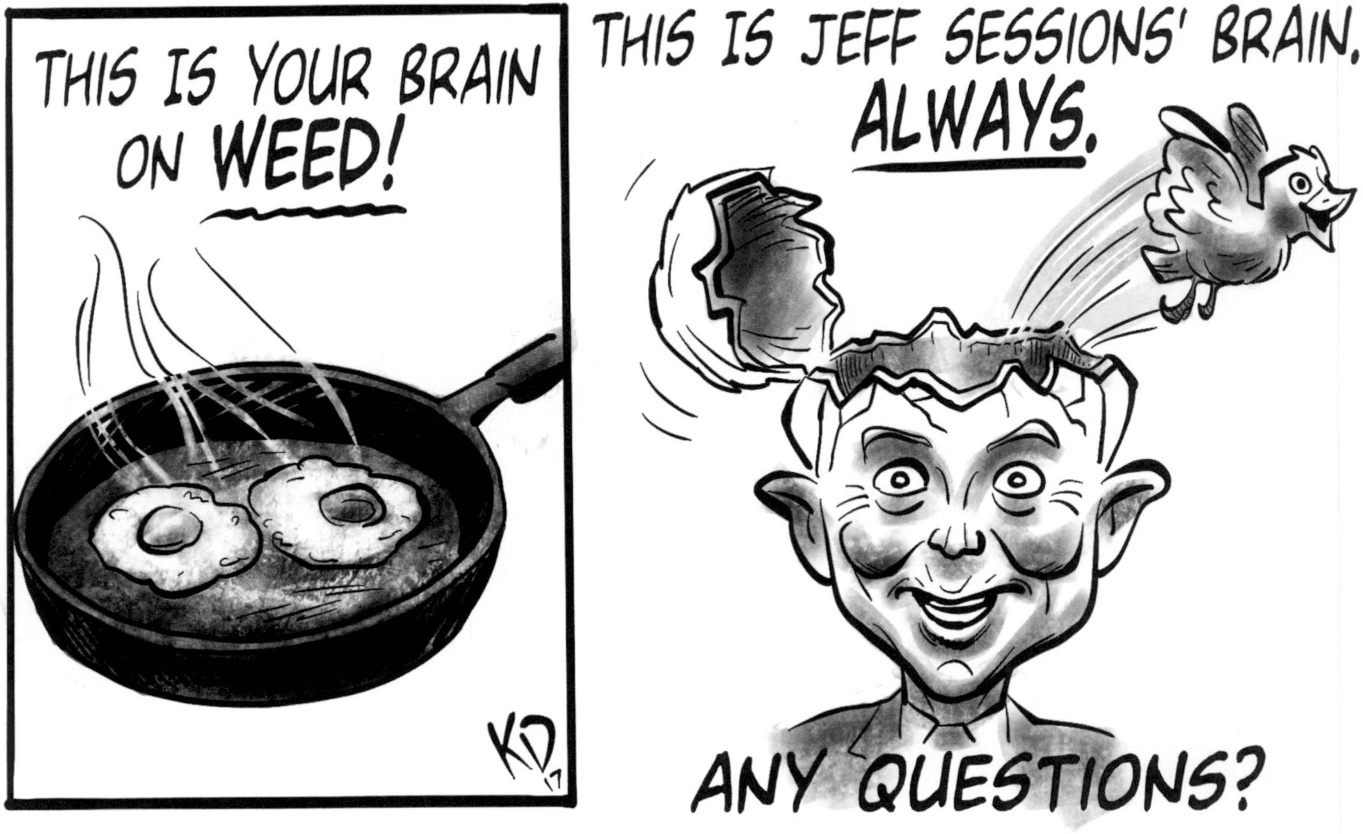
THIS IS YOUR BRAIN ON WEED!
KD '17
THIS IS JEFF SESSIONS' BRAIN. ALWAYS.
ANY QUESTIONS?

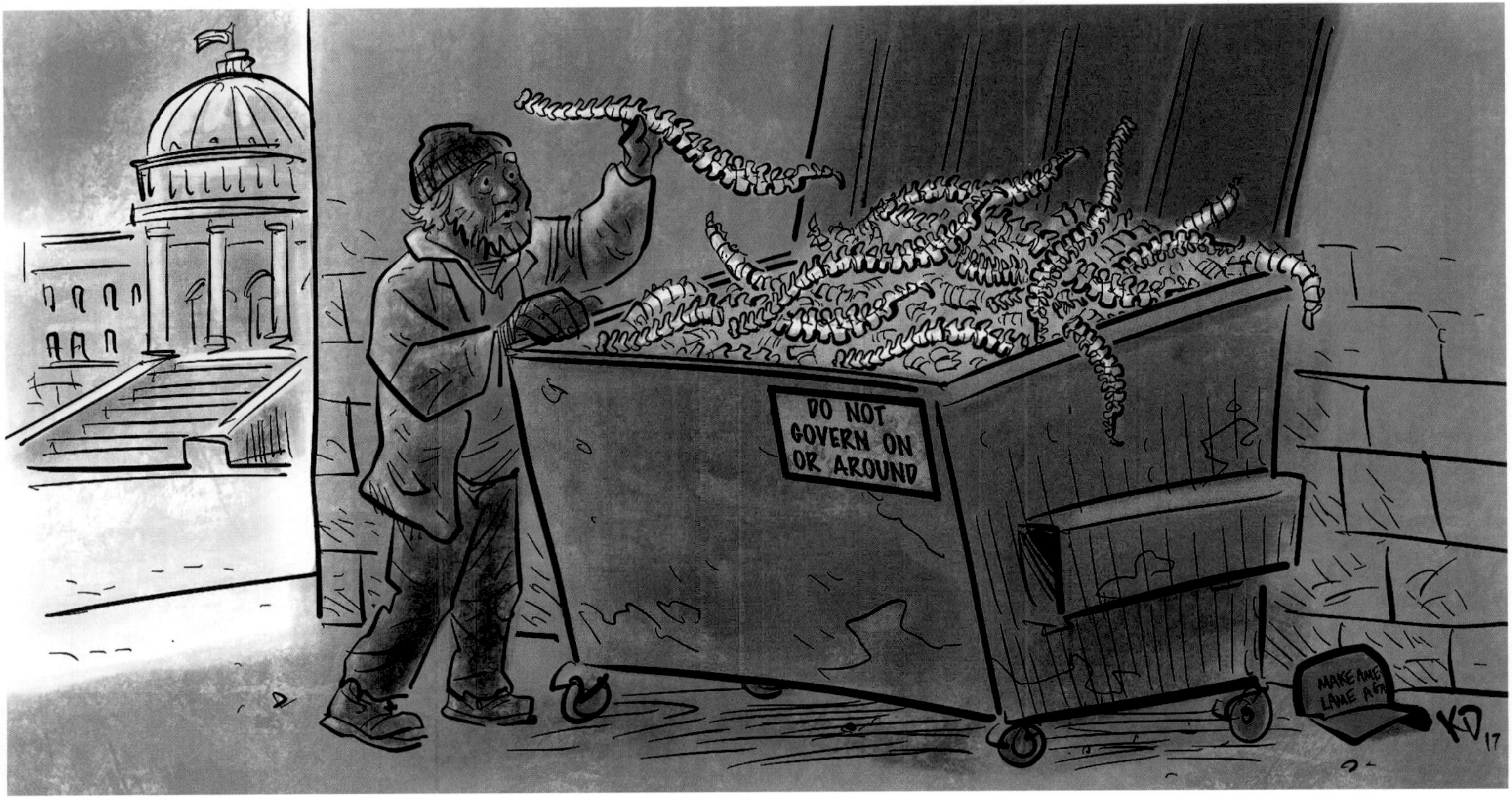
DO NOT
GOVERN ON
OR AROUND
MAKE AME
LAME AGA
KD 17

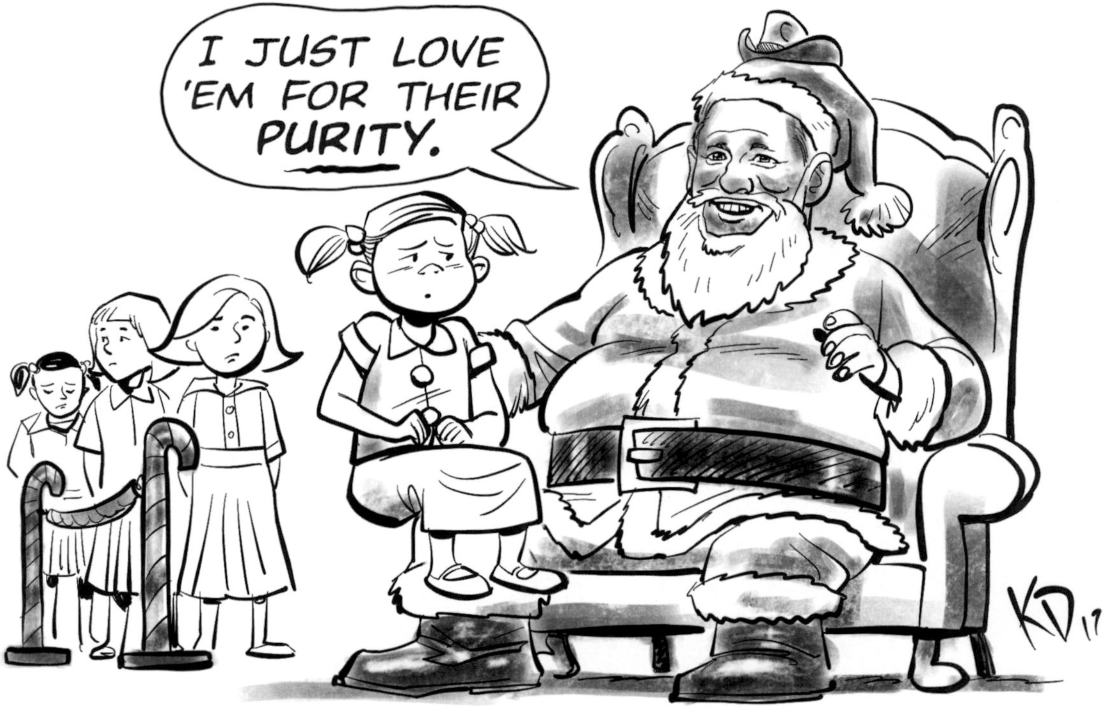
I JUST LOVE 'EM FOR THEIR PURITY.
KD 17

*Judge Roy Moore finds a way around his ban from the local mall...*

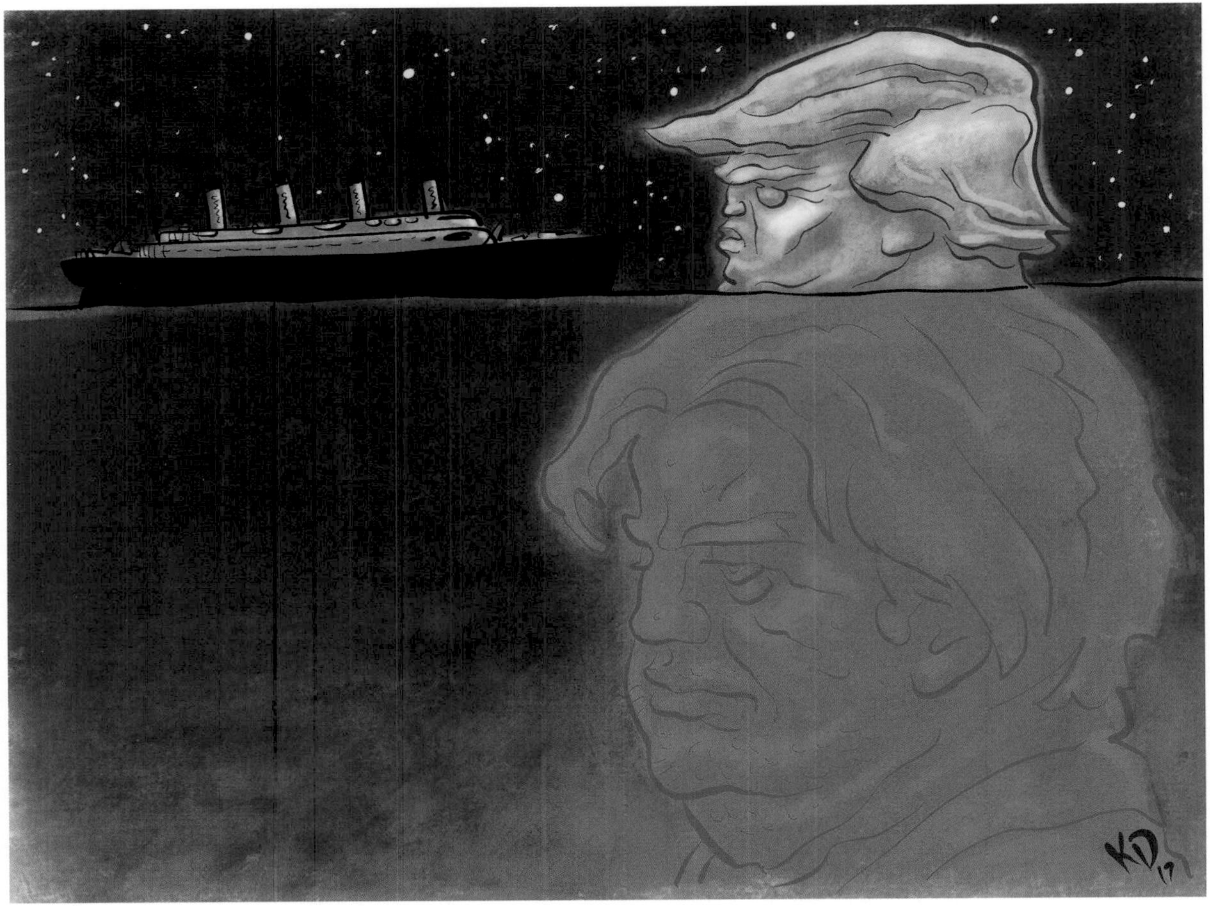
KD 17

*Titanic Mistake*

COWARDLY LYIN'

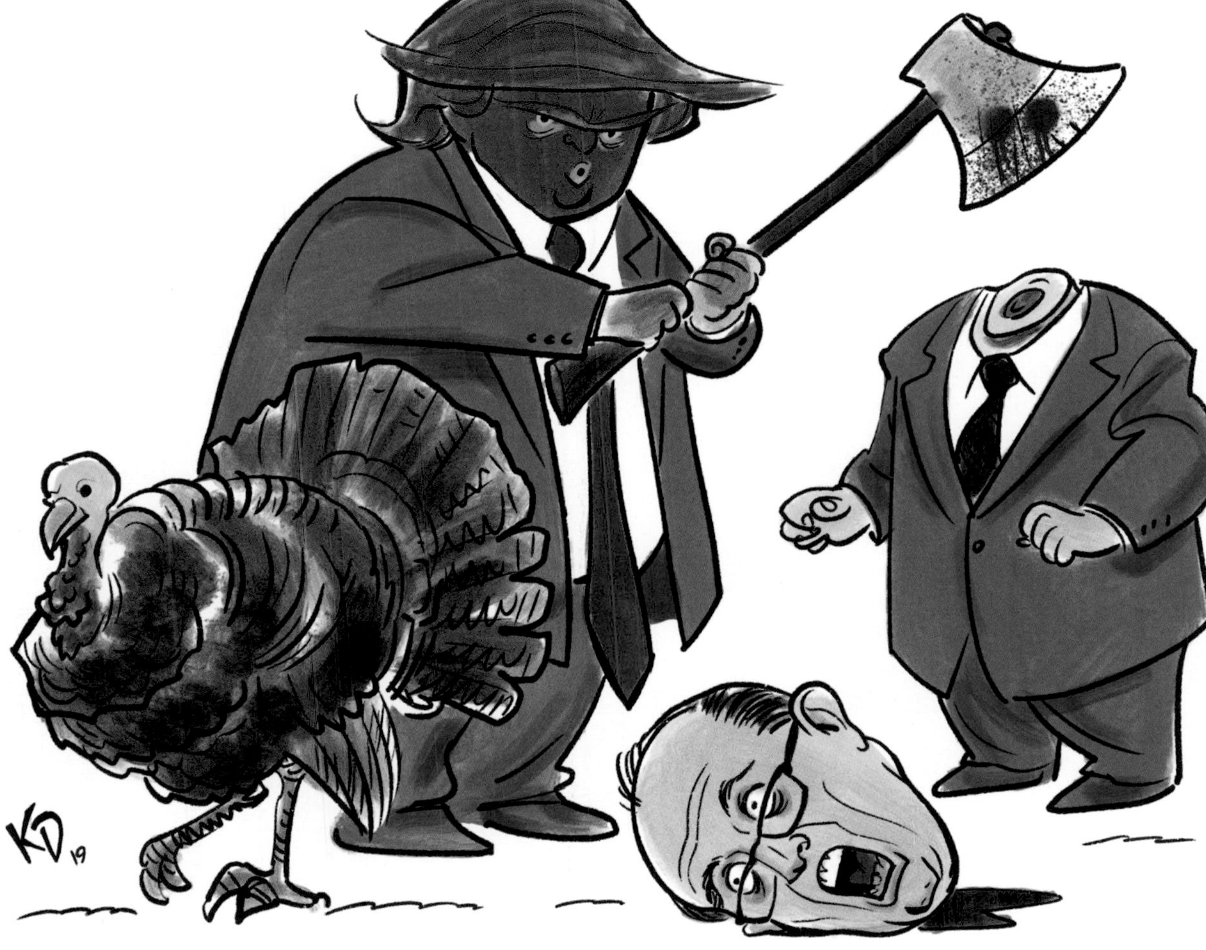
KD 19

*"Oops. Wrong turkey."*

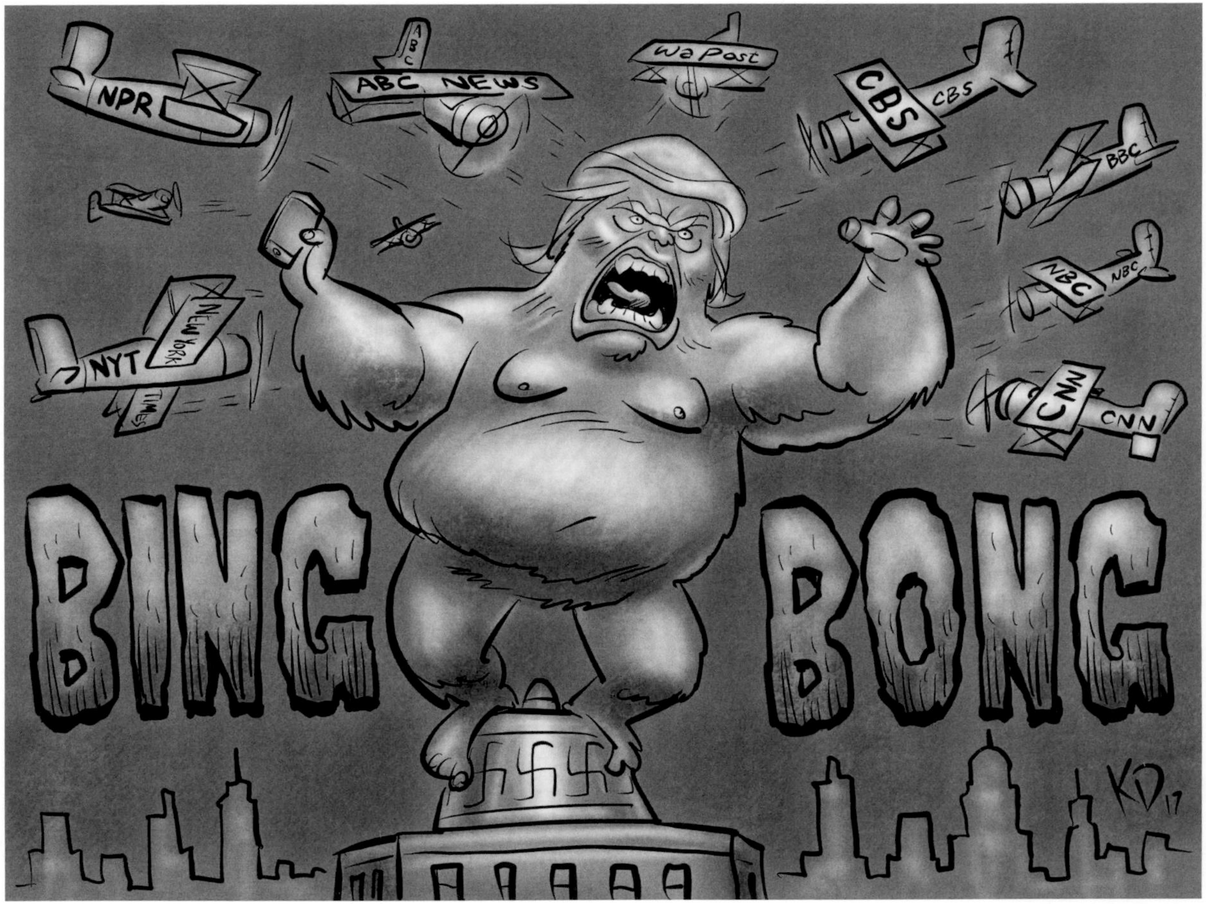
NPR
ABC
ABC NEWS
WaPost
CBS
CBS
BBC
NBC
NBC
NEW YORK
NYT
TIMES
CNN
CNN
BING BONG
KD 17

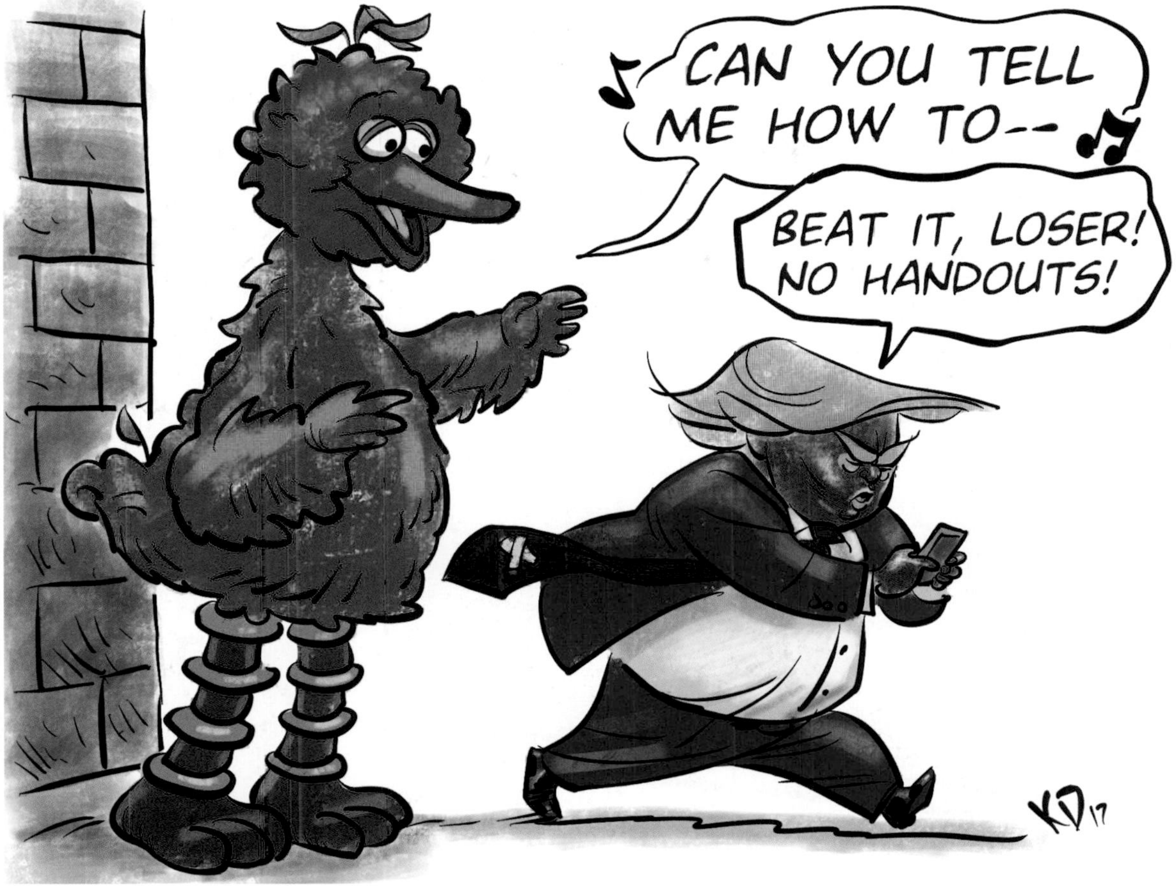
CAN YOU TELL ME HOW TO--
BEAT IT, LOSER! NO HANDOUTS!
KD 17

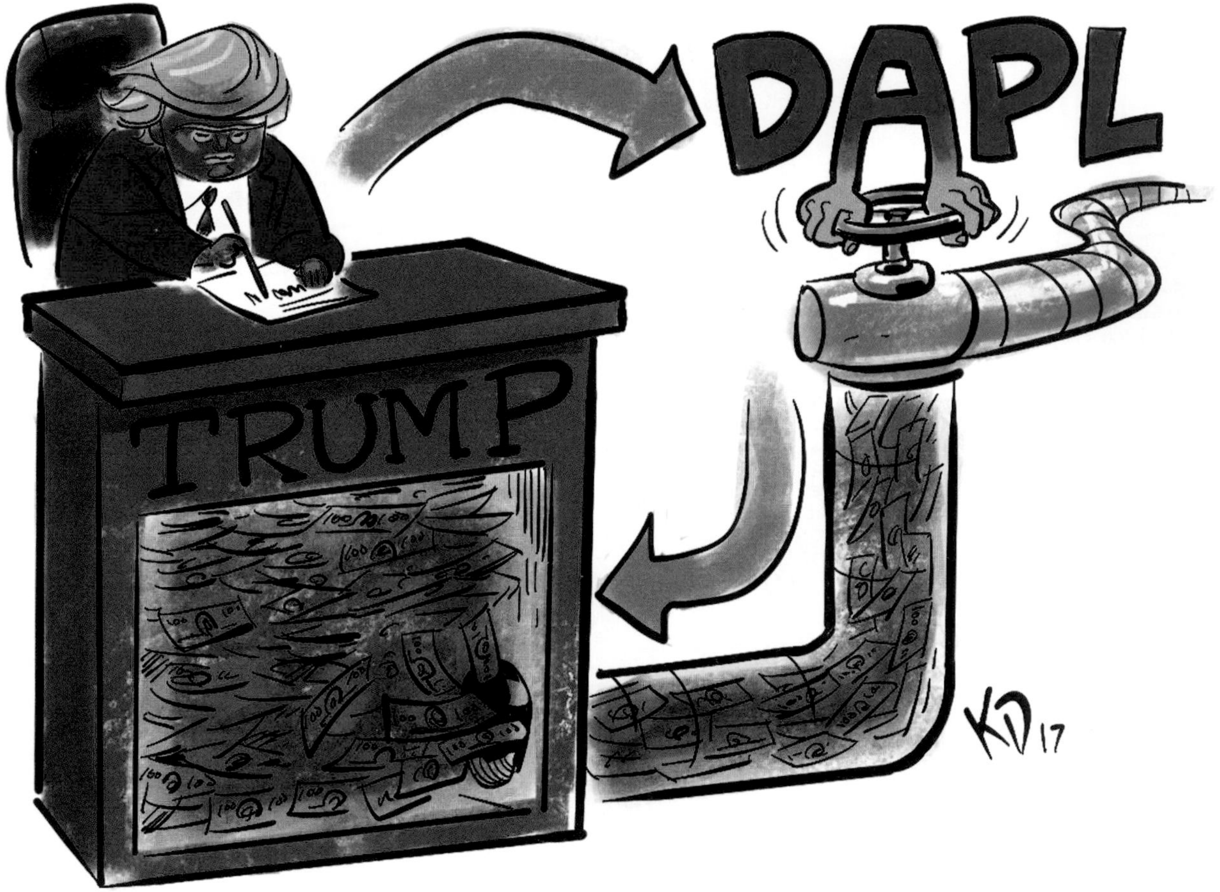
DAPL
TRUMP
KD 17

*DAPL: Donald Access Payment Line*

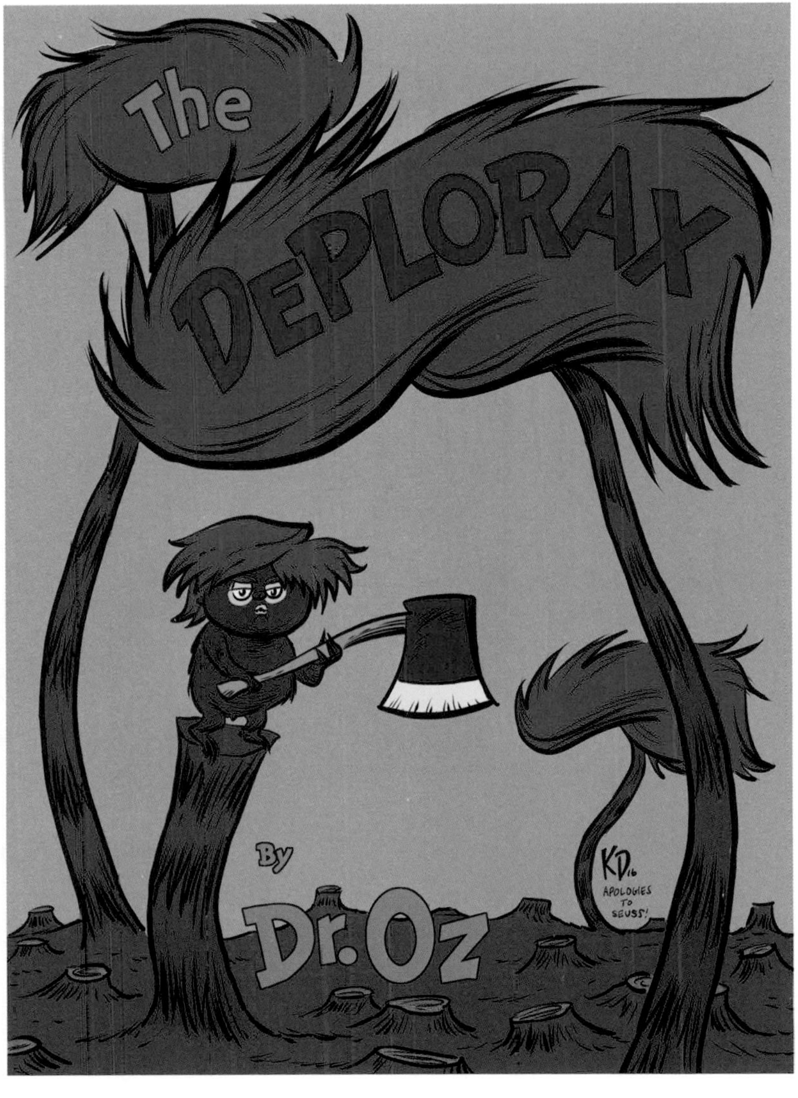
The
DEPLORAX
By
Dr. Oz
KD 16
APOLOGIES TO SEUSS!

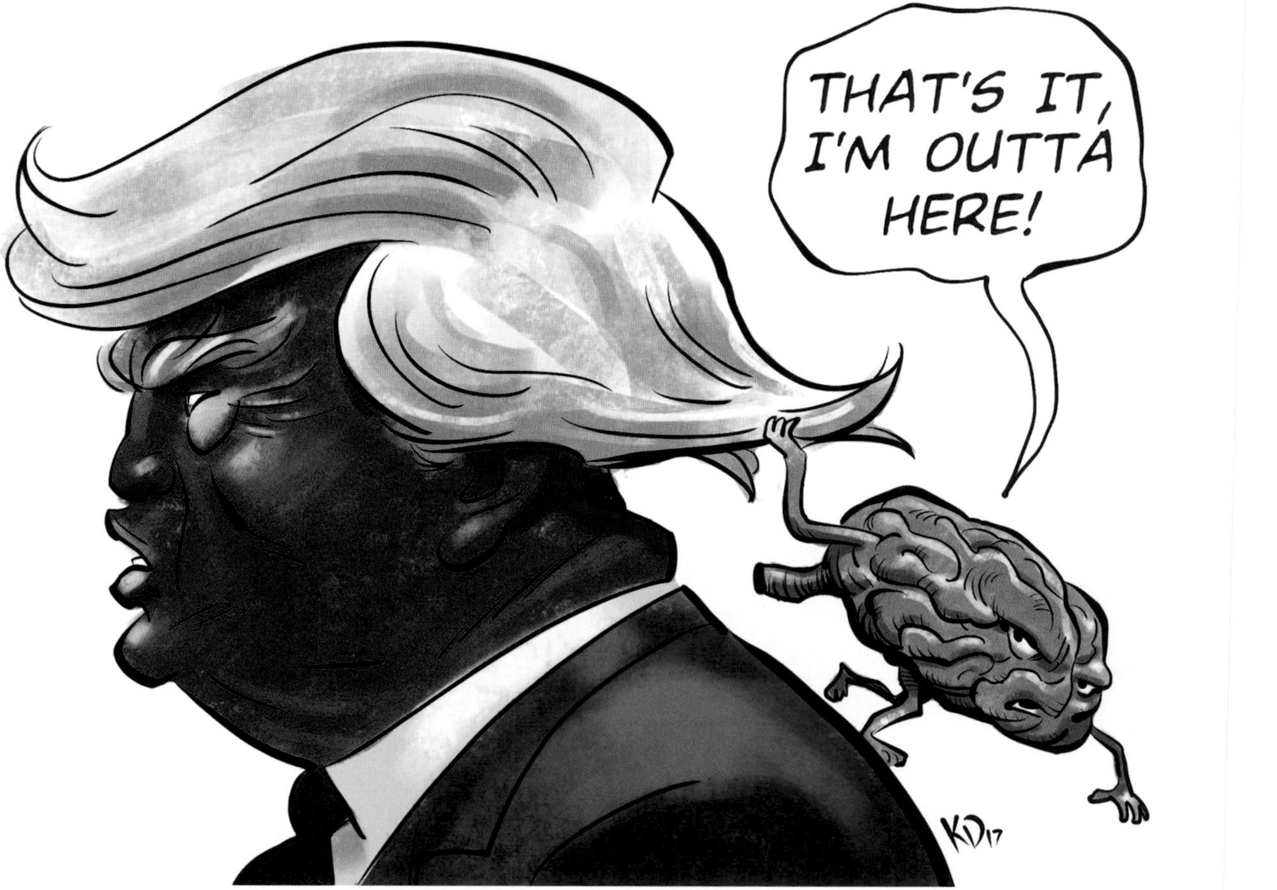
THAT'S IT, I'M OUTTA HERE!
KD17

*Brain Break*

*Narcissyphus*

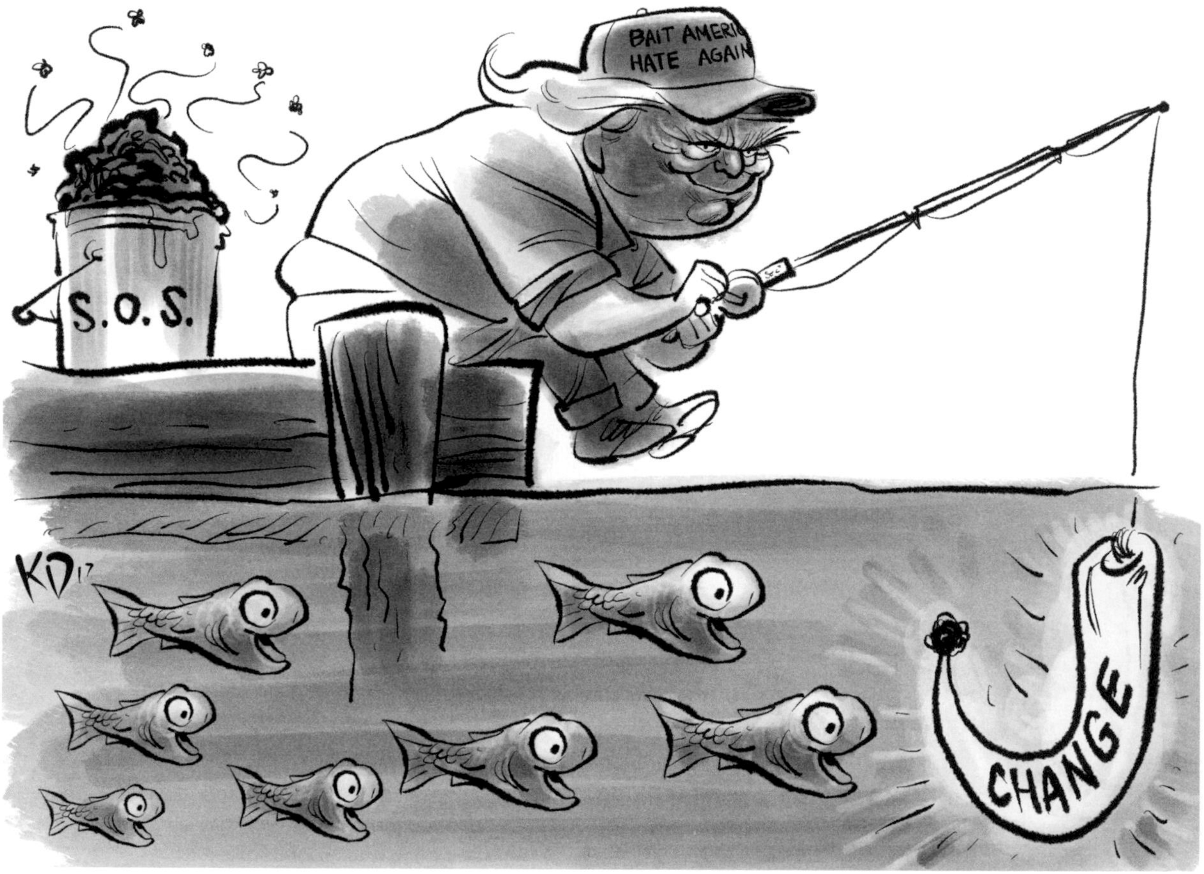
BAIT AMERIC
HATE AGAIN
S.O.S.
KD17
CHANGE

*Hook, Line, and Stinker*

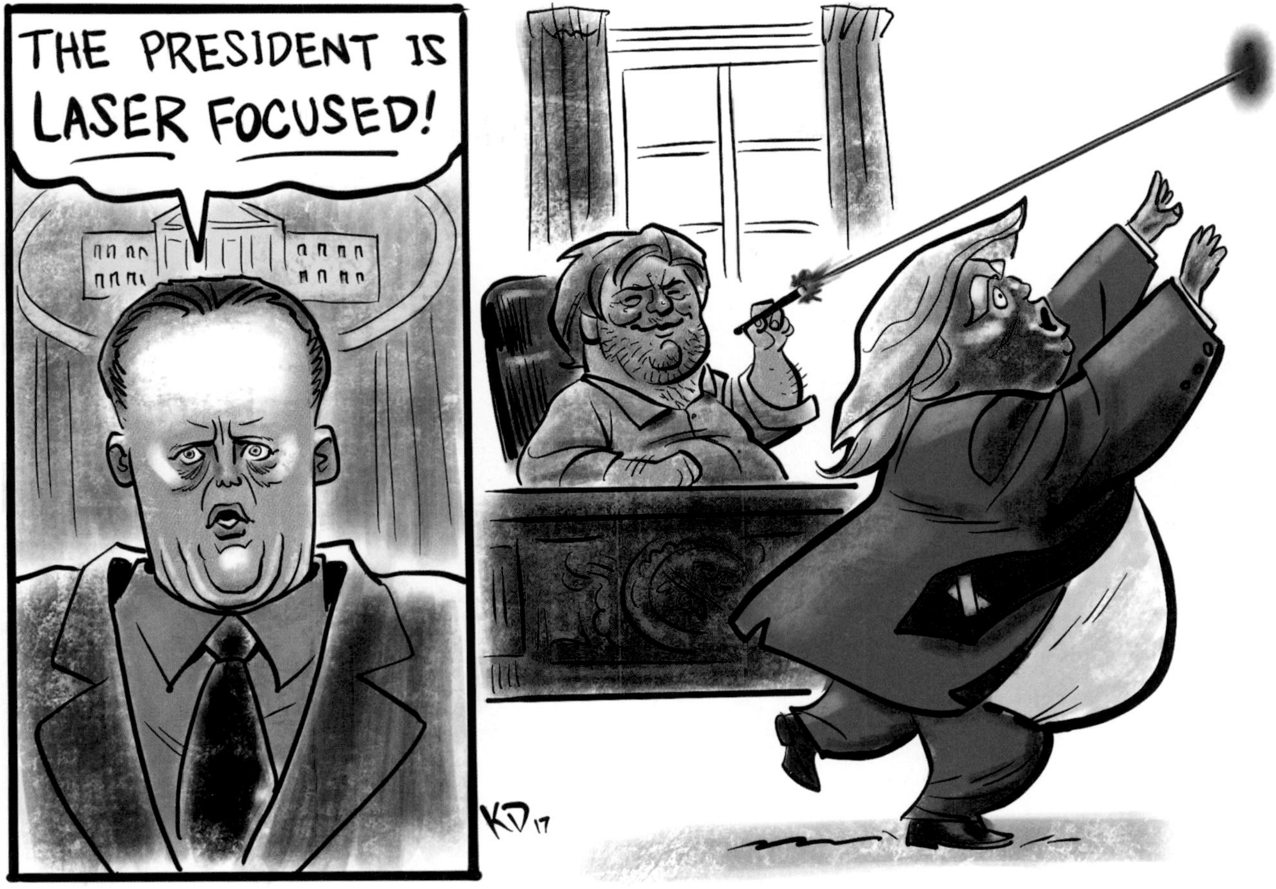
THE PRESIDENT IS LASER FOCUSED!
KD 17

NEA
FUNDING
I DON'T KNOW ART BUT I KNOW WHAT I HATE.
KD 17

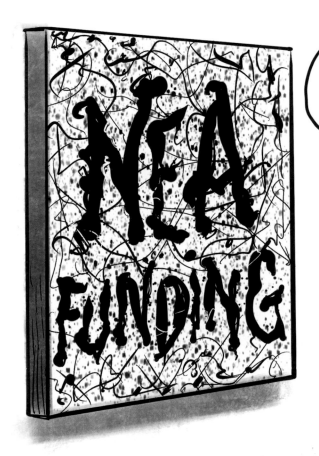

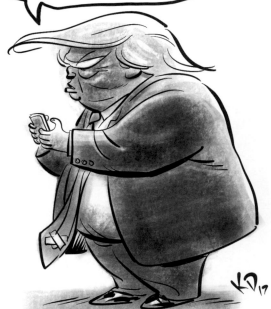

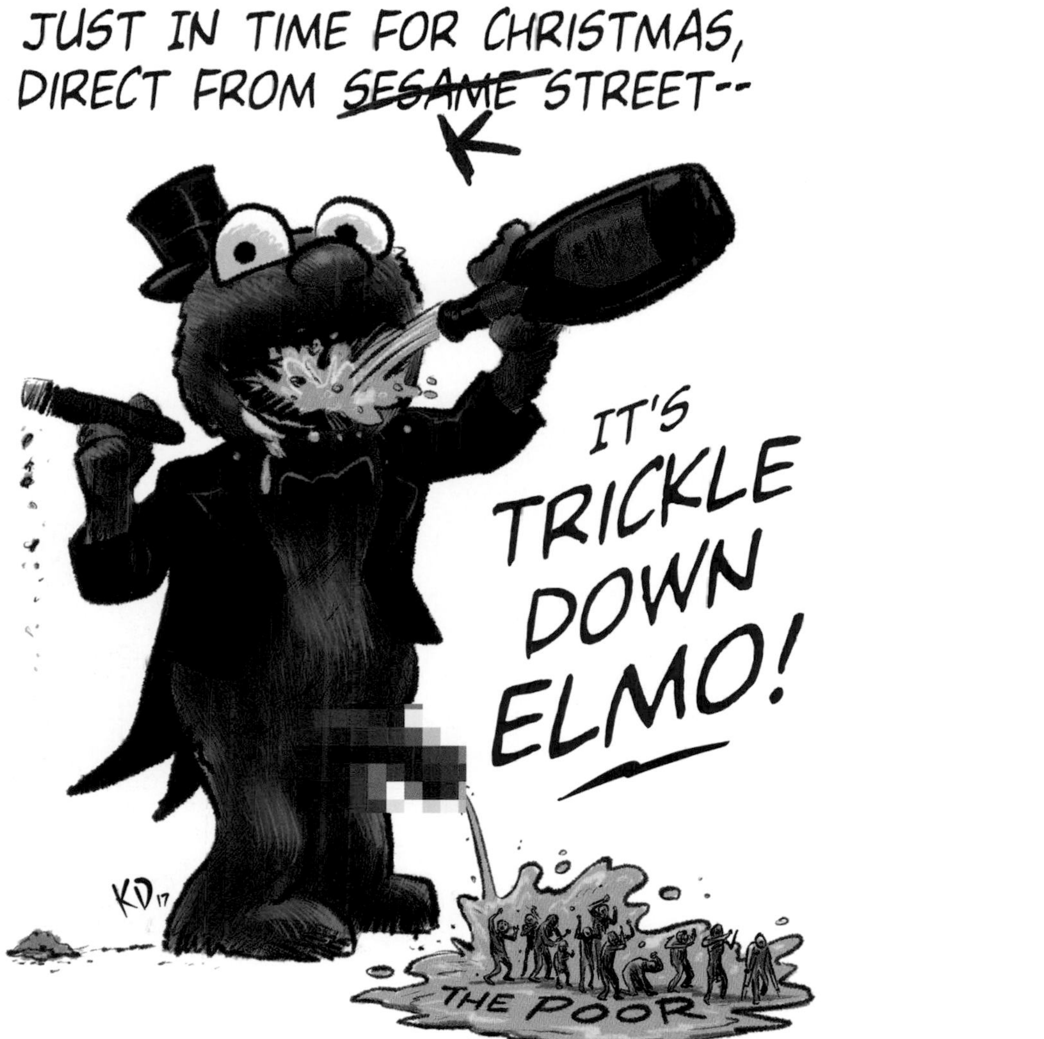
JUST IN TIME FOR CHRISTMAS,
DIRECT FROM ~~SESAME~~ STREET--
K
IT'S
TRICKLE
DOWN
ELMO!
THE POOR
KD 17

# STATUESQUE

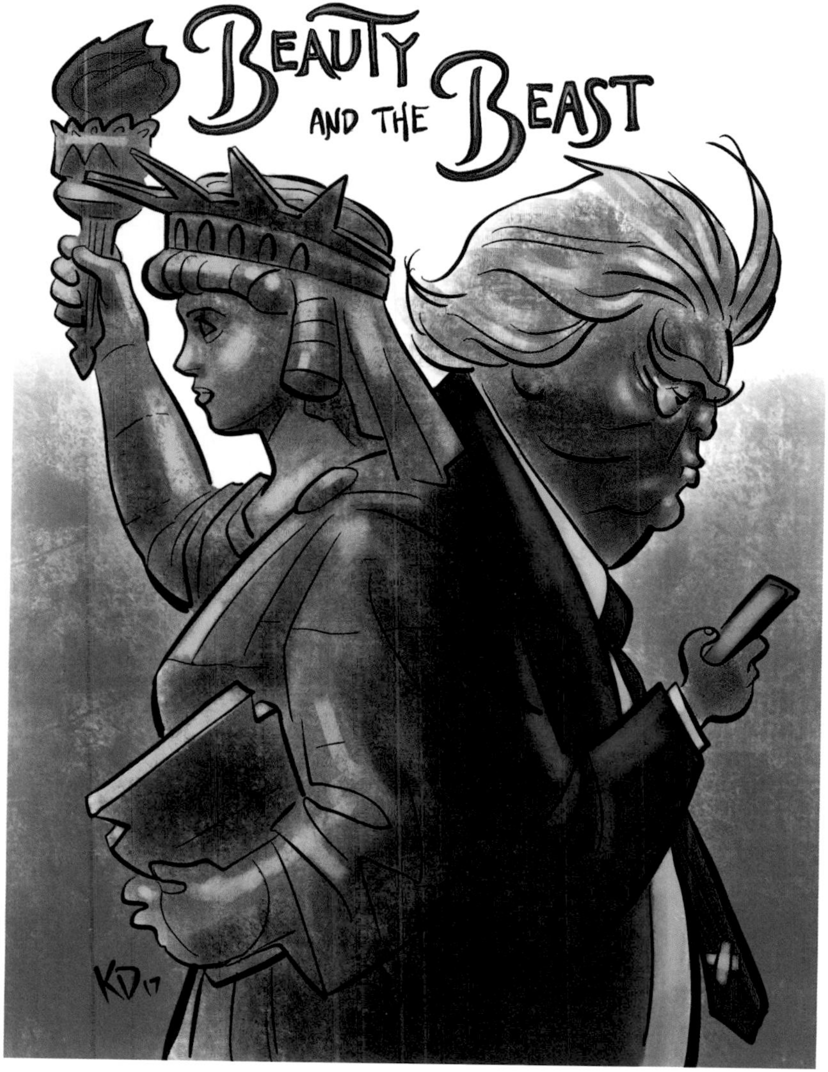
BEAUTY AND THE BEAST
KD 17

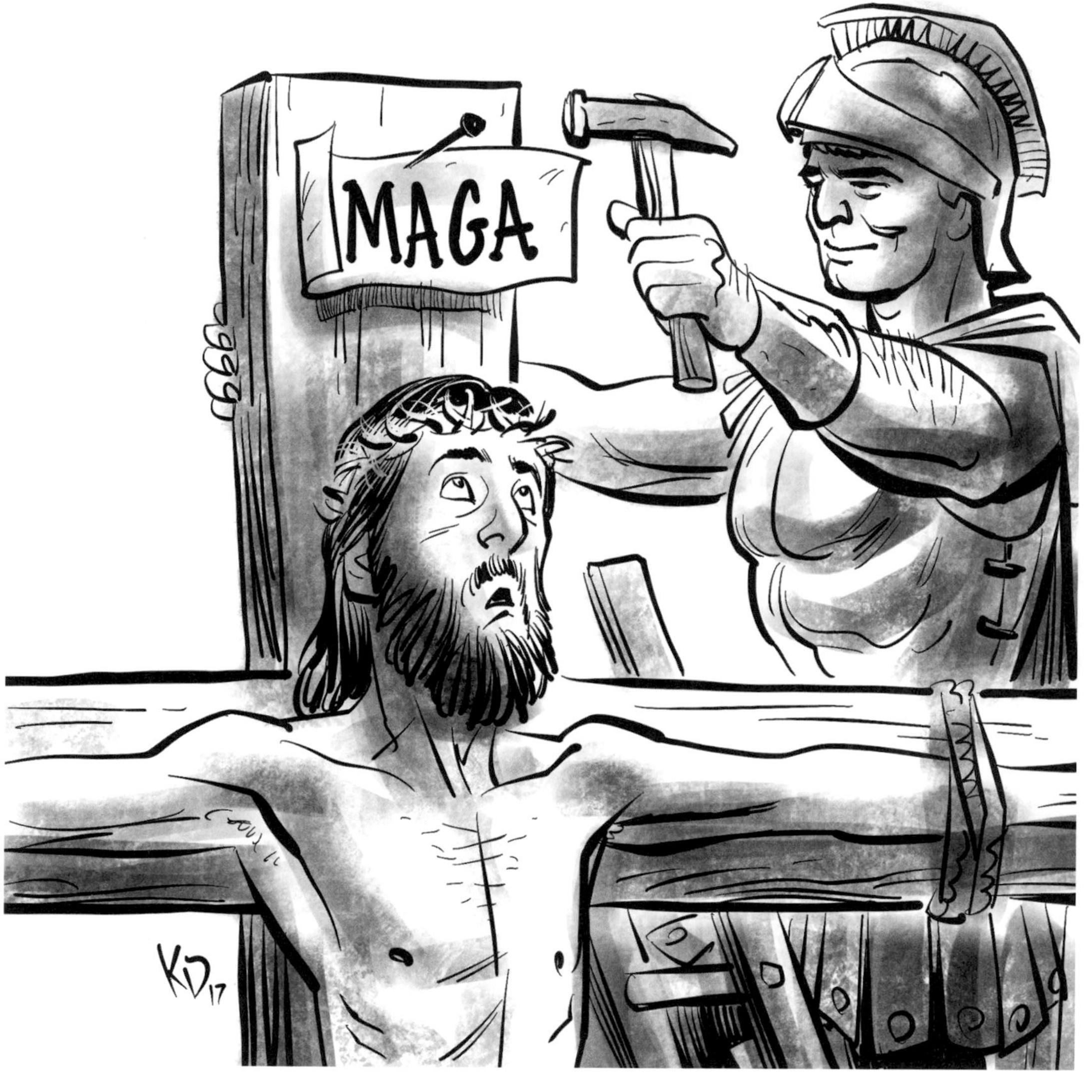
MAGA
KD 17

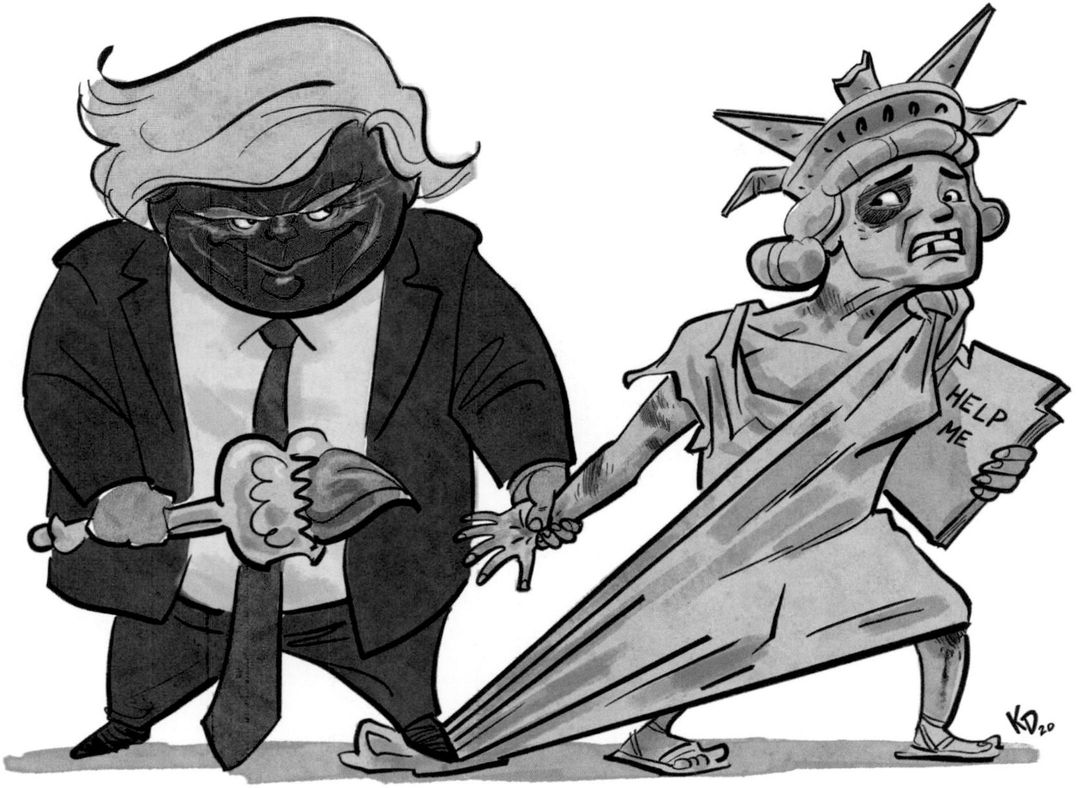
HELP
ME
KD20

#UStoo

# HEALTHSCARE

FIRST RULE OF GOP HEALTH CLUB:
THERE IS NO HEALTH CLUB!
KD '17

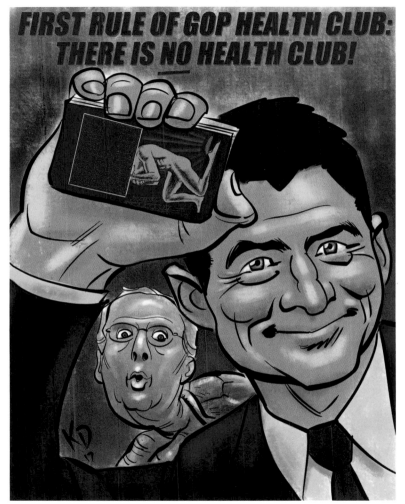

*Alt-Right Club*

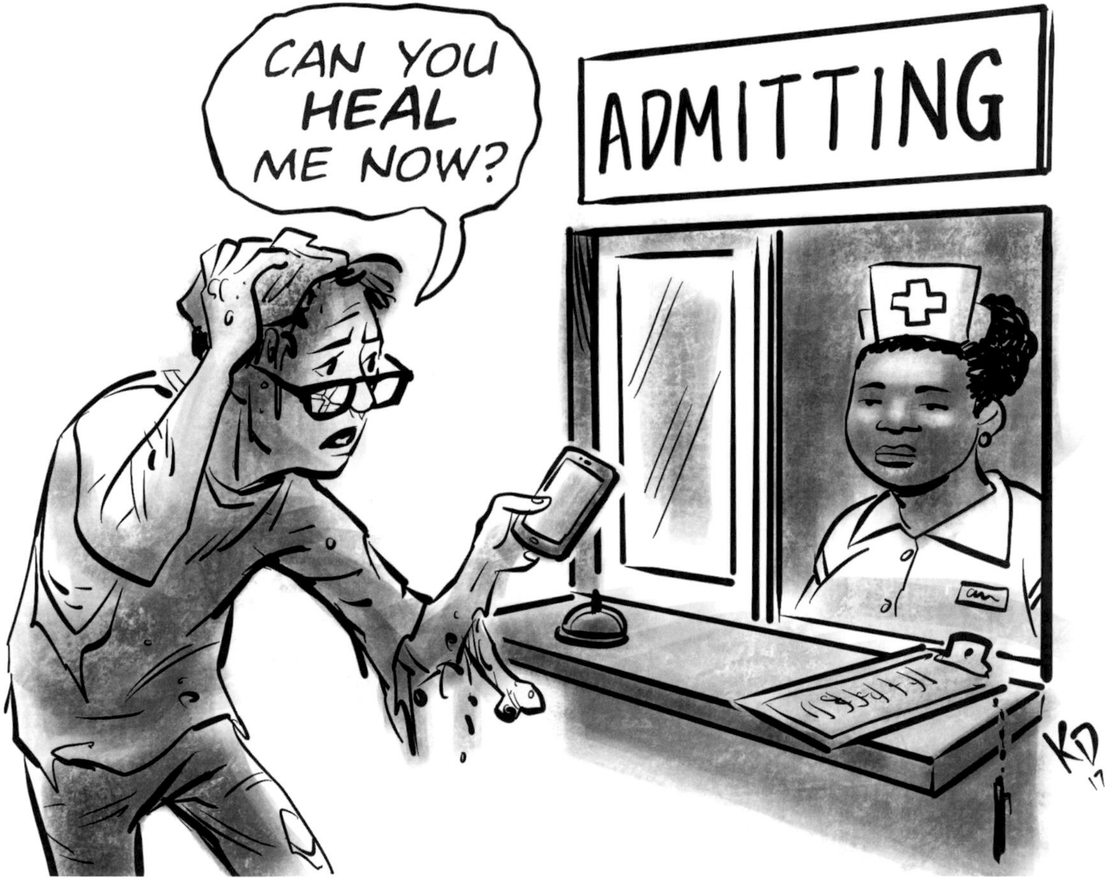
CAN YOU HEAL ME NOW?
ADMITTING
KD 17

*Rep. Chaffetz (R-UT): "Rather than get that new iPhone, maybe they should invest in their own healthcare."*

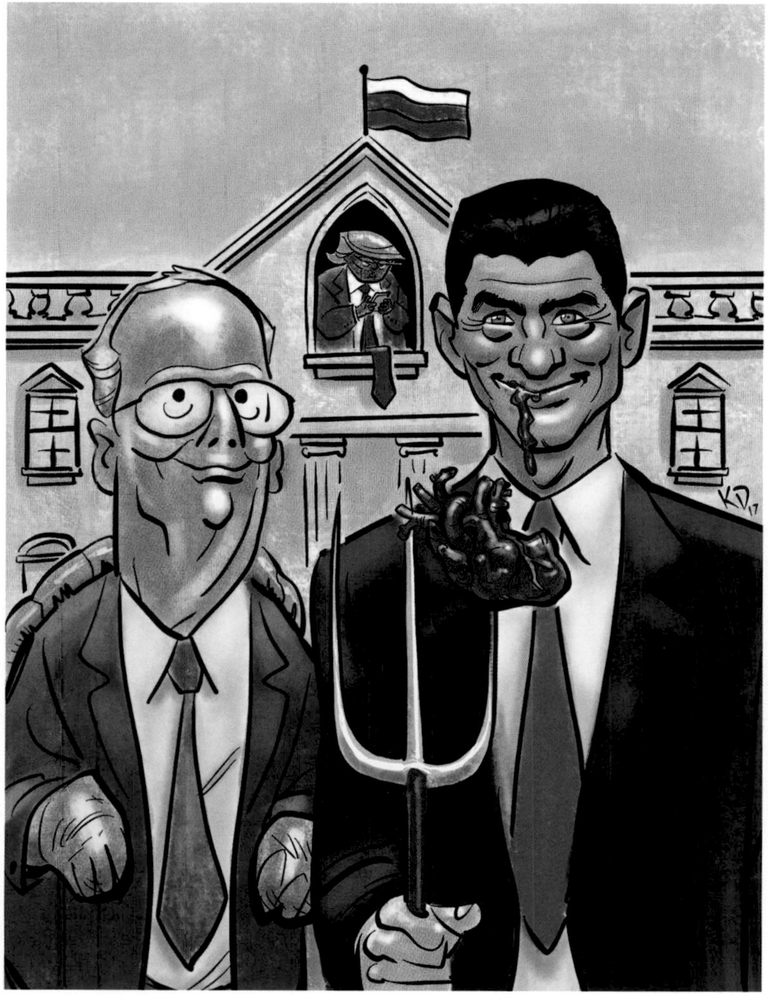
KD '17

*Mitch and Paul: Unamerican Gothic*

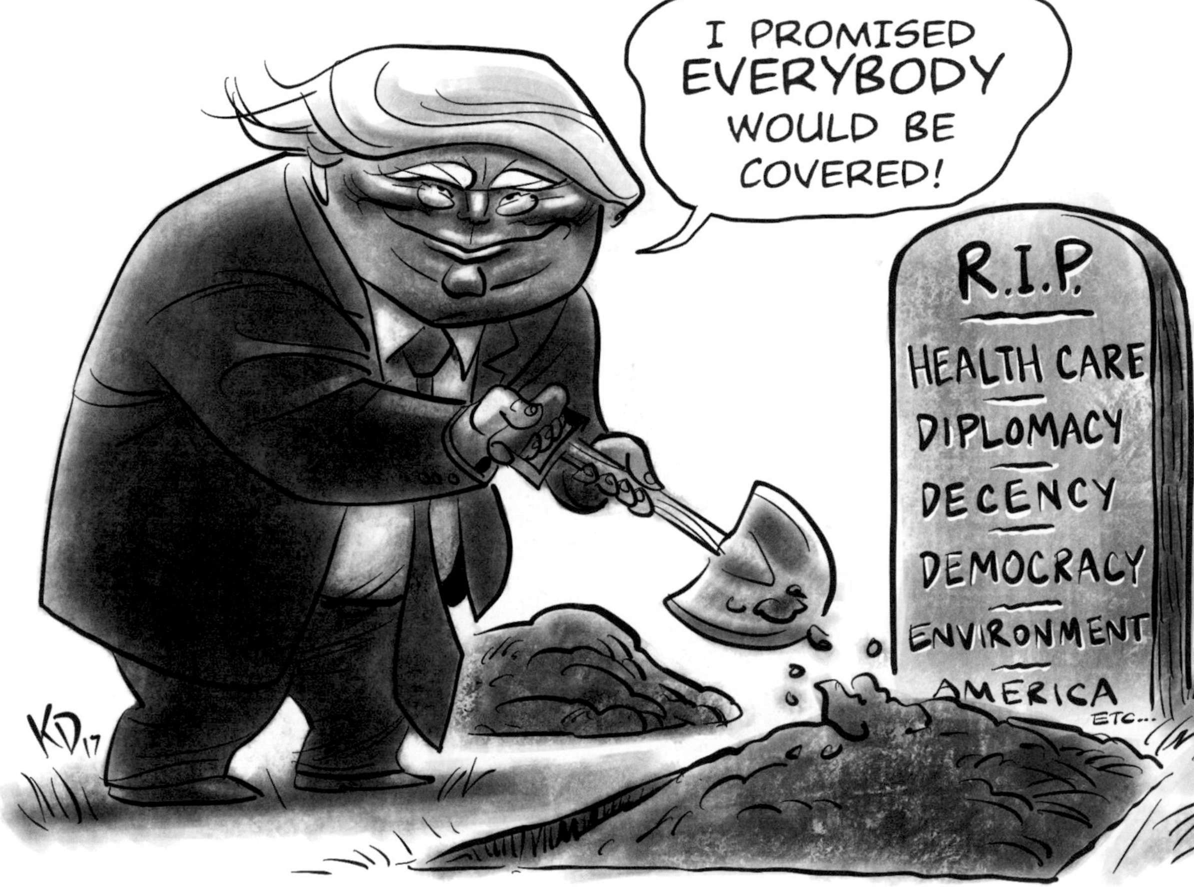
I PROMISED EVERYBODY WOULD BE COVERED!
R.I.P.
HEALTH CARE
DIPLOMACY
DECENCY
DEMOCRACY
ENVIRONMENT
AMERICA
ETC...
KD17

# PAUL RYAN, BOY SCOUT

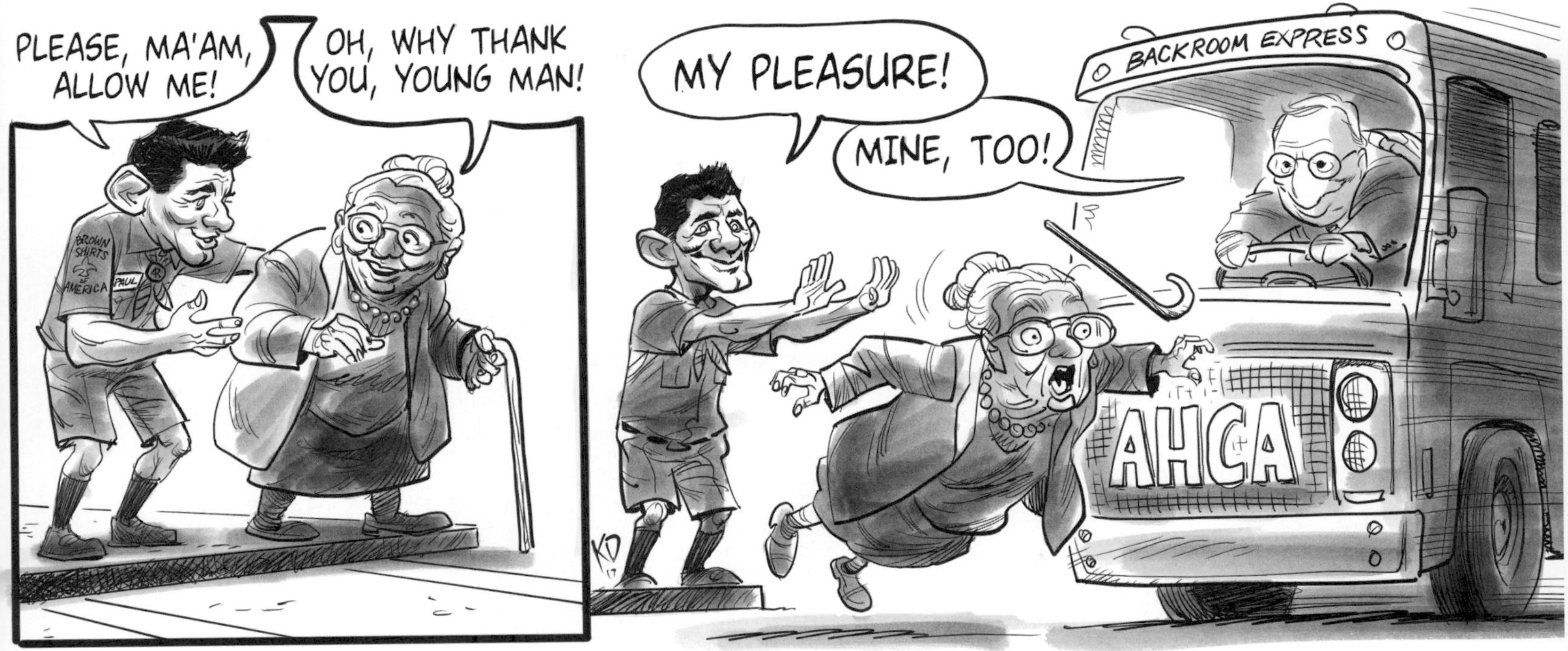
PLEASE, MA'AM, ALLOW ME!
OH, WHY THANK YOU, YOUNG MAN!
BROWN SHIRTS OF AMERICA
PAUL
MY PLEASURE!
MINE, TOO!
BACKROOM EXPRESS
AHCA

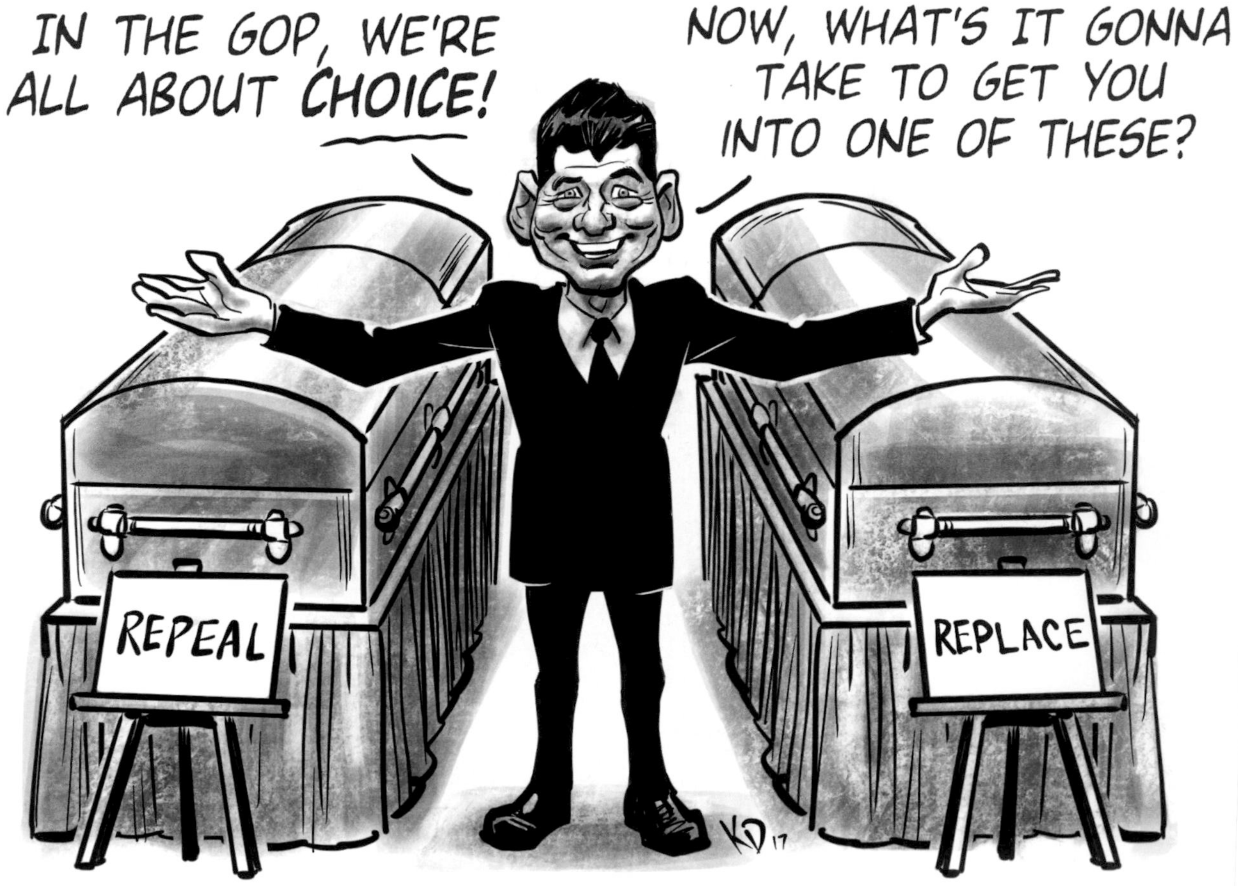
IN THE GOP, WE'RE ALL ABOUT CHOICE!
NOW, WHAT'S IT GONNA TAKE TO GET YOU INTO ONE OF THESE?
REPEAL
REPLACE
KD 17

*Paul Ryan, Used Health Salesman*

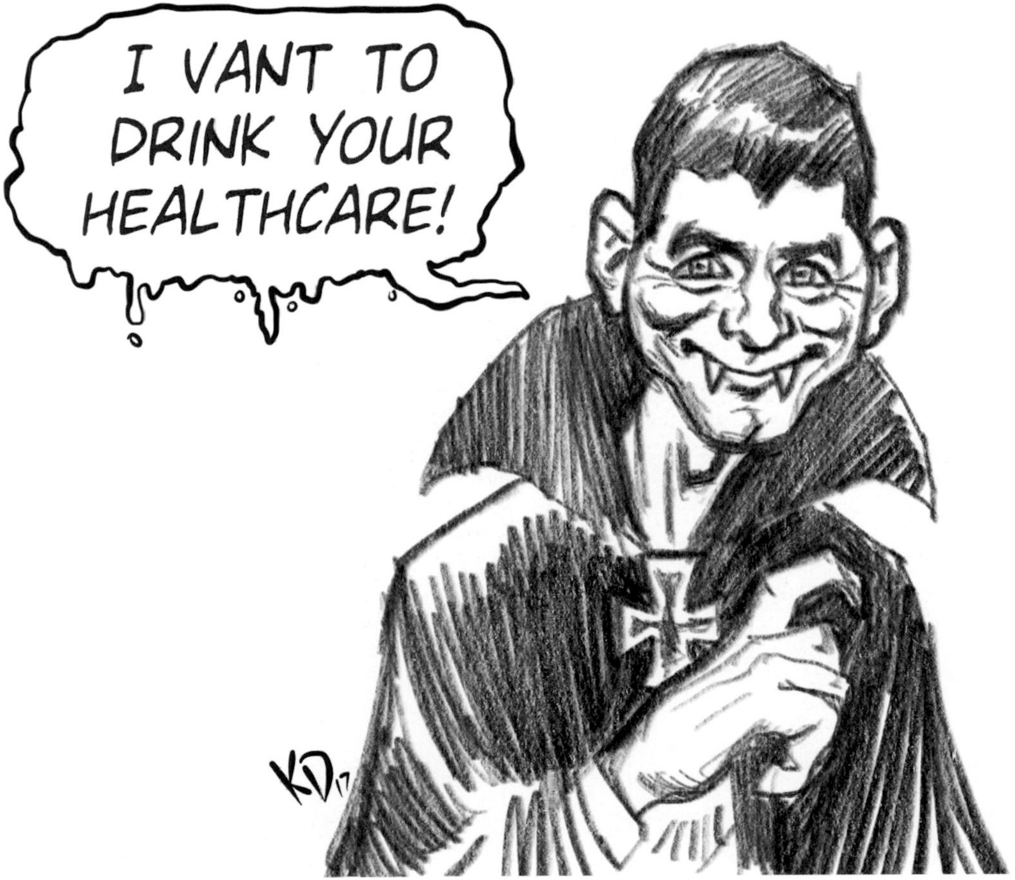
I VANT TO DRINK YOUR HEALTHCARE!
KD17

*Paul Ryan, Bloodsucker*

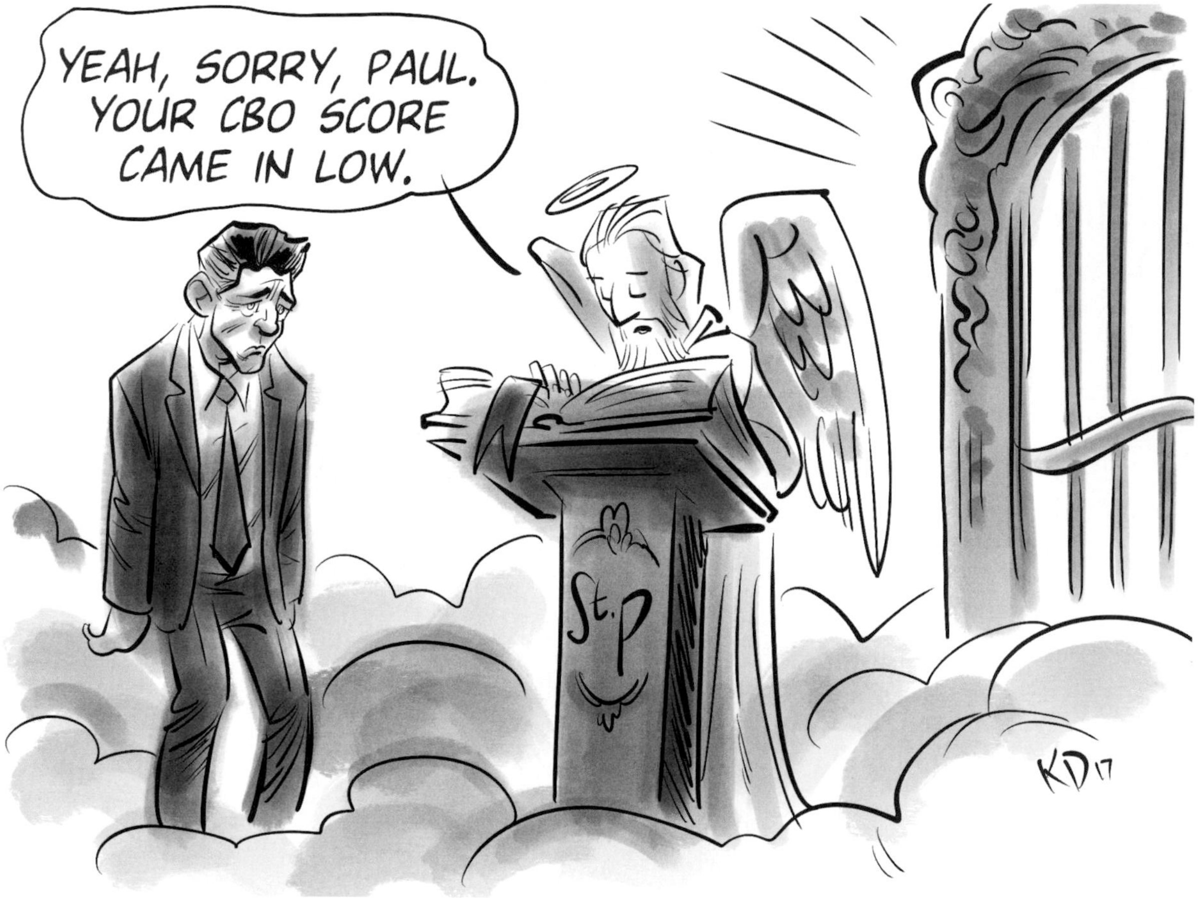
YEAH, SORRY, PAUL. YOUR CBO SCORE CAME IN LOW.
St. P
KD 17

*Karma's a bitch.*

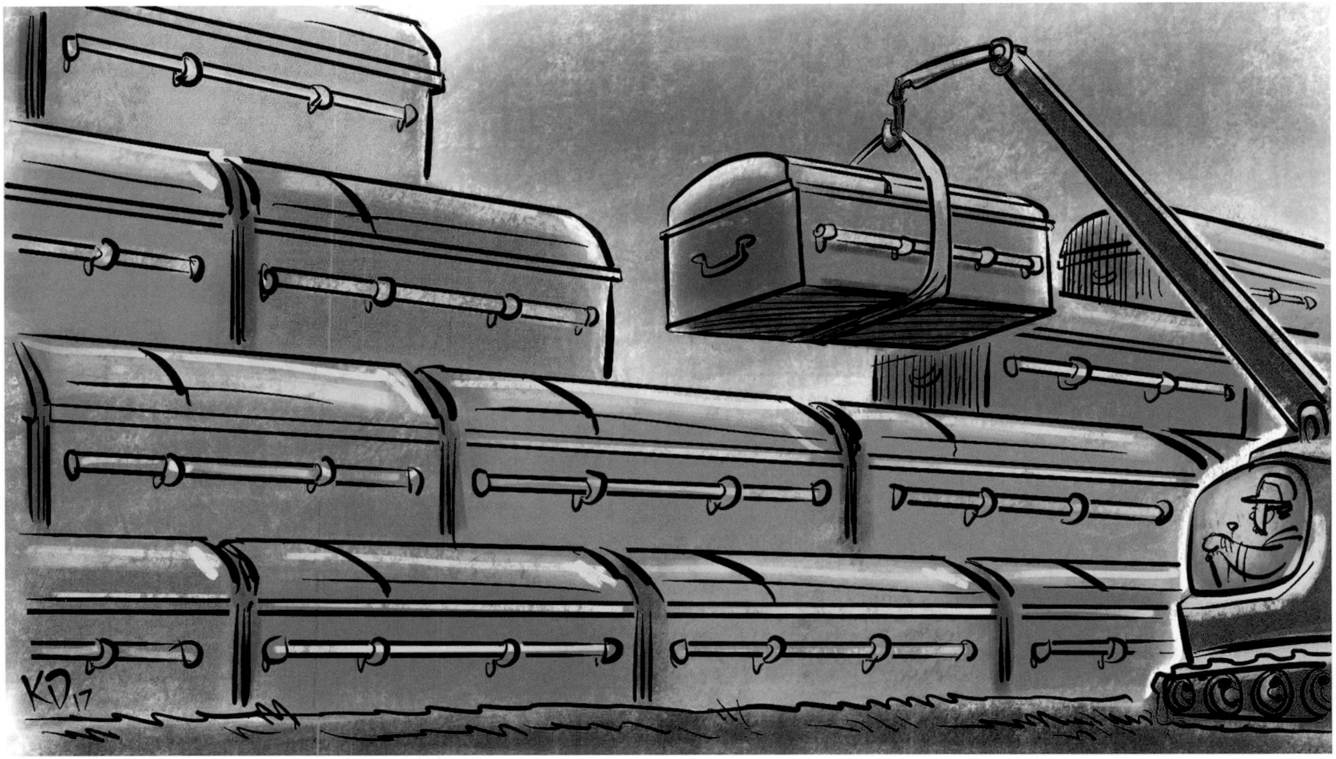

*Win-Win, GOP-style: Kill Obamacare AND build tRump's Wall*

# AMERICAN IDIOT

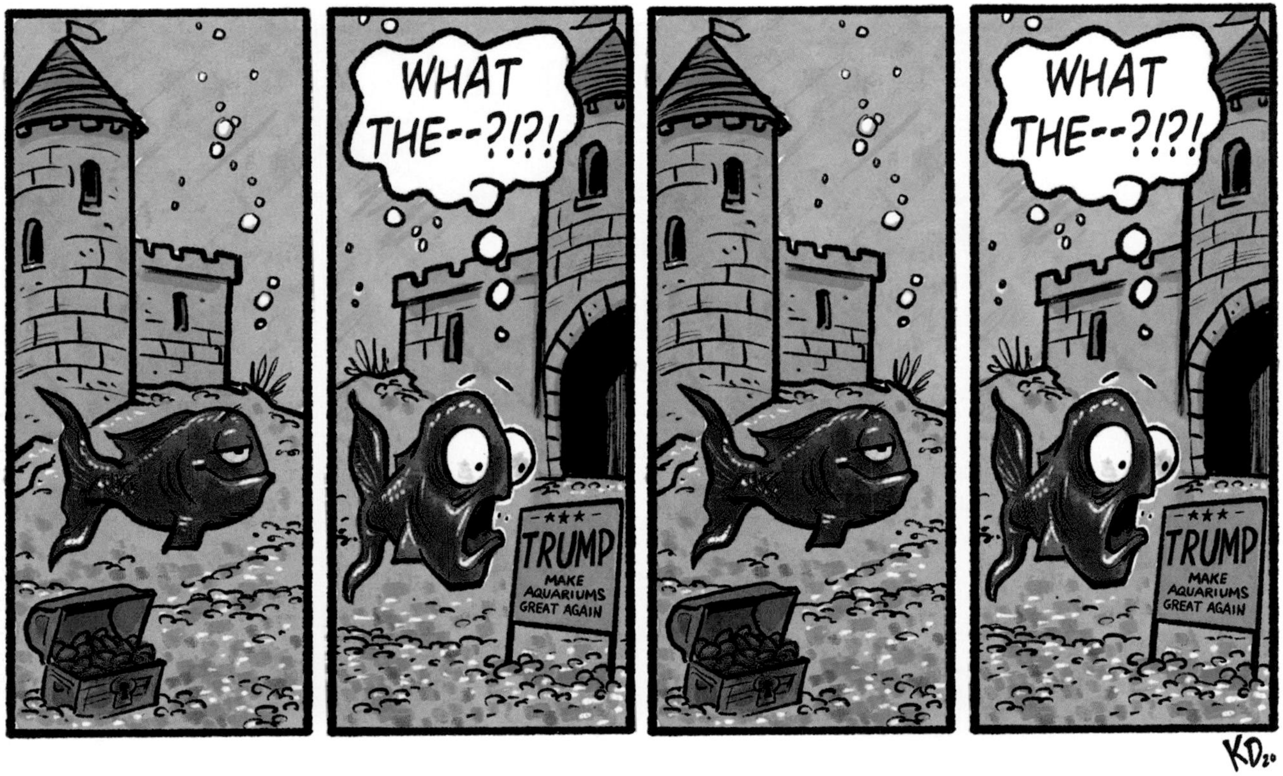
WHAT THE--?!?!
TRUMP
MAKE AQUARIUMS GREAT AGAIN
WHAT THE--?!?!
TRUMP
MAKE AQUARIUMS GREAT AGAIN
KD20

*EVERY. DAY.*

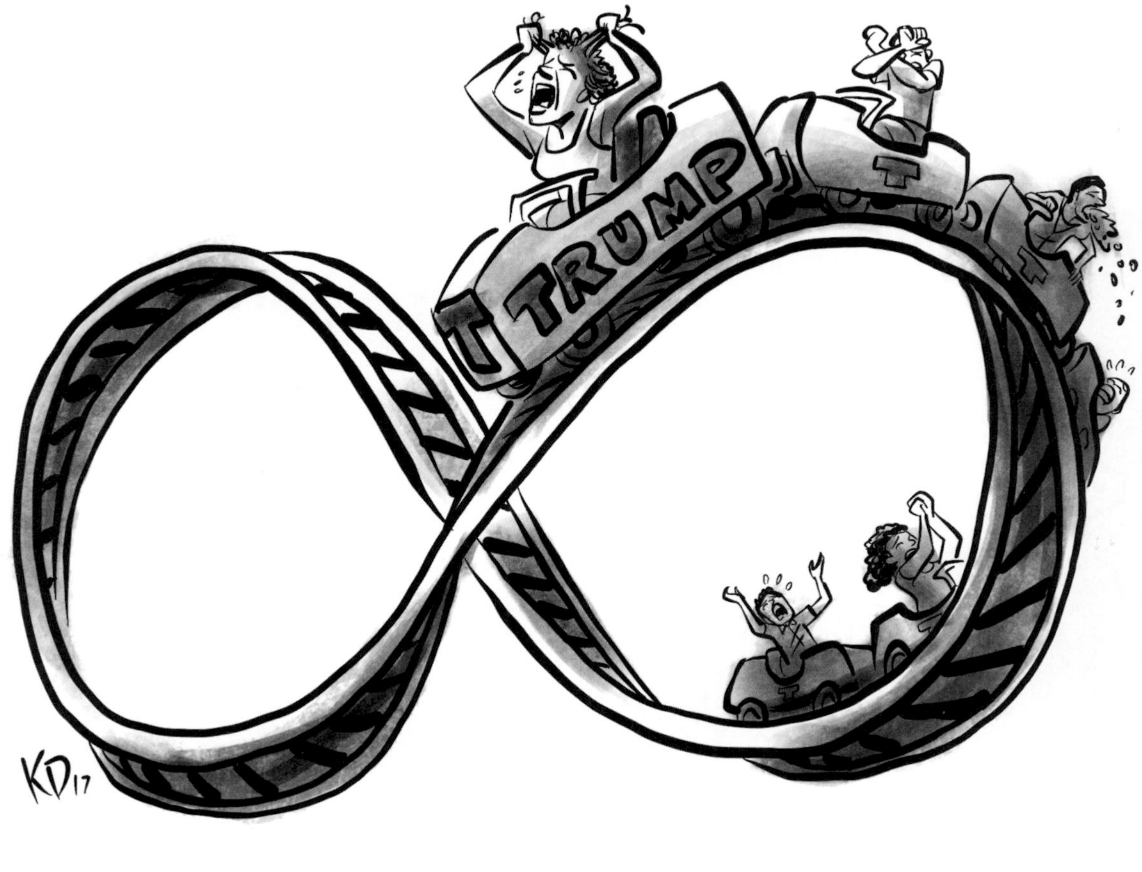
TRUMP
KD17

*Stop the ride, we want to get off.*

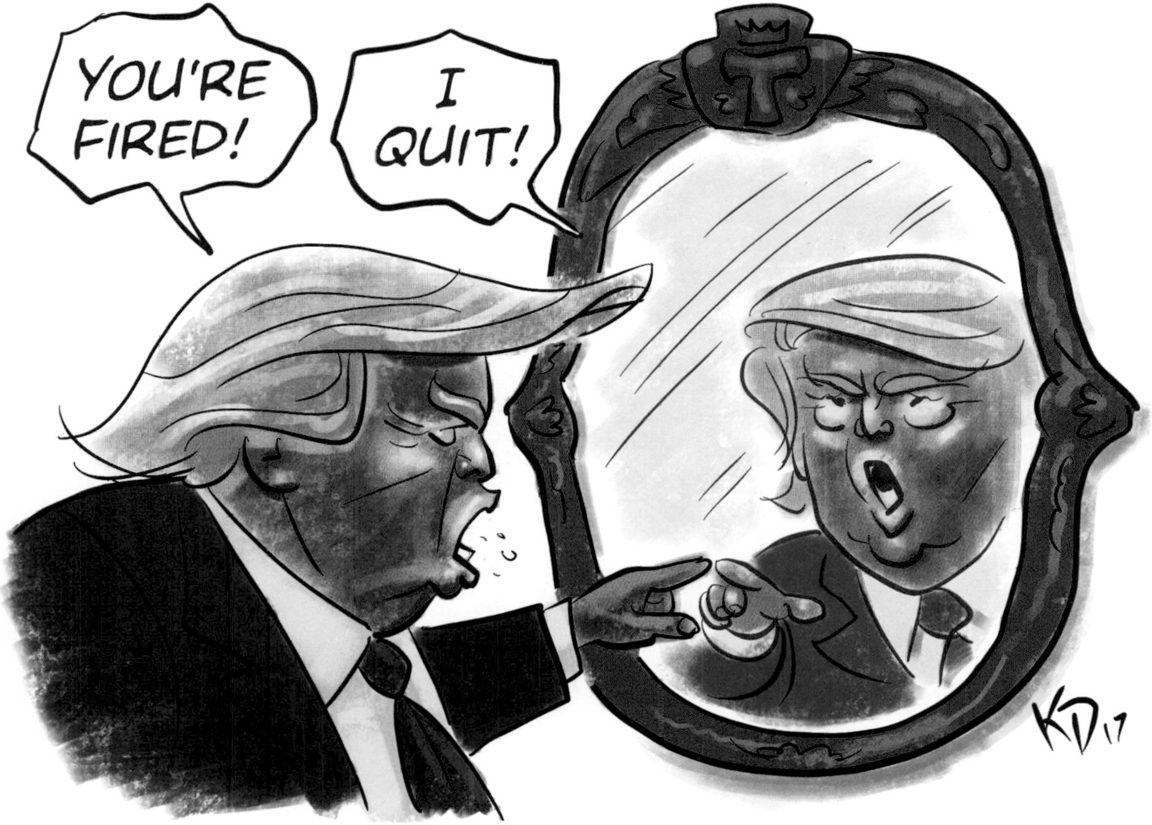
YOU'RE FIRED!
I QUIT!
KD'17

*Fairly Unbalanced of Them All*

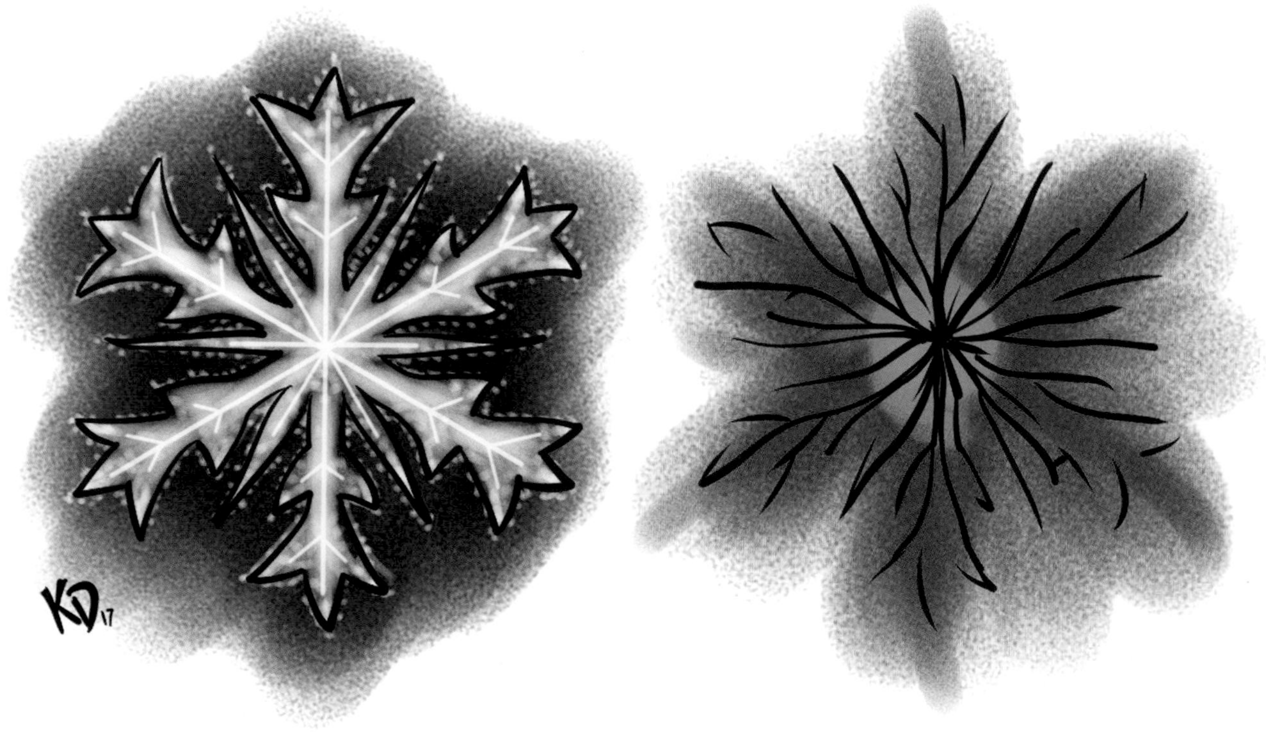
KD17

*Better to be a tiny snowflake than a giant asshole.*

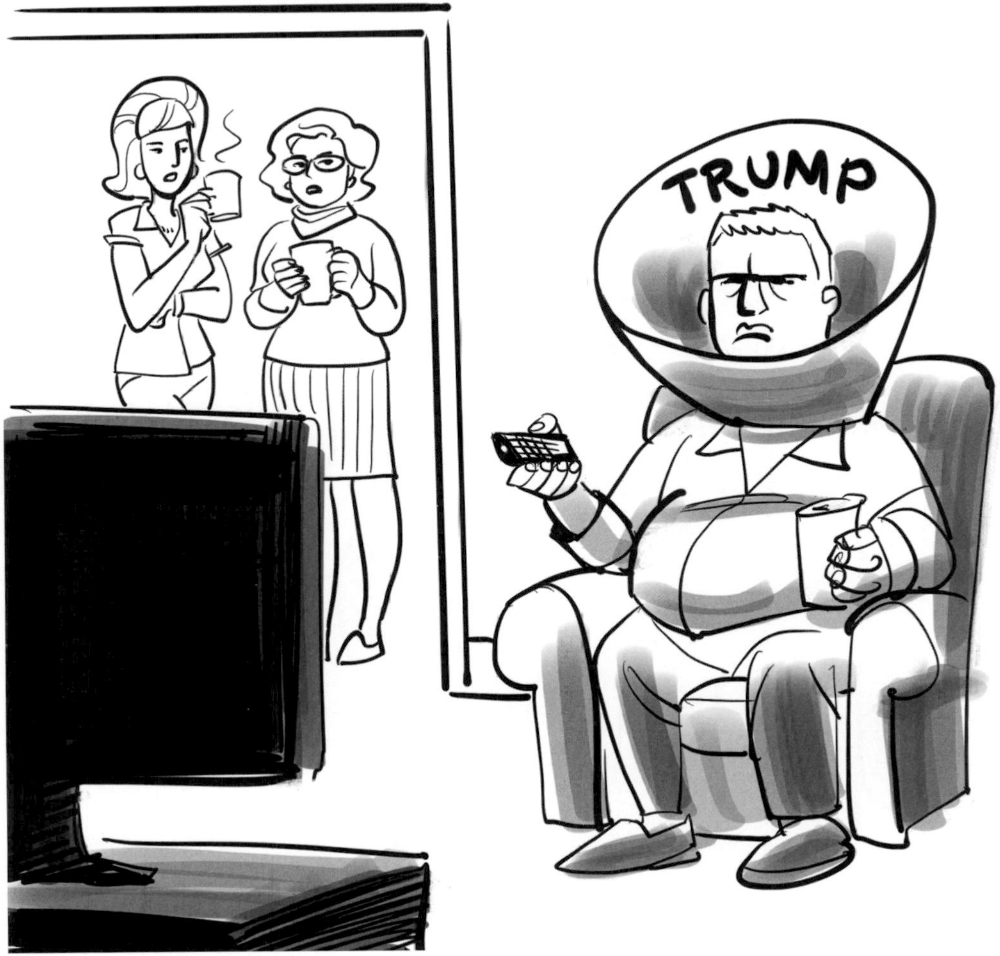
TRUMP

*"He has to wear it for the next four years, at least."*

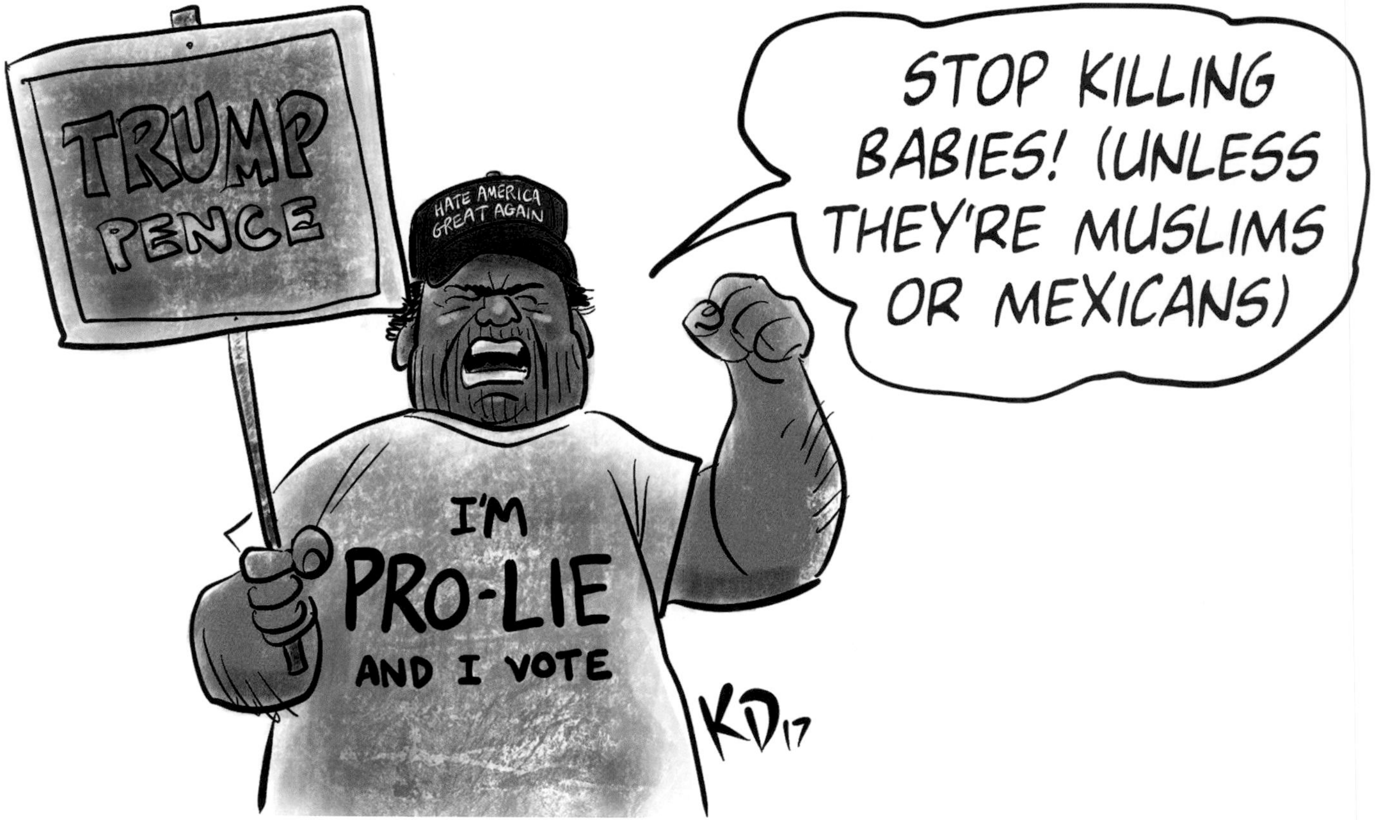
TRUMP
PENCE
HATE AMERICA GREAT AGAIN
STOP KILLING BABIES! (UNLESS THEY'RE MUSLIMS OR MEXICANS)
I'M PRO-LIE AND I VOTE
KD17

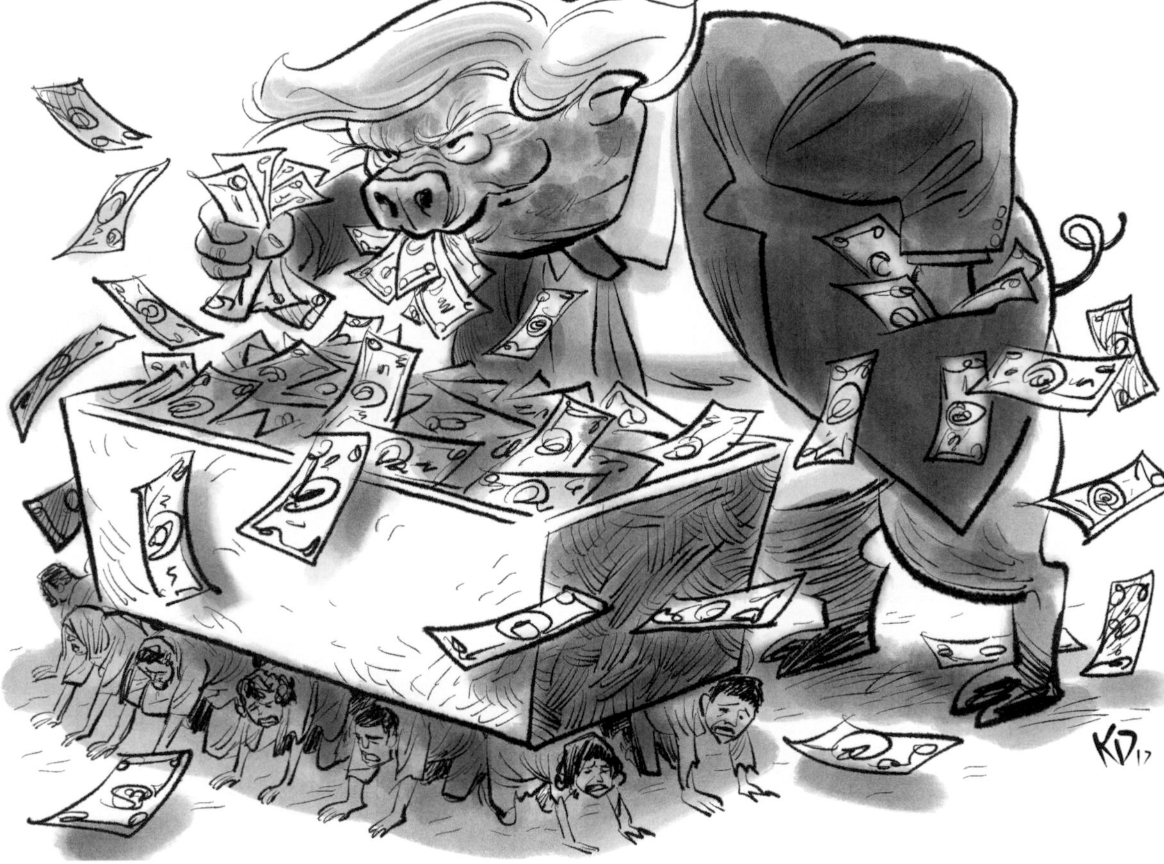
KD17

*Too Pig to Fail*

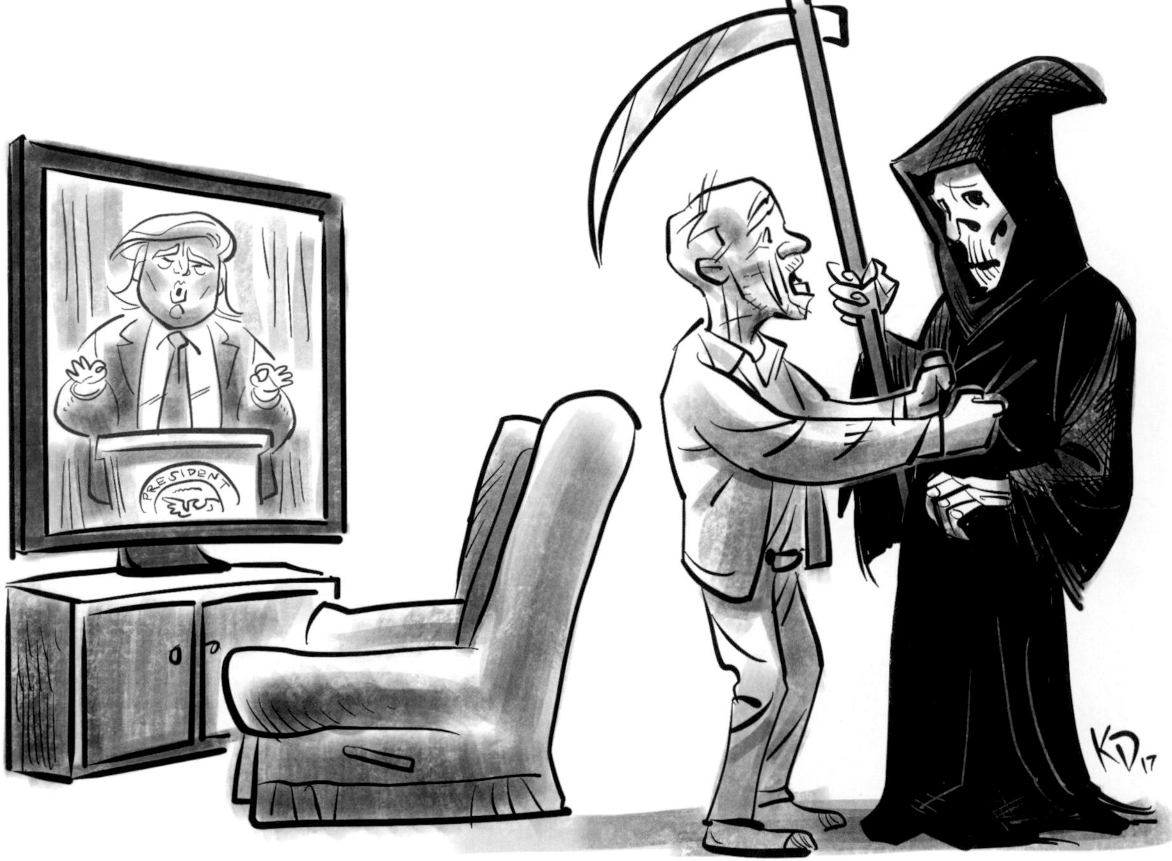
PRESIDENT
KD 17

*"What took you so long?!"*

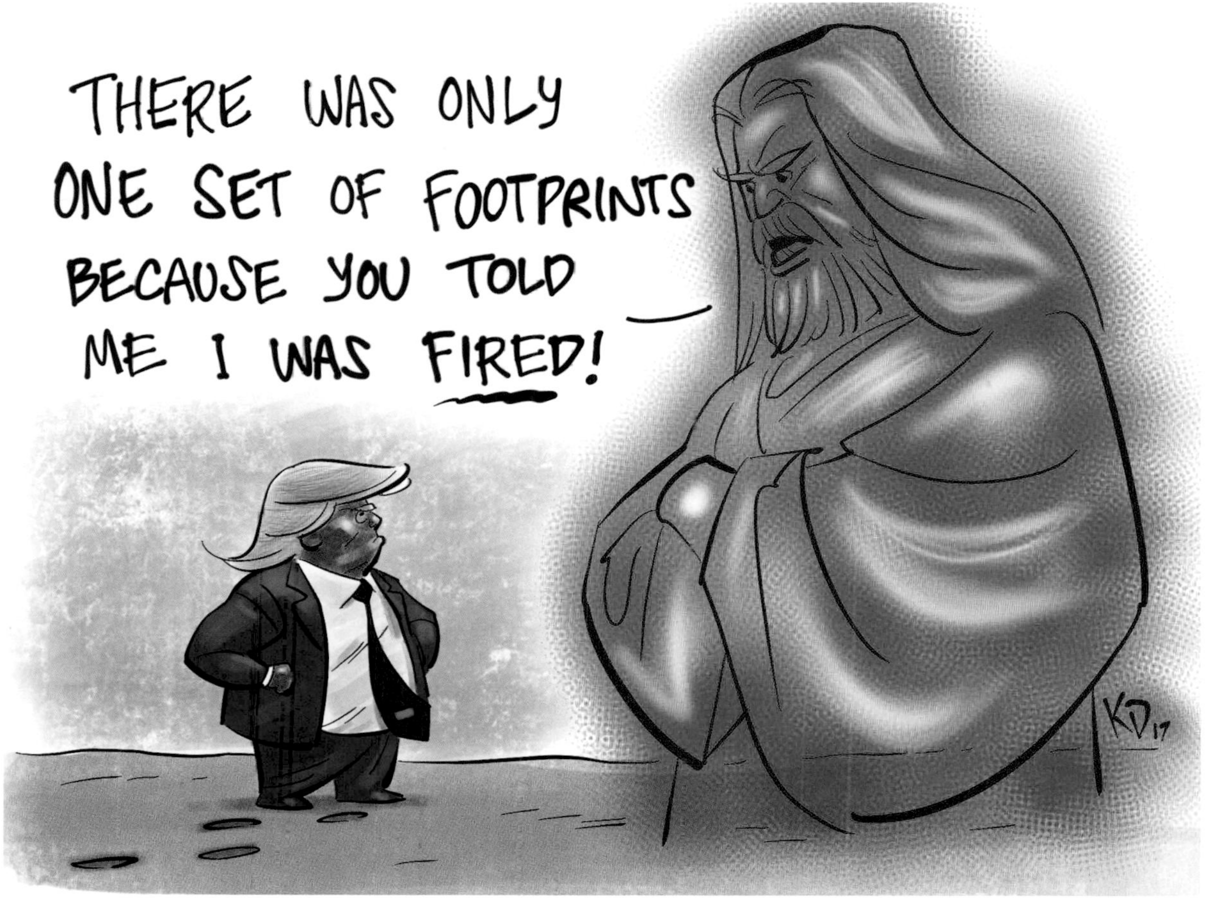
THERE WAS ONLY ONE SET OF FOOTPRINTS BECAUSE YOU TOLD ME I WAS FIRED!
KD 17

WHAT CONSTITUTIONAL CRISIS?

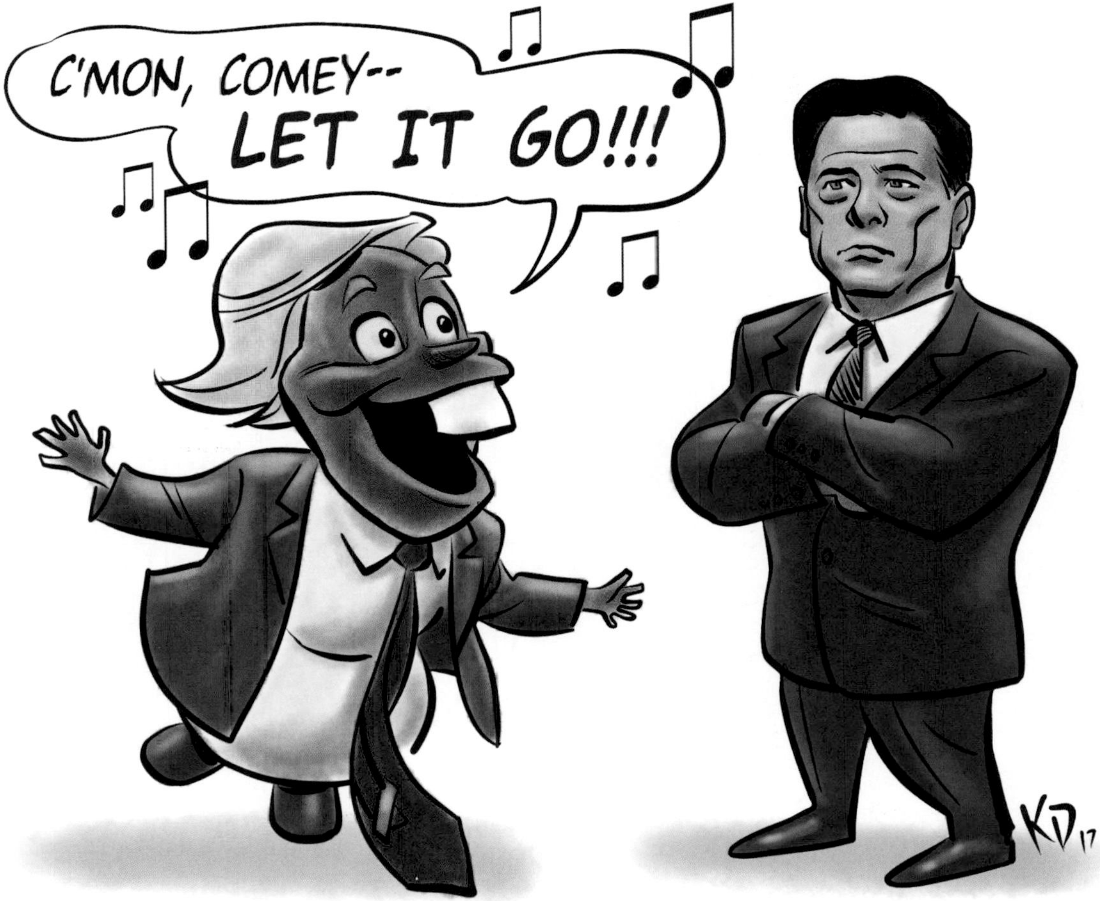
C'MON, COMEY--
LET IT GO!!!
KD 17

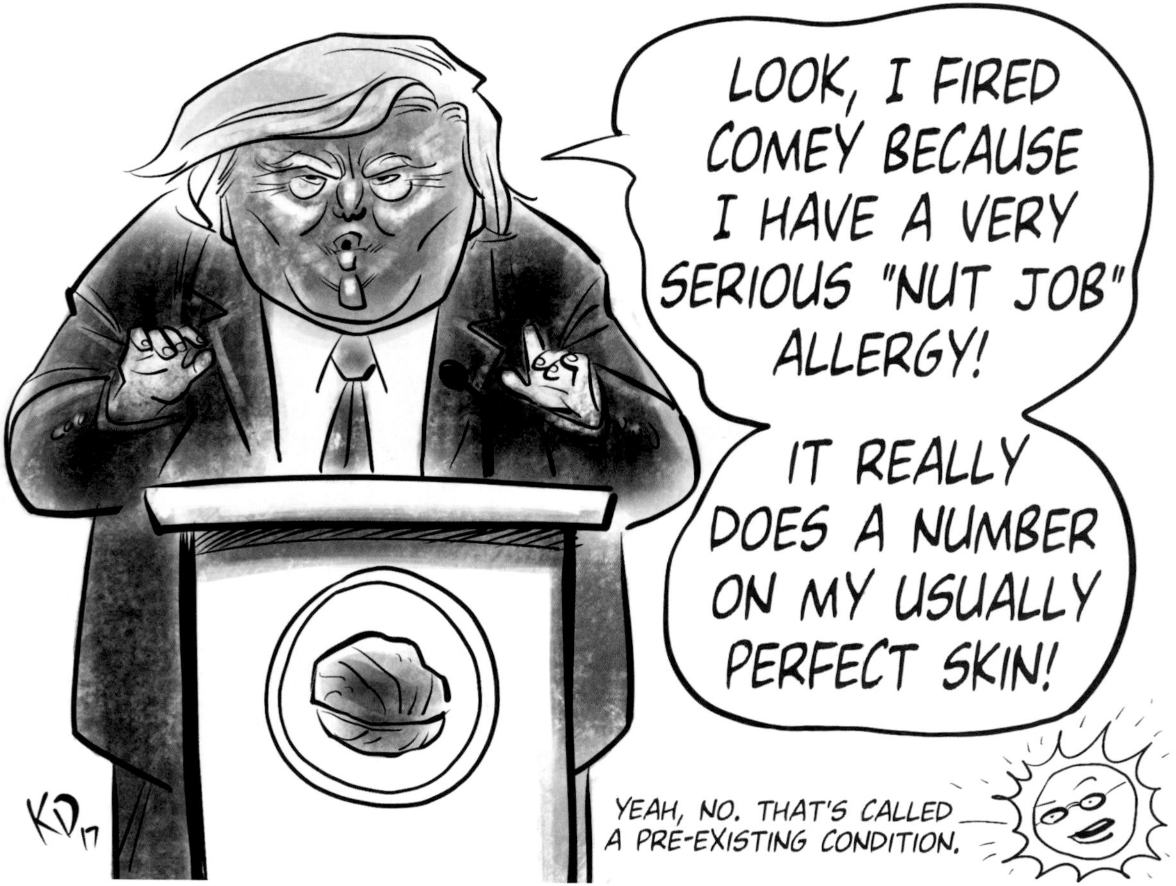
LOOK, I FIRED COMEY BECAUSE I HAVE A VERY SERIOUS "NUT JOB" ALLERGY!
IT REALLY DOES A NUMBER ON MY USUALLY PERFECT SKIN!
YEAH, NO. THAT'S CALLED A PRE-EXISTING CONDITION.
KD 17

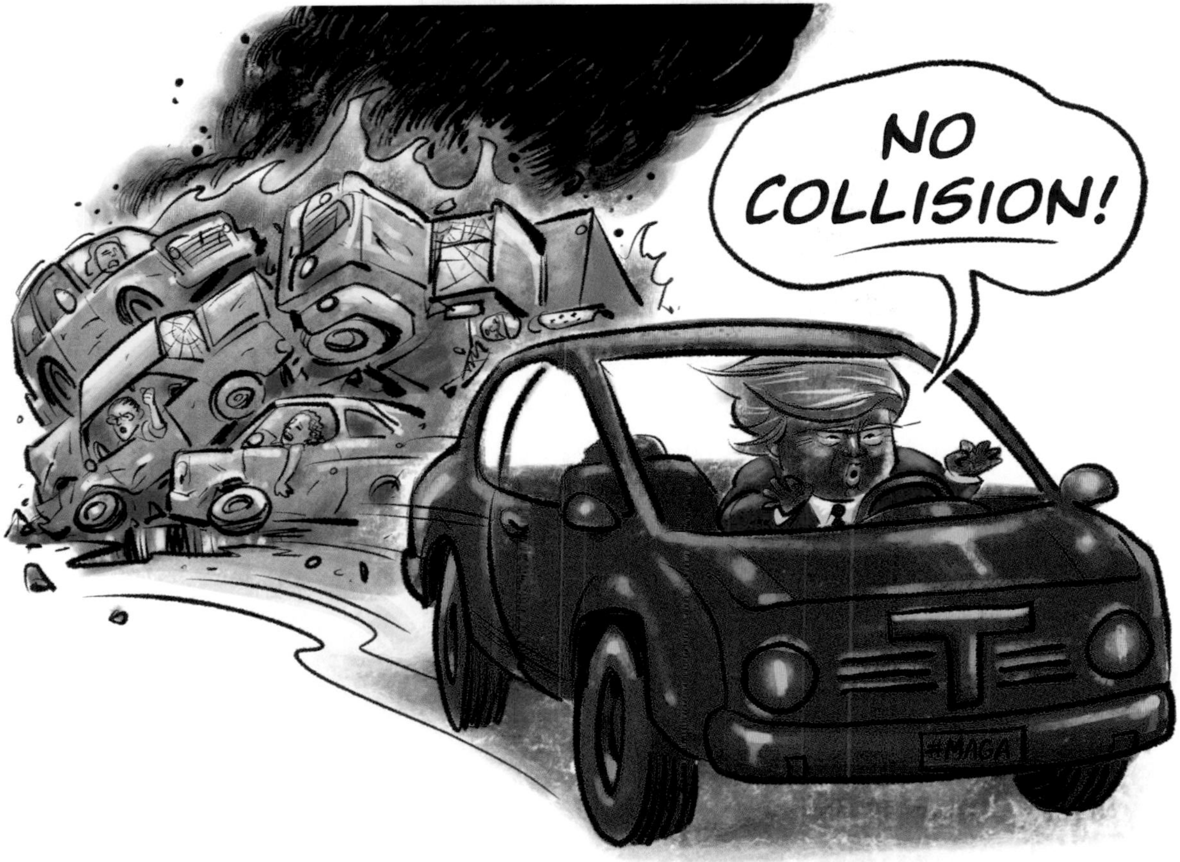
NO COLLISION!
T
#MAGA

*The best driver.*

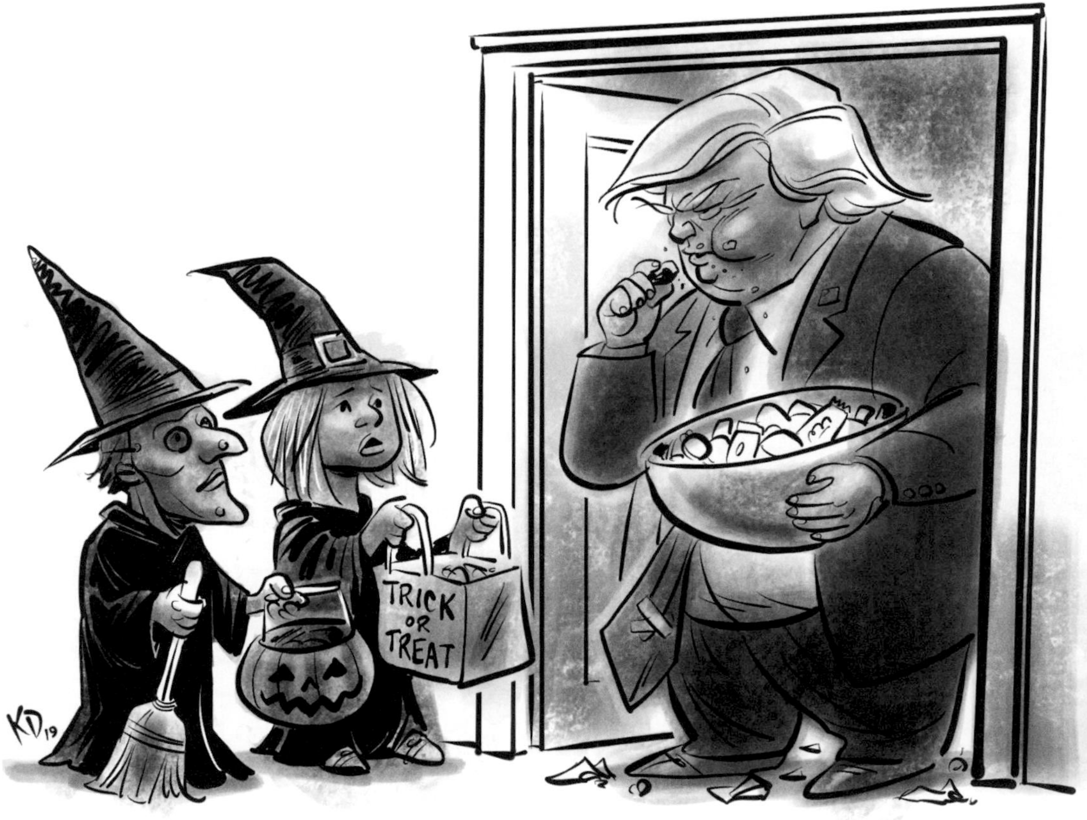
TRICK
OR
TREAT
KD 19

*"How many times do I have to say it? No Quid Pro Quo!"*

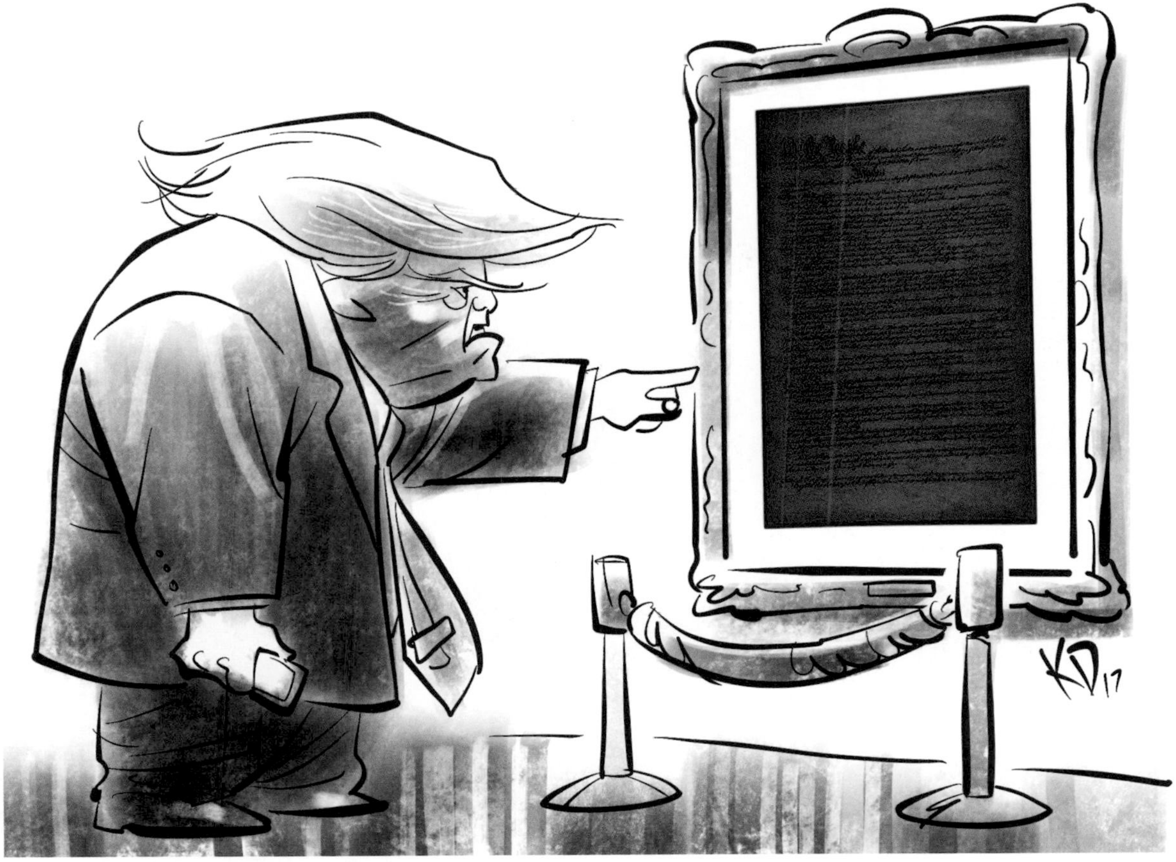

*"You're fired."*

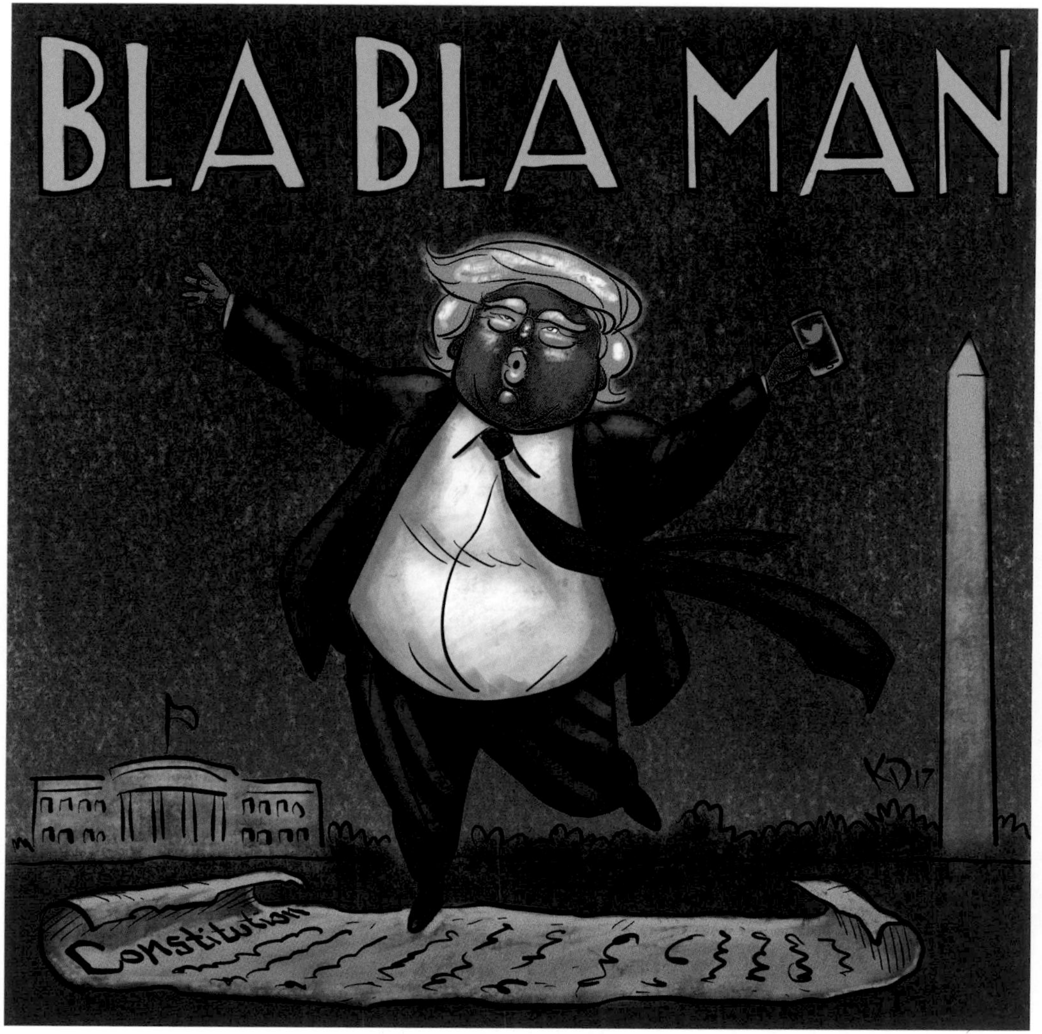
BLA BLA MAN
Constitution
KD17

"He's just not that into you..."

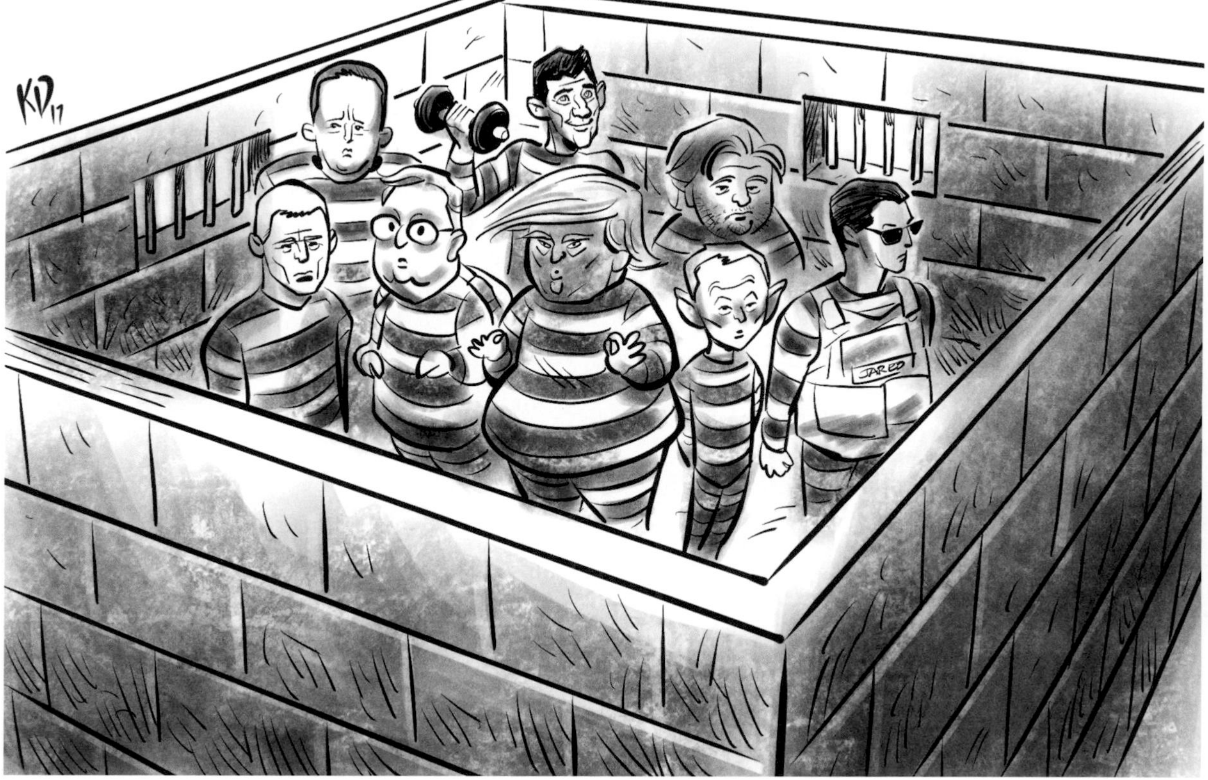
KD 17
JARED

*Wall the President's Men*

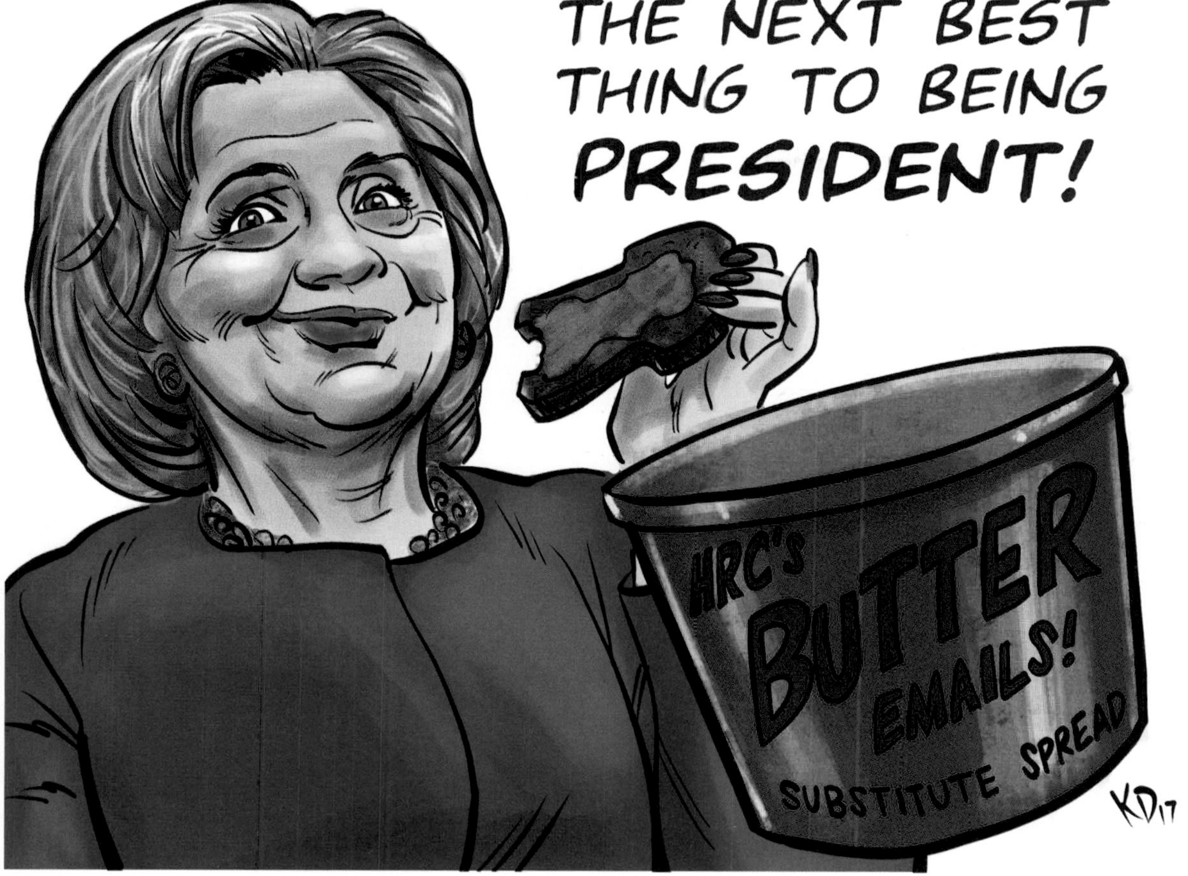
THE NEXT BEST
THING TO BEING
PRESIDENT!
HRC'S
BUTTER
EMAILS!
SUBSTITUTE SPREAD
KD17

# UNCLE SHAM

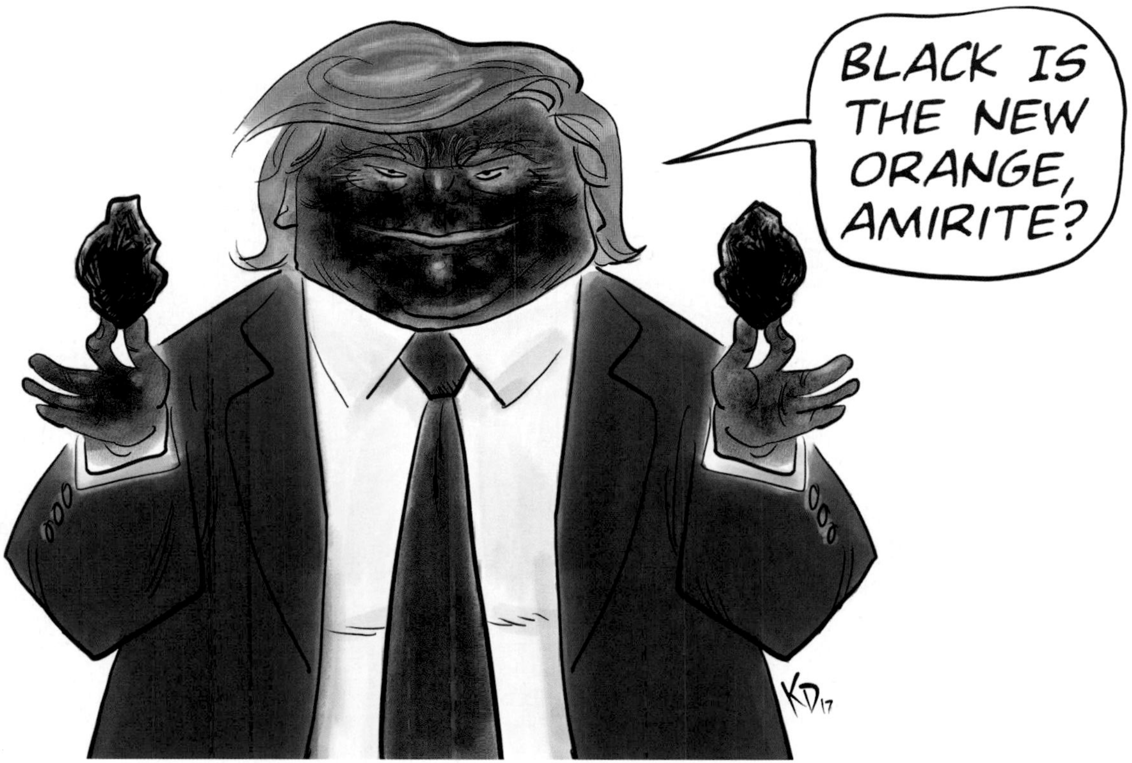
BLACK IS THE NEW ORANGE, AMIRITE?
KD 17

*Nut King (of) Coal*

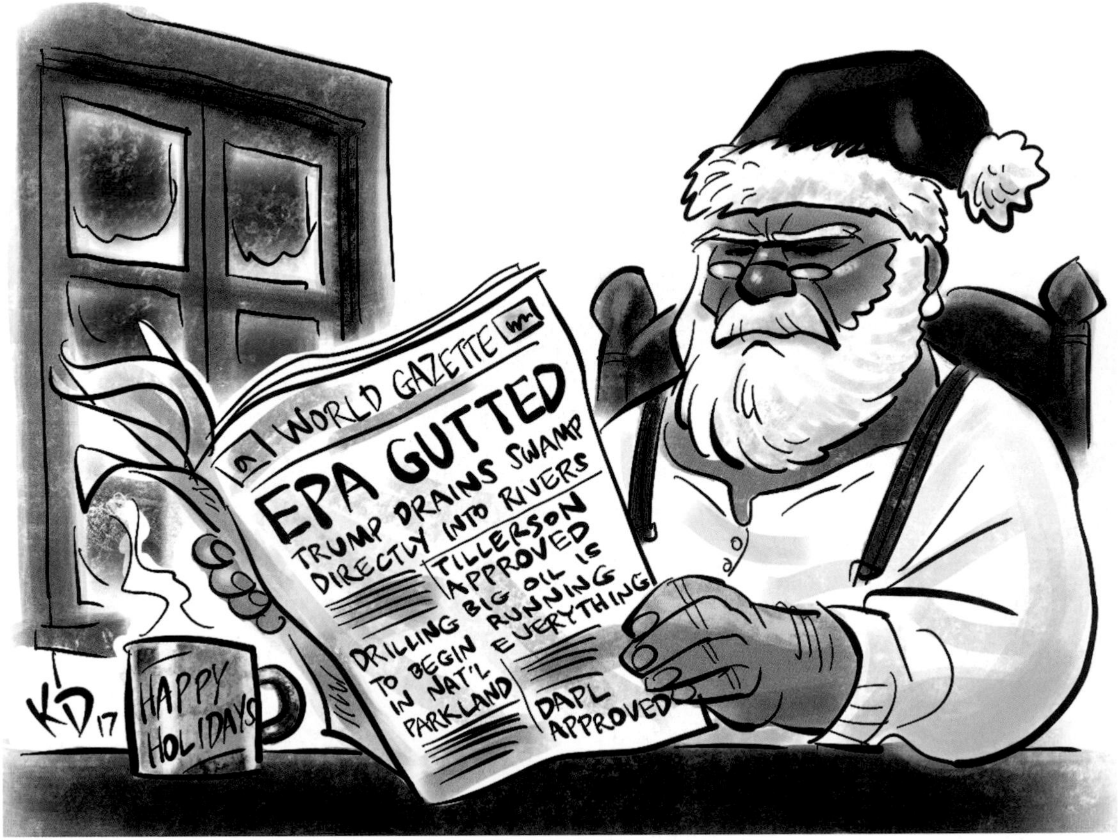
WORLD GAZETTE
EPA GUTTED
TRUMP DRAINS SWAMP DIRECTLY INTO RIVERS
TILLERSON APPROVED
BIG OIL IS RUNNING EVERYTHING
DRILLING TO BEGIN IN NAT'L PARKLAND
DAPL APPROVED
HAPPY HOLIDAYS
KD 17

*"#@$% it, EVERYBODY gets coal this year."*

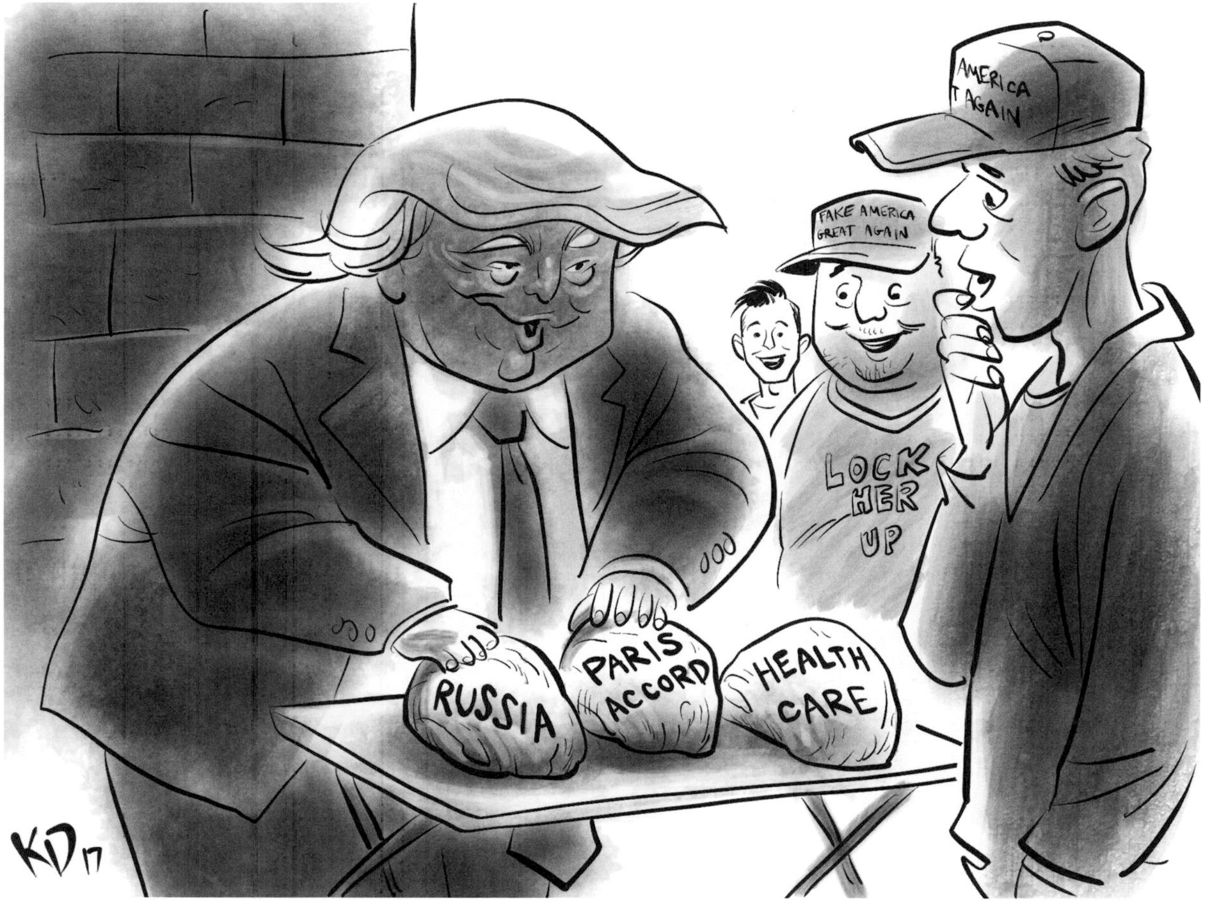
AMERICA
T AGAIN
FAKE AMERICA GREAT AGAIN
LOCK HER UP
RUSSIA
PARIS ACCORD
HEALTH CARE

*"Nothing to covfefe here."*

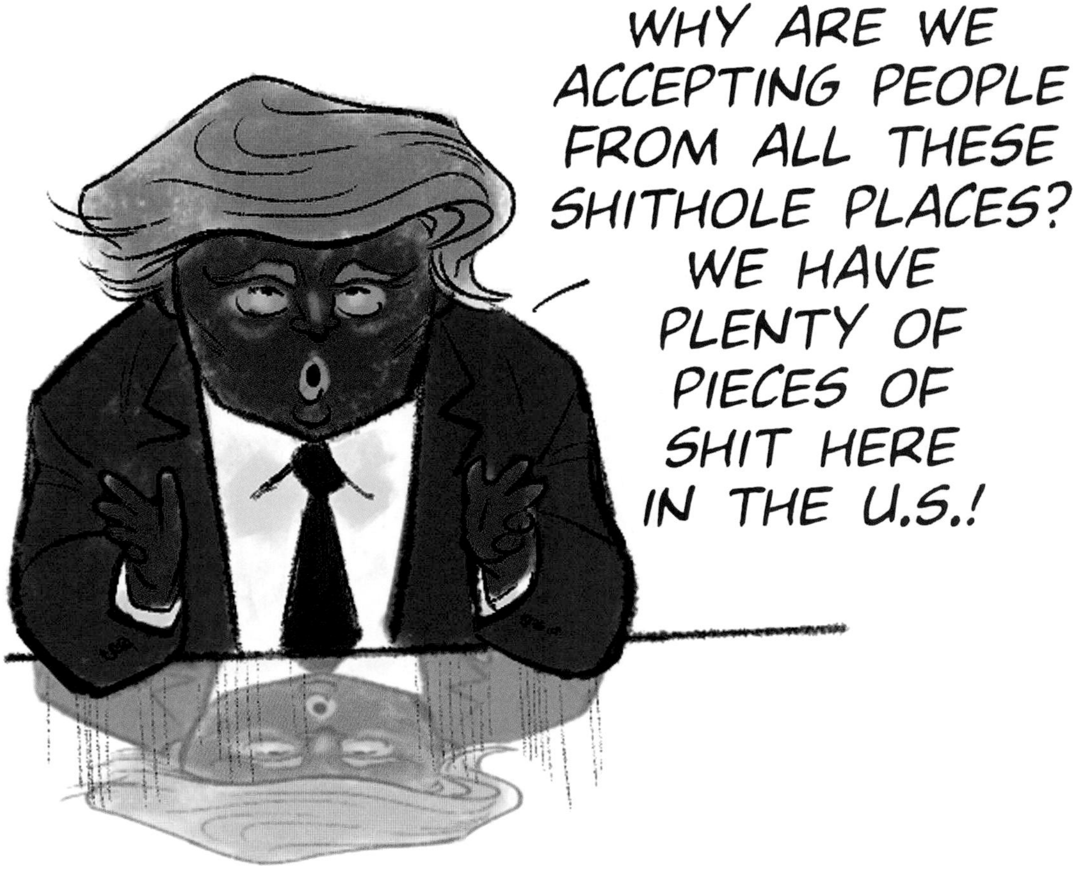
WHY ARE WE ACCEPTING PEOPLE FROM ALL THESE SHITHOLE PLACES? WE HAVE PLENTY OF PIECES OF SHIT HERE IN THE U.S.!

*Mirror, mirror...*

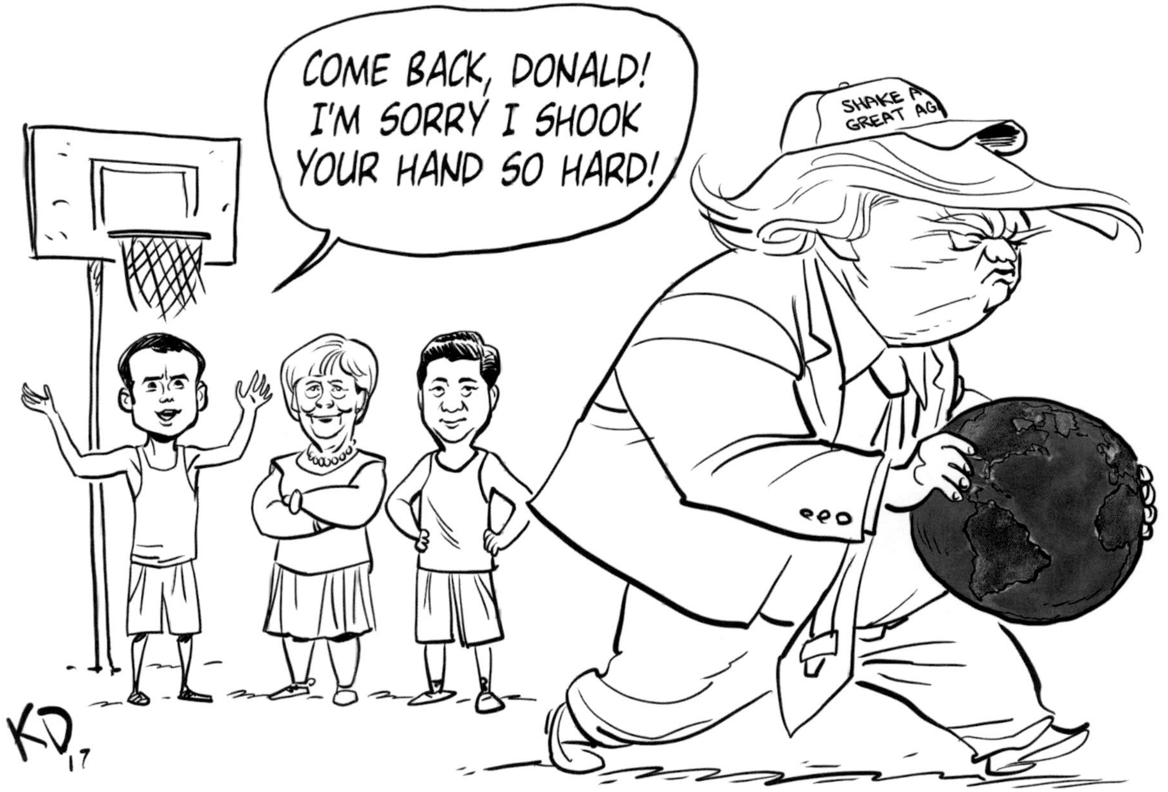
COME BACK, DONALD! I'M SORRY I SHOOK YOUR HAND SO HARD!
SHAKE A
GREAT AG
KD 17

*Playground Politics: tRump takes his ball and goes home.*

*Shit-Hole-in-One*

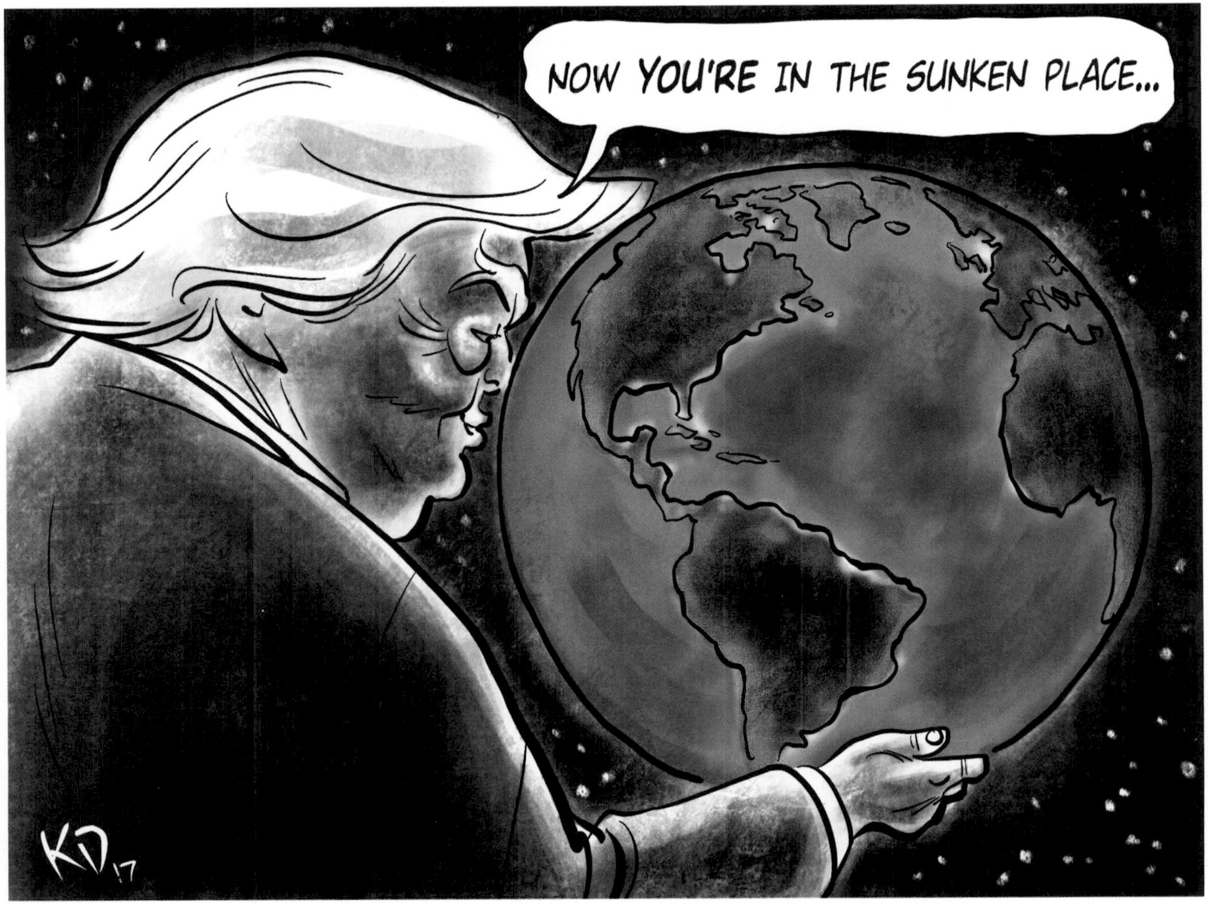
NOW YOU'RE IN THE SUNKEN PLACE...
KD 17

PARDONED.
UNPARDONABLE.
KD 17

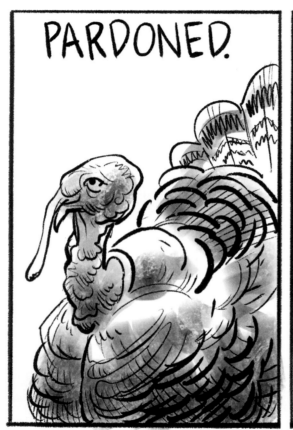

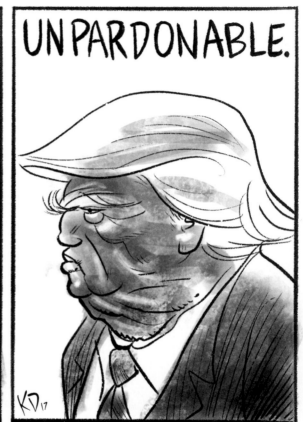

*A Tale of Two Turkeys*

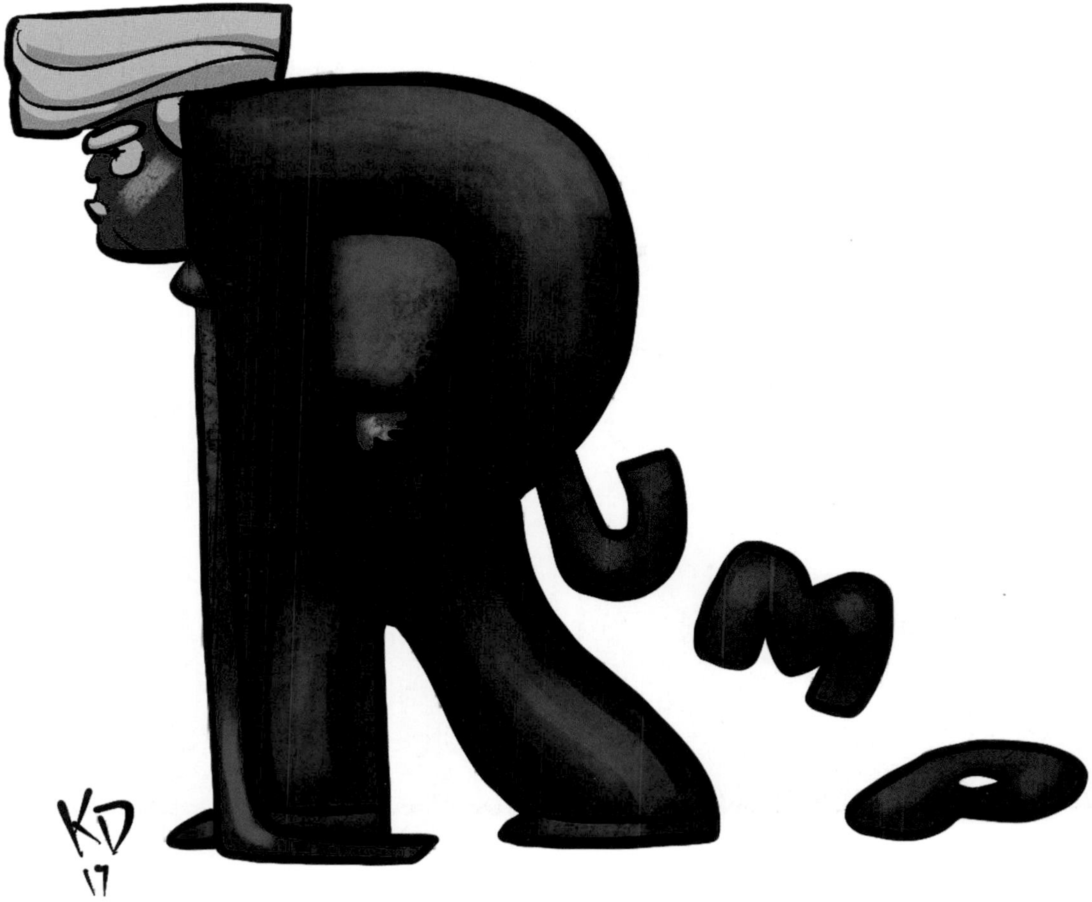
RUMP
KD 17

GUN WRONGS

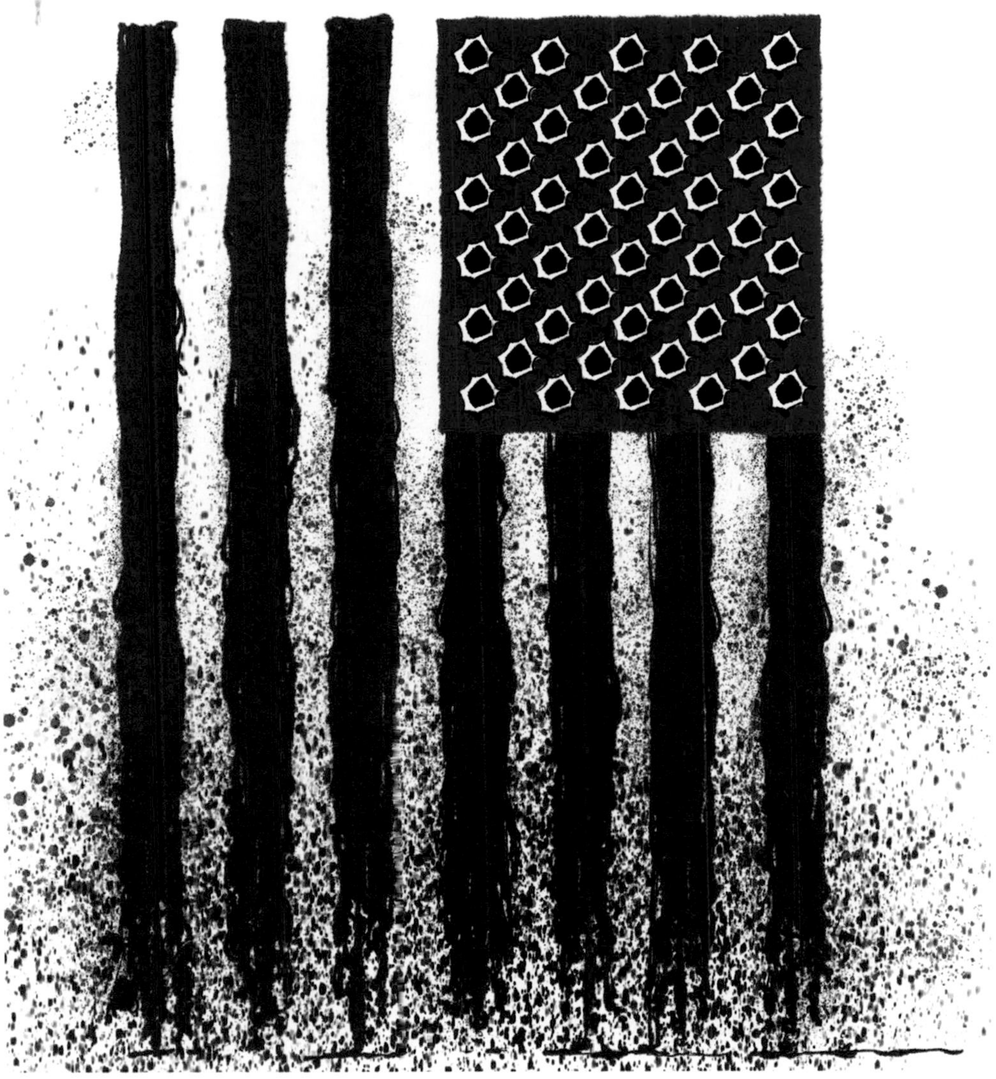

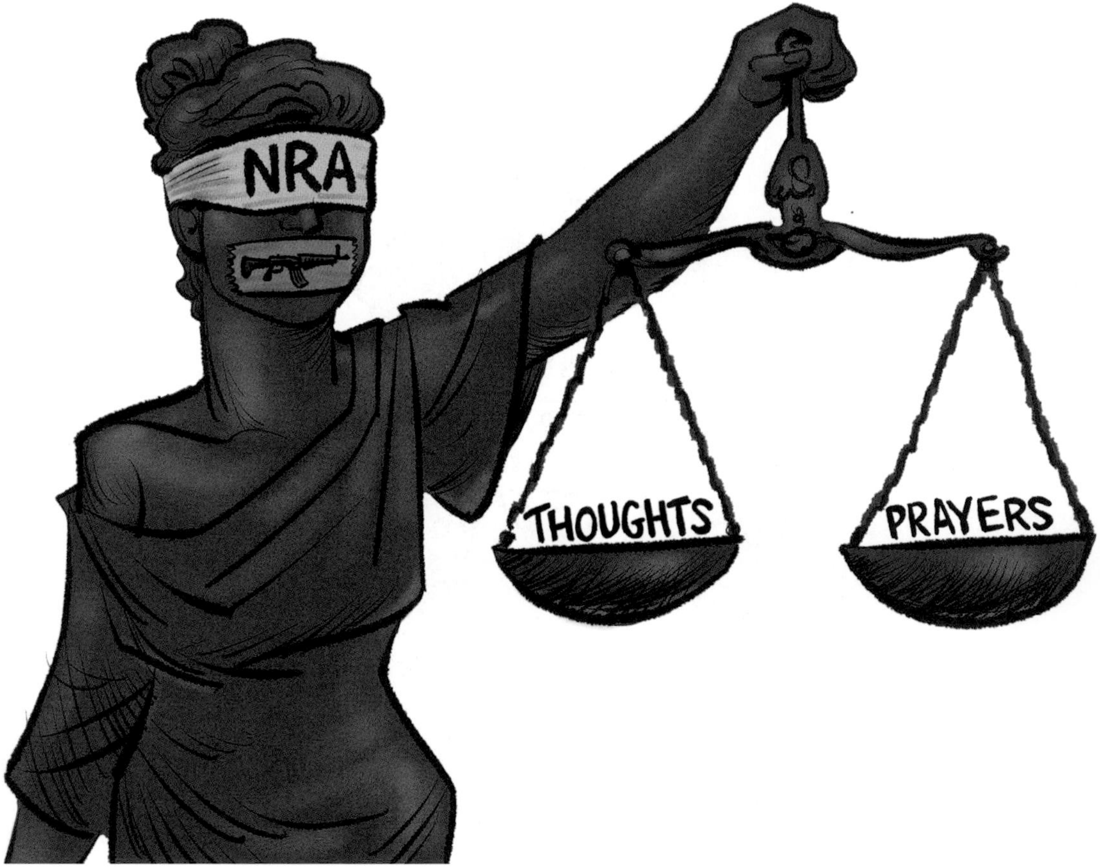
NRA
THOUGHTS
PRAYERS

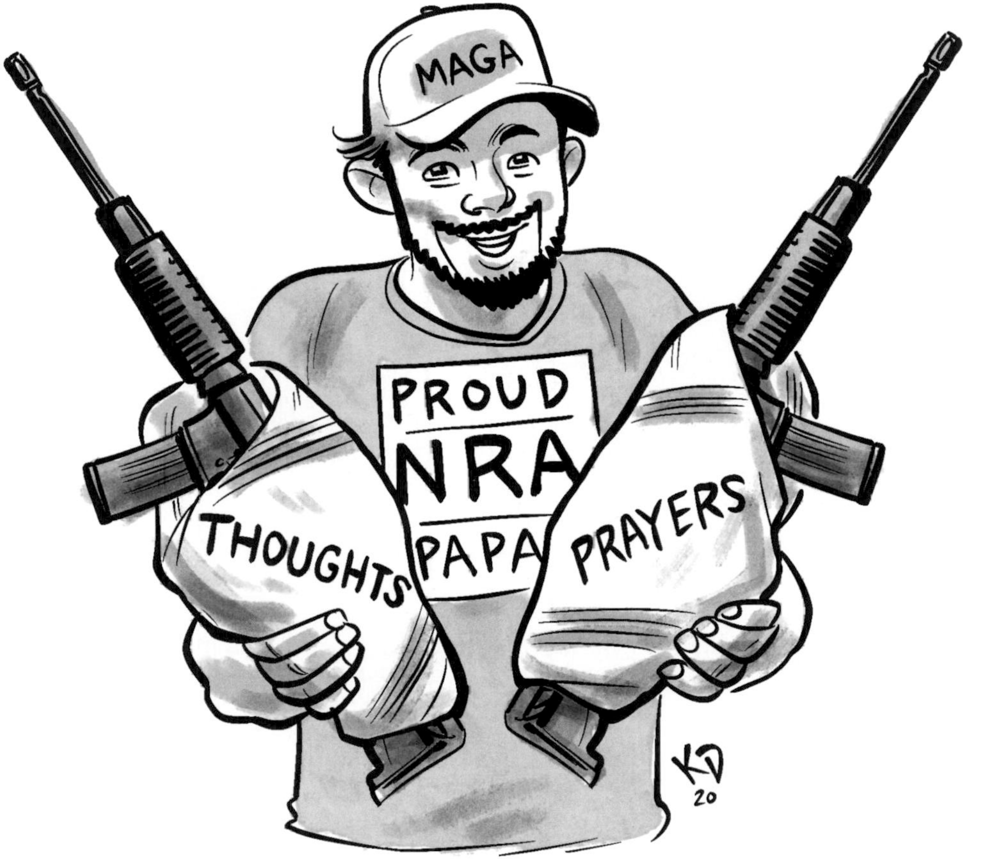
MAGA
PROUD
NRA
PAPA
THOUGHTS
PRAYERS
KD
20

*"We've gotta protect our babies."*

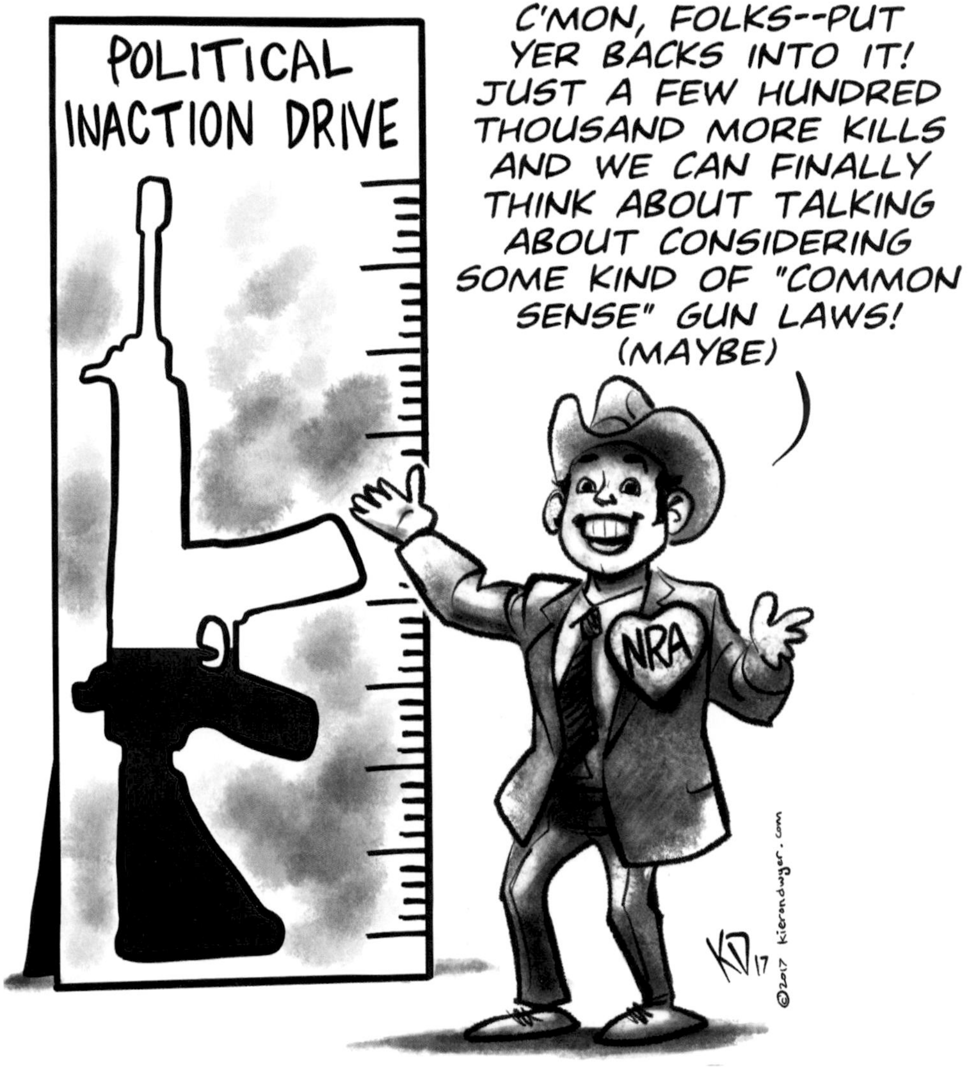
POLITICAL INACTION DRIVE
C'MON, FOLKS--PUT YER BACKS INTO IT! JUST A FEW HUNDRED THOUSAND MORE KILLS AND WE CAN FINALLY THINK ABOUT TALKING ABOUT CONSIDERING SOME KIND OF "COMMON SENSE" GUN LAWS! (MAYBE)
NRA
©2017 kierondwyer.com

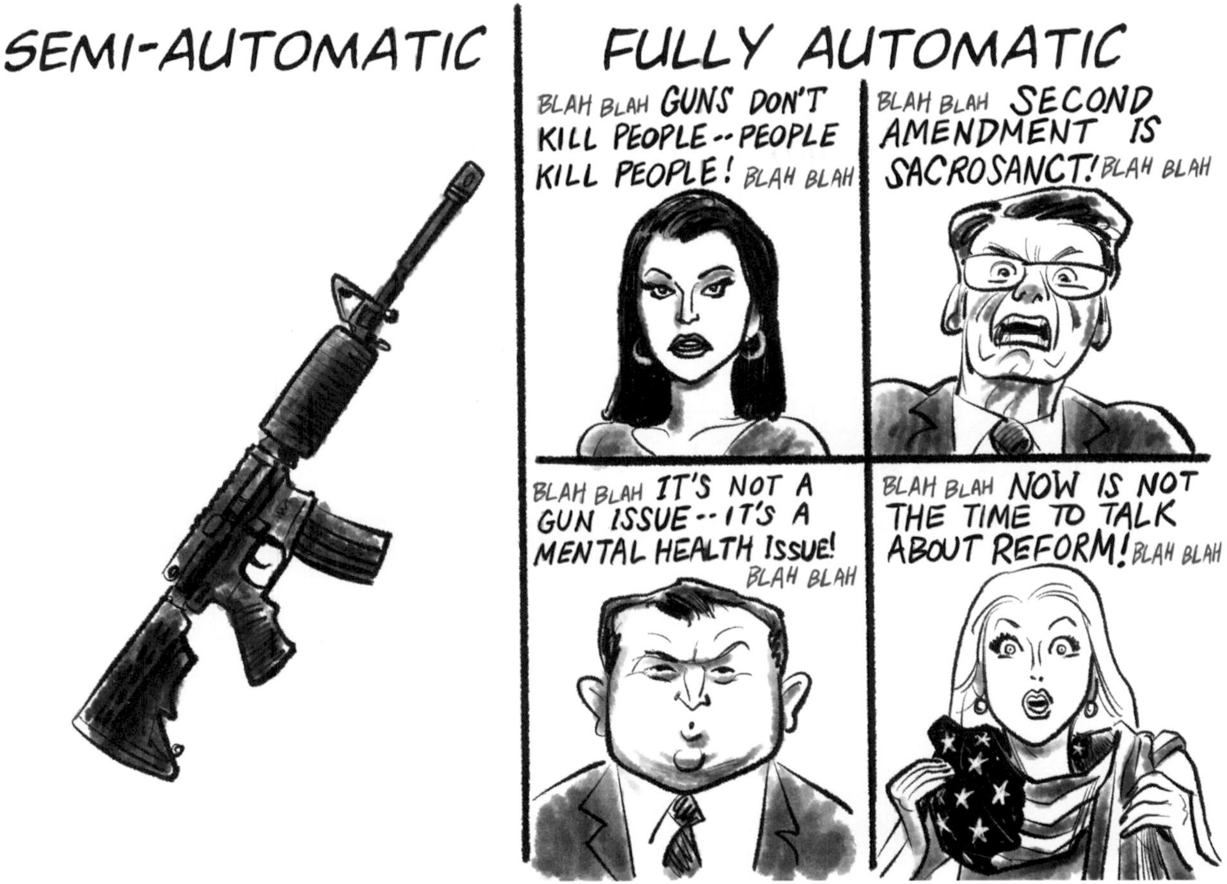

SEMI-AUTOMATIC
FULLY AUTOMATIC
BLAH BLAH GUNS DON'T KILL PEOPLE--PEOPLE KILL PEOPLE! BLAH BLAH
BLAH BLAH SECOND AMENDMENT IS SACROSANCT! BLAH BLAH
BLAH BLAH IT'S NOT A GUN ISSUE--IT'S A MENTAL HEALTH ISSUE! BLAH BLAH
BLAH BLAH NOW IS NOT THE TIME TO TALK ABOUT REFORM! BLAH BLAH

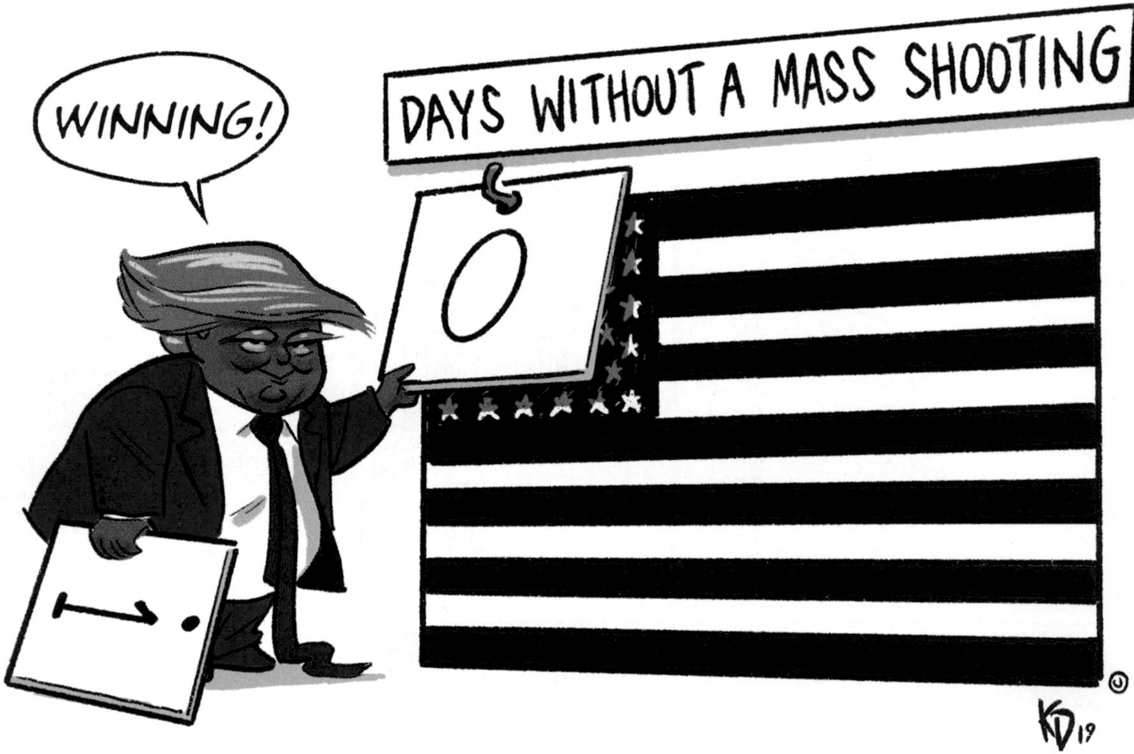
WINNING!
DAYS WITHOUT A MASS SHOOTING
0

*# AmericaFirst*

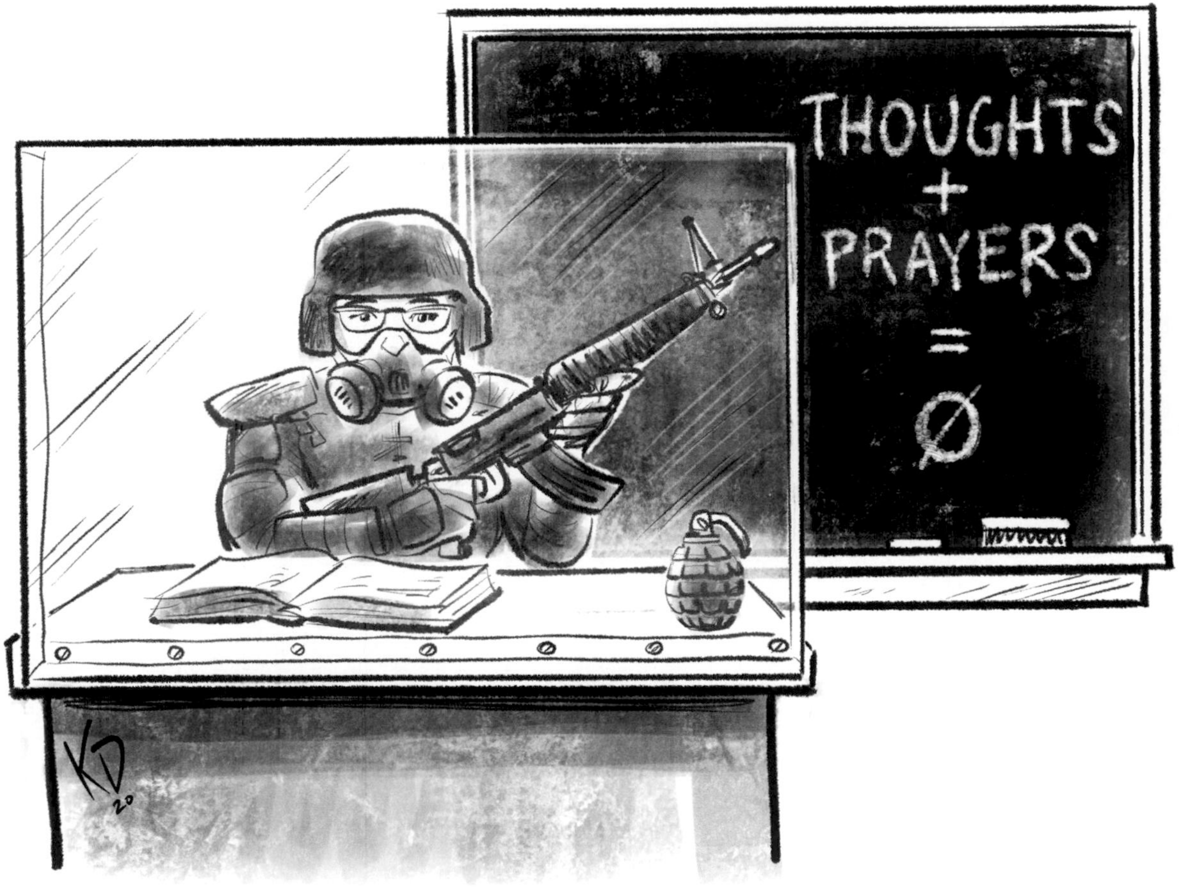
THOUGHTS
+
PRAYERS
=
Ø
KD
20

*Basic Math*

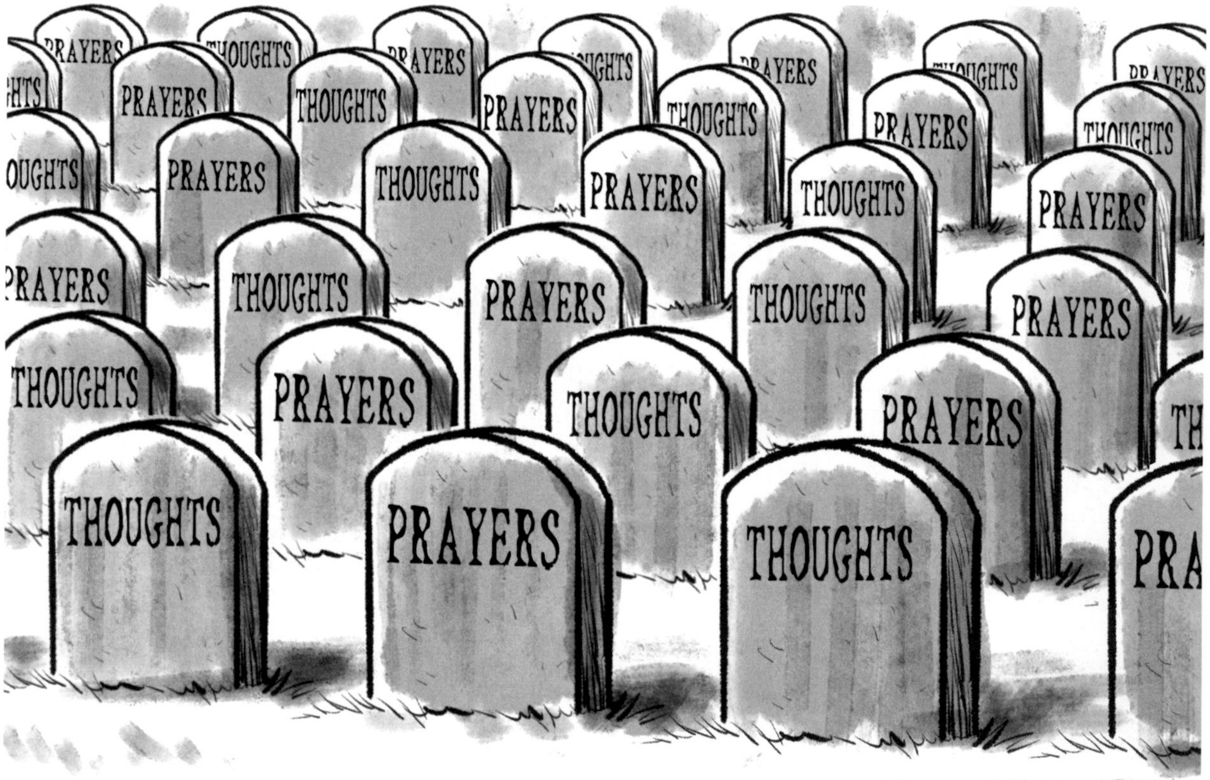
PRAYERS
THOUGHTS
PRAYERS
THOUGHTS
PRAYERS
THOUGHTS
PRAYERS
THOUGHTS
PRAYERS
THOUGHTS
PRAYERS
THOUGHTS
PRAYERS
THOUGHTS
PRAYERS
THOUGHTS
PRAYERS
THOUGHTS
PRAYERS
THOUGHTS
PRAYERS
THOUGHTS
PRAYERS
THOUGHTS
PRAYERS
THOUGHTS

*We're gonna need a bigger graveyard.*

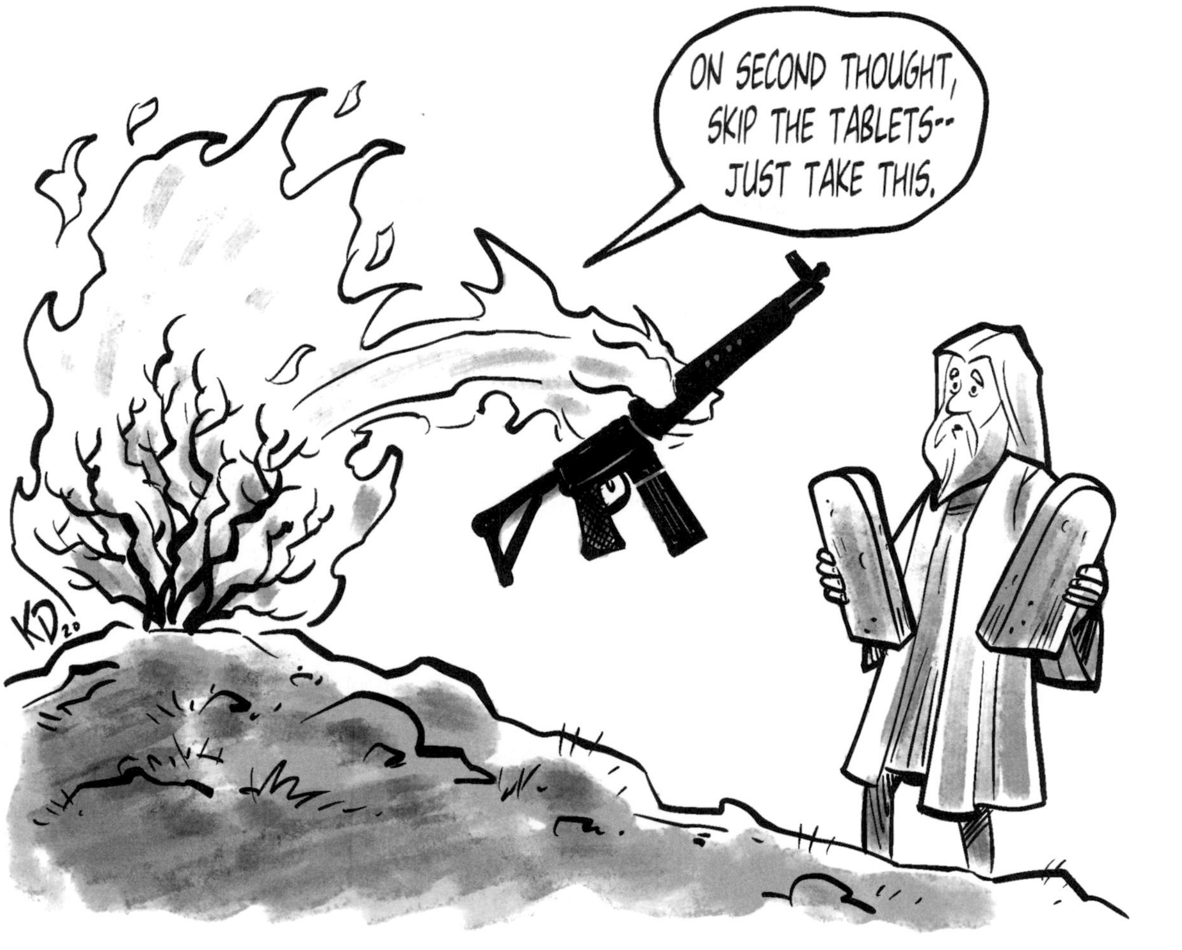
ON SECOND THOUGHT, SKIP THE TABLETS-- JUST TAKE THIS.
KD 20

*Lost Biblical Moments, no. 847*

I'M PEACHY

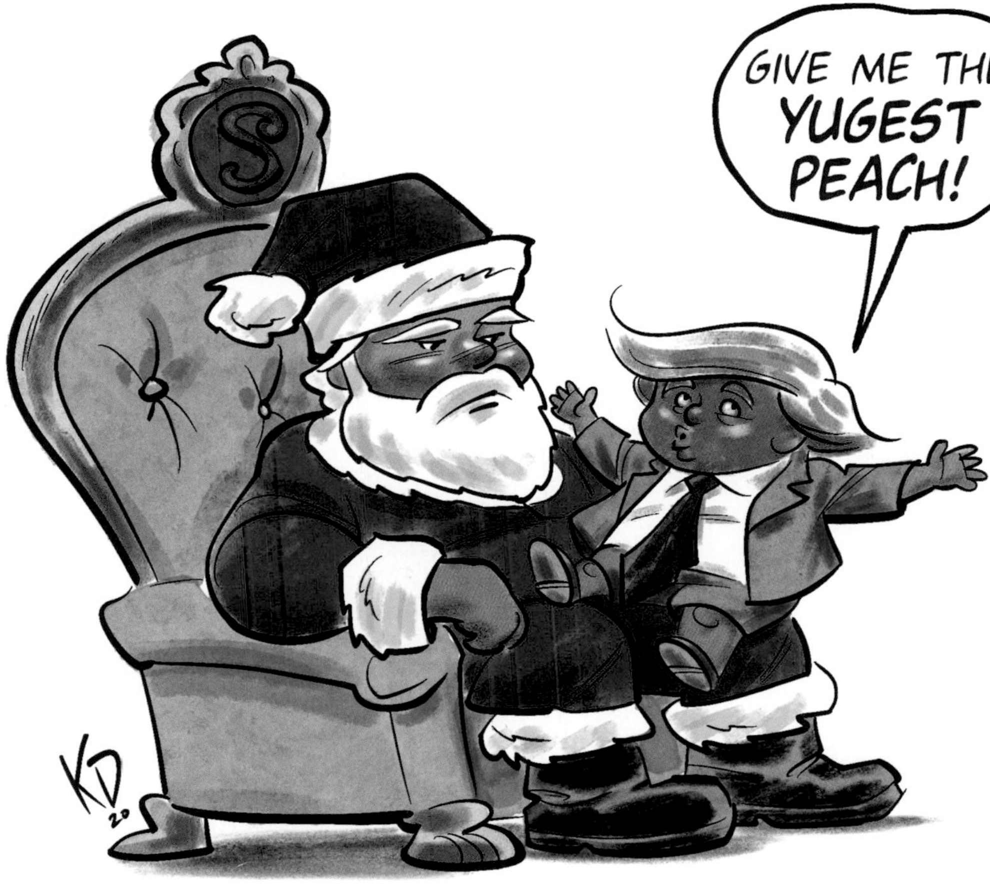
GIVE ME THE YUGEST PEACH!
KD 20

*Careful what you wish for.*

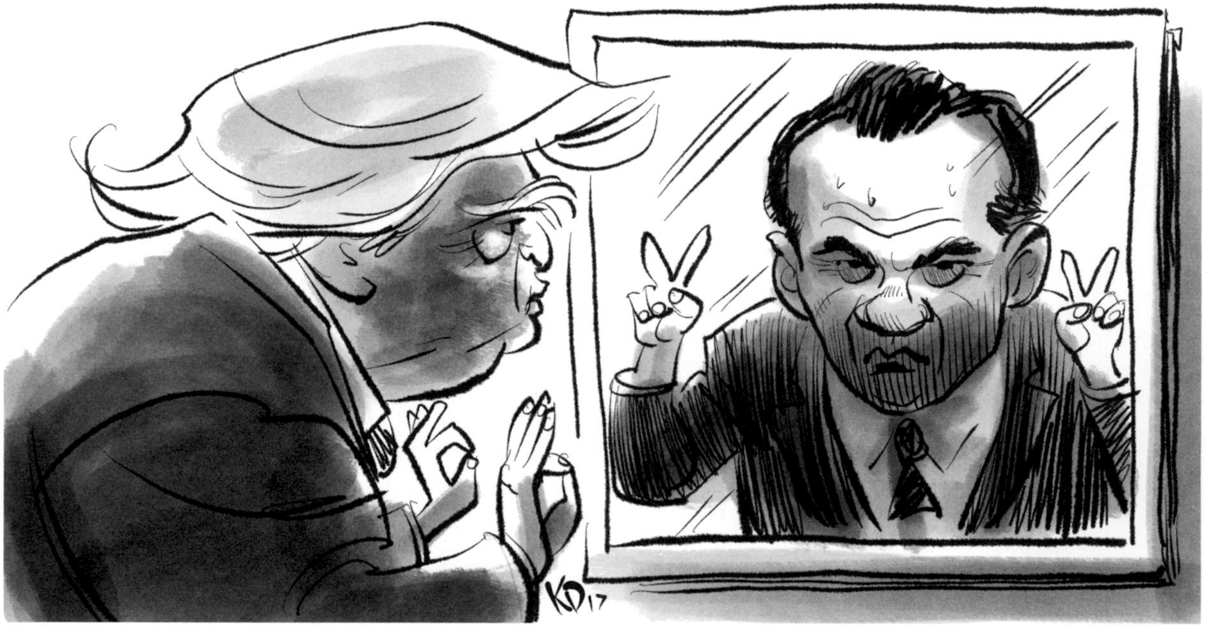
KD 17

*When the president sees his 5 o'clock shadow, just 5 more weeks 'til impeachment!*

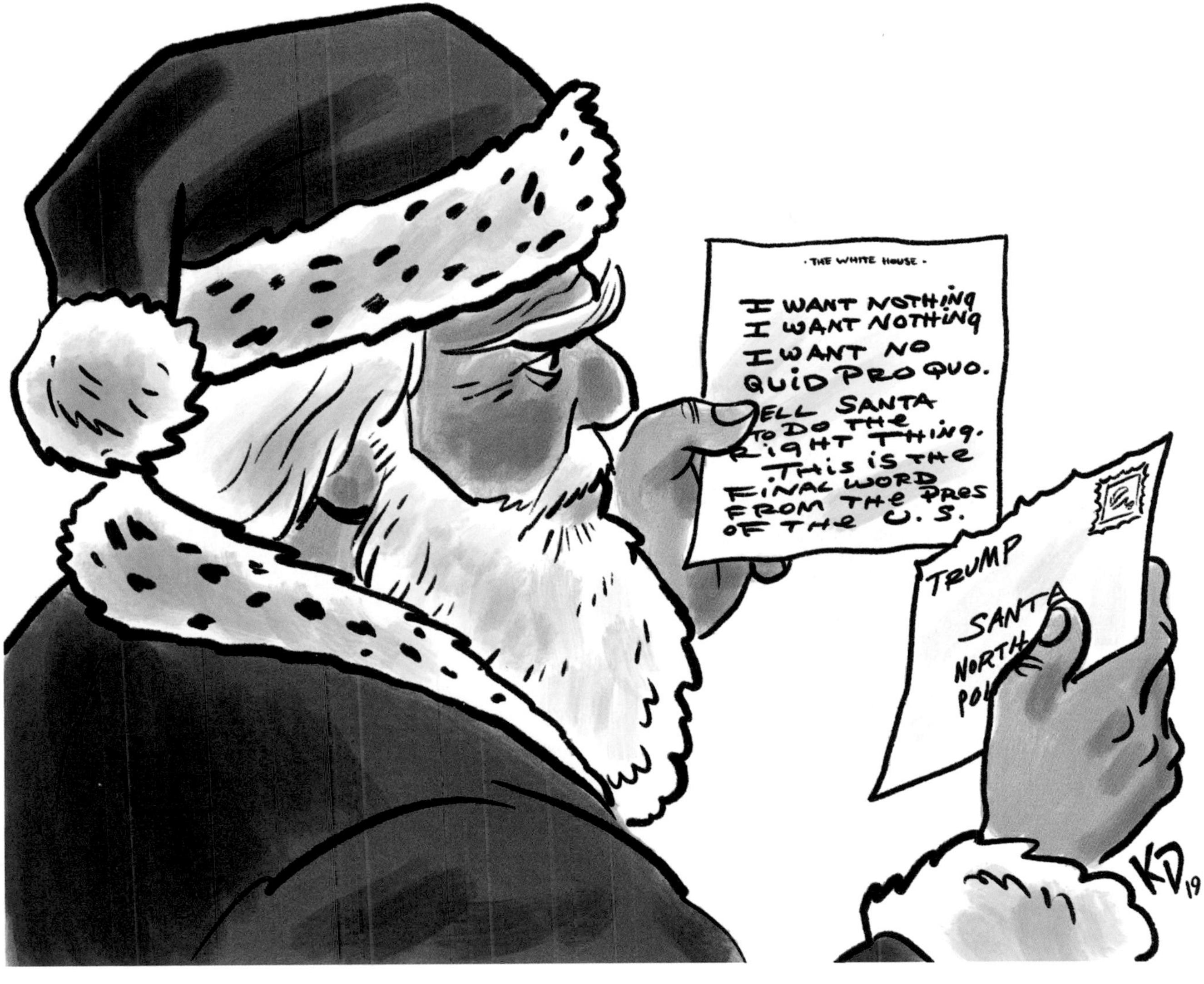
· THE WHITE HOUSE ·
I WANT NOTHING
I WANT NOTHING
I WANT NO
QUID PRO QUO.
ELL SANTA
TO DO THE
RIGHT THING.
THIS IS THE
FINAL WORD
FROM THE PRES
OF THE U.S.
TRUMP
SANT
NORTH
PO
KD 19

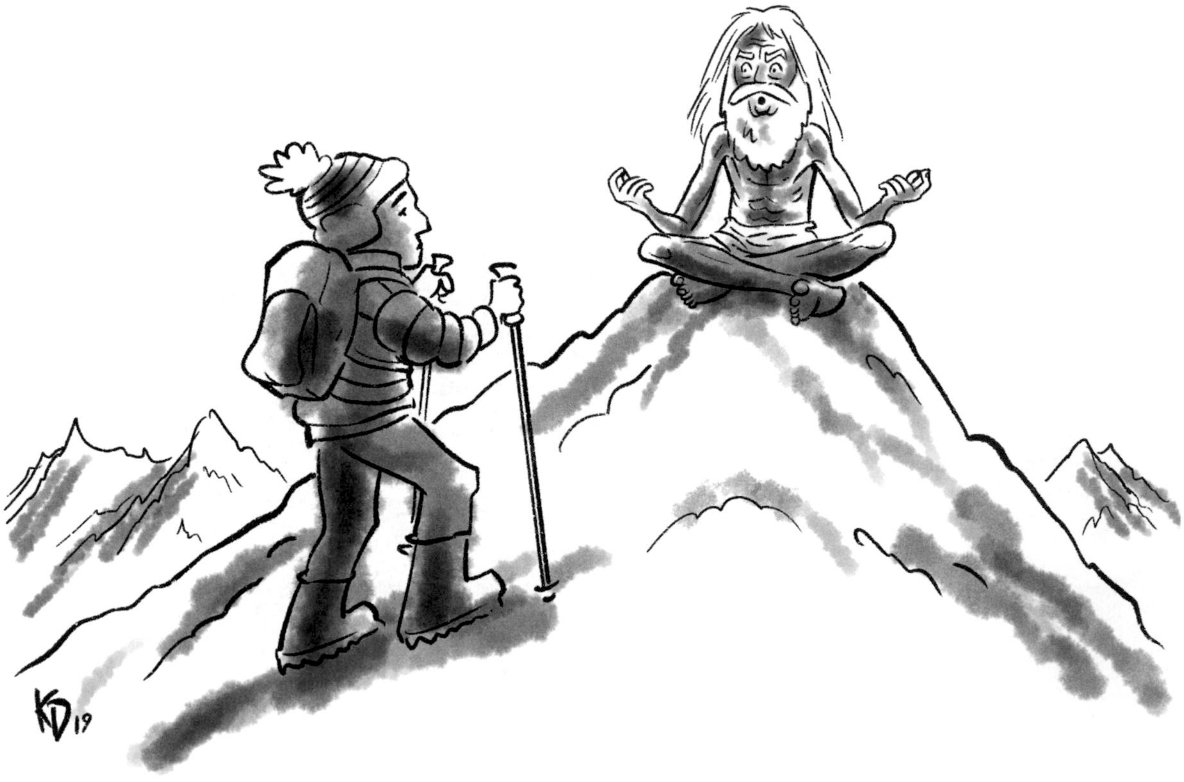
KD 19

*"Did they impeach the mother****er yet?"*

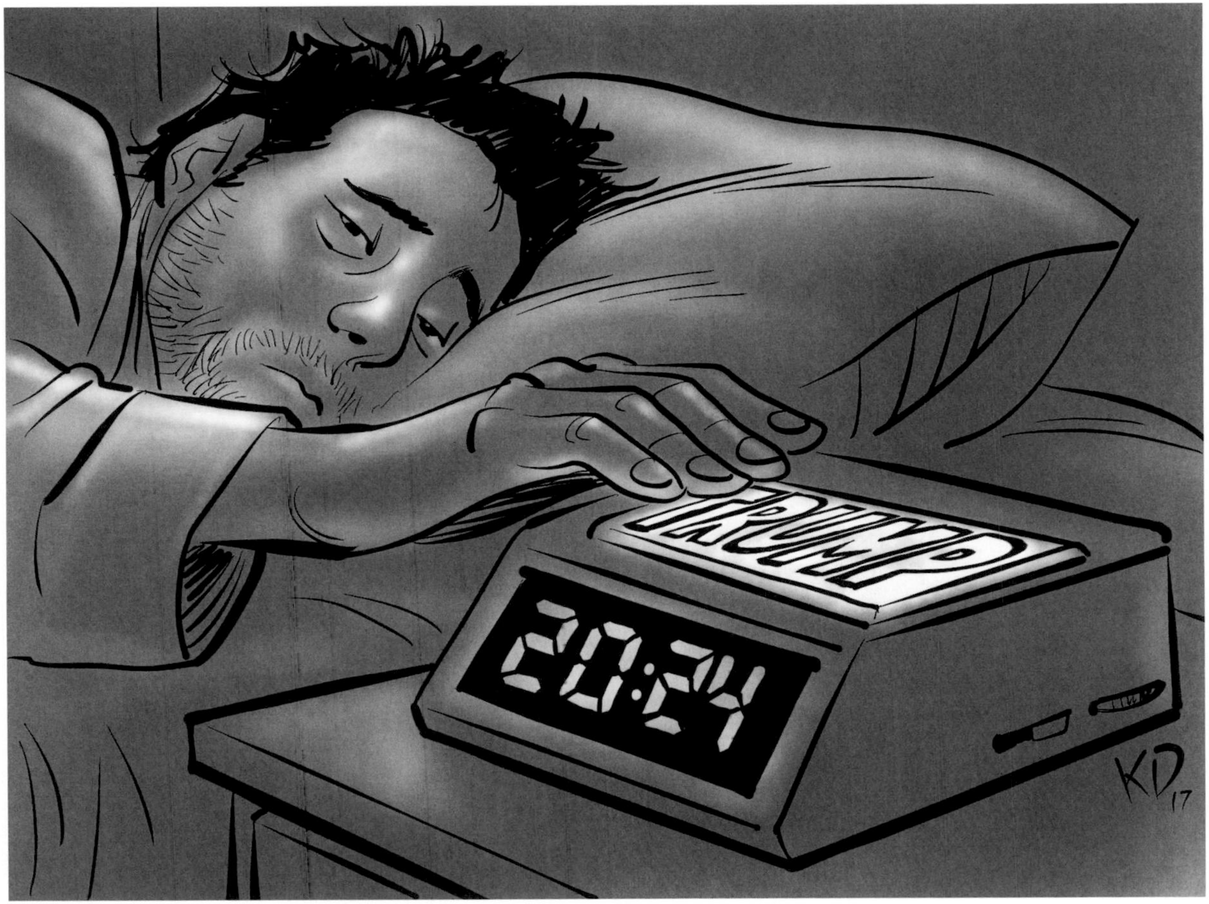
TRUMP
20:24
KD 17

*Wake me when it's over...?*

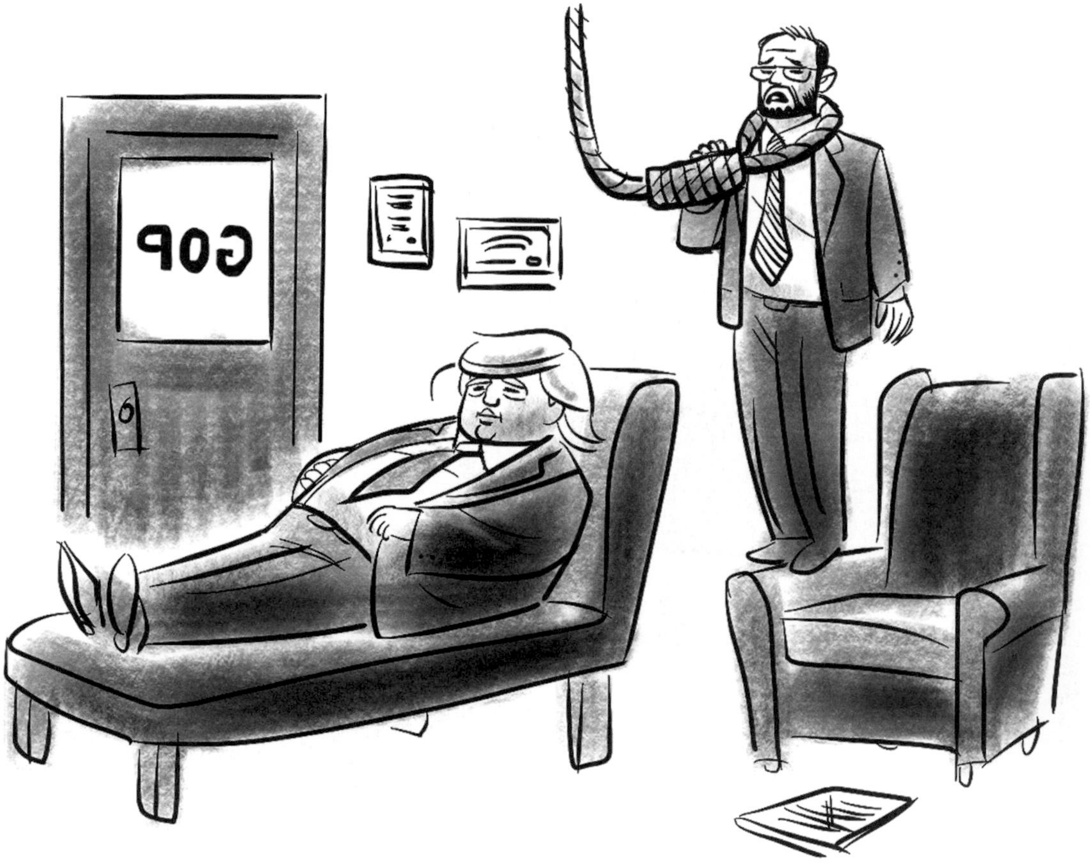
GOP

*"I'm sorry, Mr. Trump, but our time is up."*

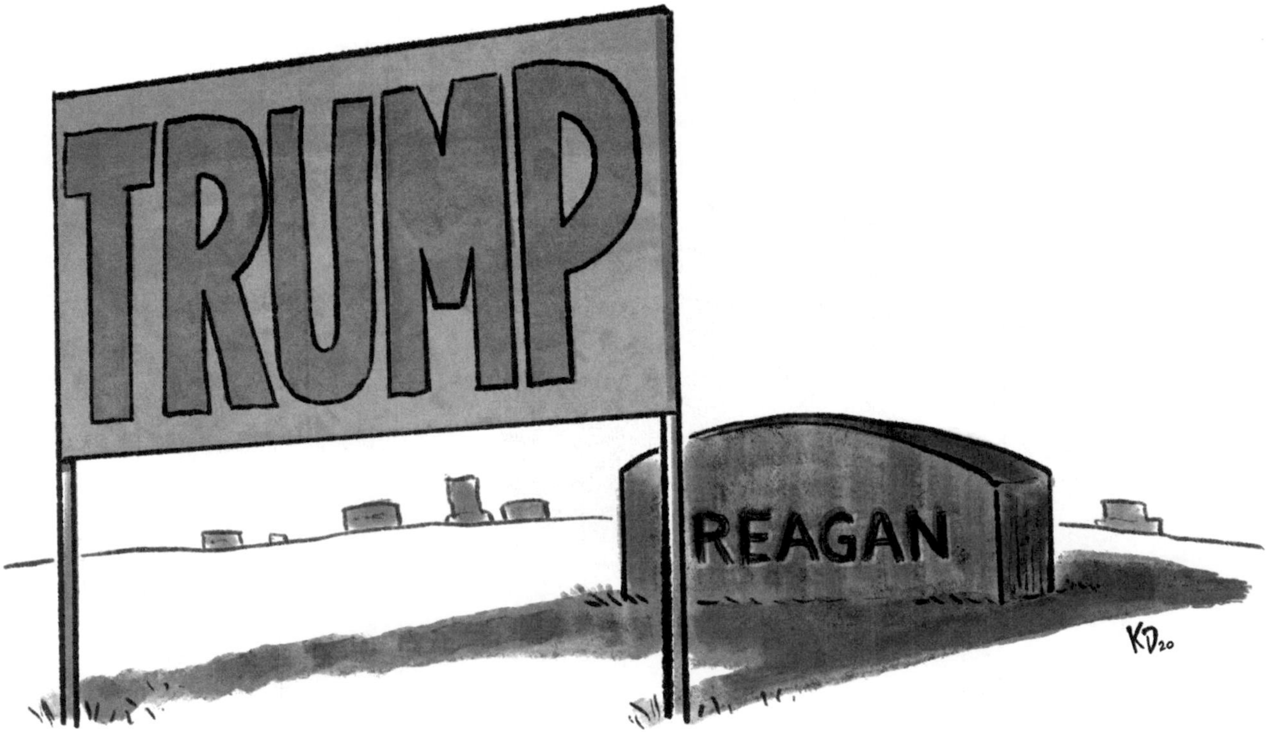
TRUMP
REAGAN
KD20

*Mourning in America*

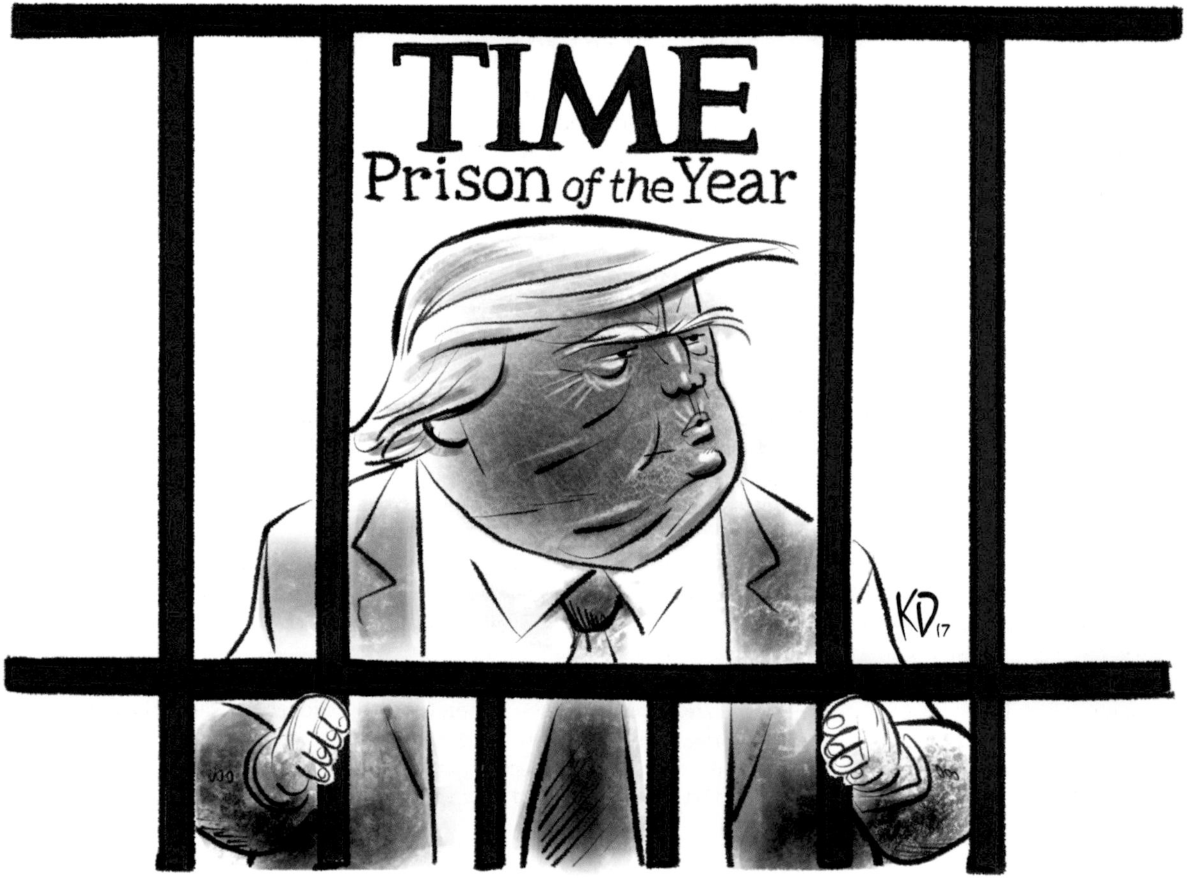
TIME
Prison of the Year
KD 17

*The ending we all deserve.*

# AFTERWORD
## by Kieron Dwyer

Even when I was a very young kid, I've always been drawn to editorial and political cartoons, both in style and substance. The exaggerated yet loose qualities of them appealed to me much in the same way that the work of Mort Drucker and Jack Davis did in MAD Magazine, another touchstone of my youth, along with the erudite crassness of National Lampoon, the incredible cartoonists in Playboy magazine and the New Yorker (notably the late great Gahan Wilson, who was frequently in both), and the amazing books of B. Kliban. Even with my bent towards drawing the adventures of costumed crimefighters, I knew there was something special about the particular abilities of the editorial cartoonists, something to which I aspired.

The economy of information in an excellent editorial cartoon is, in my opinion, the highest form of graphic storytelling. In most ways, that is what I strive for in all my illustration work: simplicity and essence; true communication. Even before my professional comics career, my first "published" works were the editorial cartoons I did for my high school newspapers, both the official one and the anti-establishment underground one put out by myself and several friends. None of my cartoons were as clever or bold as I would like to have believed they were, but it was a good start at taking on "The Man," speaking truth to power.

In most ways, I feel I've just been refining that storytelling craft my entire life, but events over the last few years have had a catalytic effect on me and compelled me to express my feelings in this particular medium at this crucial juncture in our country's history. It's been both exhilarating and draining, somehow. I am always pleased when struck with an idea, excited while I create it, proud (and scared) as I present it to the world, and then completely deflated. Until the next time, sometimes mere minutes later on particularly nauseating news days. I think I may know how hamsters feel, spinning on those wheels over and over again, getting nowhere.

Along those lines, one of the funniest/scariest things about many of the cartoons included here (as well as many which still remain as sketches somewhere on my iPad) is how cyclical they are in this bizarre tRumpian era. By that I mean, a cartoon I draw and release once while it is fresh will many times come back around and be useful again several weeks, months, even years later in some new context. Or a drawing I sketched out but did not complete when it seemed most relevant will eventually become relevant again. Such is this weird hamster-wheel reality we now find ourselves living in.

To be perfectly honest, the fatigue which I (and many of us) feel daily in tRumplandia is one reason I have questioned the value of adding yet another clearly partisan screed to the ever-growing pile. "Who will even want to relive these various shitty moments, let alone pay for a collection of them?" I have asked myself repeatedly. But it strikes me that the fatigue and the deliberate forgetting is part of the tRumpian playbook: draining the enemy of his enthusiasm and fight is exactly their strategy. So really, we have to keep seeing through the veneer by facing these difficult truths over and over again. We have to keep fighting, because the alternative is surrender and defeat.

Thanks to Eric Stephenson at Image for his belief in putting this book out. Thanks to you for picking it up and supporting the endeavor. Thanks to Shannon Wheeler for his friendship these many years and his lovely introduction. Thanks to my son Liam for his humor and support. Finally, yuge thanks to my wife and best friend, Birch, who is the antithesis of tRump: caring, empathetic, selfless, loving, supportive, kind. She is a wonderful partner, but I'm honestly not sure what kind of President she'd be. Better than tRump, though.

HIND
SIGHT

2020

Don't Get Fooled Again